BETTER TOGETHER

www.mascotbooks.com

Better Together: A Memoir of Persistence, Inclusion, and a Family's Power to Overcome

For more information, please contact:
Mascot Books
620 Herndon Parkway, Suite 320
Herndon, VA 20170
info@mascotbooks.com

Library of Congress Control Number: 2021910922

CPSIA Code: PFRE1021A
ISBN-13: 978-1-64543-079-7

Printed in Canada

For Nichole, Shamus, and Simon:
Thanks for showing me that together, ANYTHING
is possible!

"A dream you dream alone is only a dream. A dream you
dream together is reality."
John Lennon

Foreword

AFTER ENJOYING A FRIDAY MORNING RUN and before heading to work as a physical therapist, Shaun Evans wrote to introduce me to his then-seven-year-old son. "Shamus has spastic diplegic cerebral palsy, which limits the use of his legs; however, Shamus does not let this diagnosis slow him down. Shamus has run hundreds of miles together with me and has also recently started an adaptive ski program. Over the winter, Shamus's legs grew too long for our old stroller and we understand you can assist us with getting a running chair that will help to provide Shamus with some of the freedom that he seeks." SAY NO MORE, my new friend, as Ainsley's Angels of America stands ready to assist! For you see, my daughter Ainsley and I have also run hundreds of miles together, to include multiple Marine Corps Marathons, and we know exactly what Shamus needs in order to further his running joy . . . the amply named, Freedom Push Chair!

As I hit send on my reply, I had zero understanding of the journey to follow, for this exchange between two dads would yield tens of thousands of smiles and just as many joyful miles. Shamus and Ainsley's opportunities would open America's roadways for hundreds of exceptional people across our Ainsley's Angels family to also be included in endurance events. Prepare to be moved to your core, as Shamus's *BIG* dream inspires *you* to dream bigger, together with those you love, to accomplish so much more than one ever could alone.

Valedictorian, class president, and Superman are all great titles bestowed upon a younger Shaun Evans, but through service to others, Shaun found a sense of purpose, compassion, and joy that far surpassed the attributes associated with the aforementioned titles. From stories of Olympic dreams and nighttime predators developing his speed, to insights for how growing up on a farm can teach compassion, Shaun paints seamlessly flowing word pictures in a marathon of chapters to prepare you for the 3,205-mile journey that carried his family through fifteen states of inclusive celebration, while spreading a mission of advocacy for individuals with different abilities!

Shaun finds motivation and his stride in knowing that stiff, sore, cramped legs are a daily occurrence for Shamus. But, just like the power of a Freedom Push Chair donation can fuel hearts, so does Shamus's daily perseverance and positive mental attitude as he leads the way across America. With Freedom Push Chairs in tow, "Peggy" providing haven, and milestone moments across the map, the fabric of America cheers them on, as youngest son Simon's enthusiasm for life, wife Nichole's unwavering and never-ending support, and Shamus's optimism demonstrate how anything is possible, TOGETHER!

Major Kim "Rooster" Rossiter, USMC (Ret.)
President, Ainsley's Angels of America

PART ONE

"To give anything less than your best
is to sacrifice the gift."

—Steve Prefontaine

ONE

"Run 'til you die!" my father shouted, as I readied myself to take the baton from my fourth-grade teammate for the final leg of the one-mile relay. It was June 1988, and I had spent the previous few weeks "training" for the big day by running around our family's small, forty-acre farm in Upstate New York. My father was a physical education teacher at a neighboring school and as a result, athletics were a part of my three sisters' and my everyday lives.

I was the third born out of the four of us, and as the only son, I had a little extra attention at times. Part of the reason for the increased attentiveness was the trouble I caused, which commanded additional scrutiny from my parents. When we were young, I was the one coming home with notes from teachers about my misbehavior in the classroom. I was the one getting in trouble on the bus, and I was the one throwing tantrums if I didn't get my way. I recall, on several occasions, being sent to my room as punishment for fighting with my sisters, and then climbing up on my desk, taking the screen out of my window, jumping out, and then sliding down the siding of our house. My mother then watched as I sprinted across the field to my tree house at the back of our property.

To help reign in my extra energy, my parents would often give me the task of running around the house twenty times. When I was done, I'd come back inside and they'd say, "Great job. Now do it again, faster this time!" I'd happily accept the challenge, to see if I could appease them with faster and faster laps. My sisters soon caught on to the idea and would send me out for a run around the house when they wanted me out of their hair. Their special addition to the routine was to lock me out of the house while I was running.

My sister Jen is the oldest, five years my senior, and plays the role of oldest child well. When we were young, she looked out for the rest of us and, to a degree, still does to this day by checking in on each of us younger siblings on a regular basis.

Jodie is next in line. She is three years older than me and was my rival in our youth. Though I can't say for sure, I am quite confident it was her idea to lock the door behind me when they'd send me out for my laps around the house.

Jyll is the youngest and was my closest playmate and best friend when we were young. She's two years younger than me, and frequently tagged along with my buddies and me. Through the years we've remained close. She even served as the best "man" in my wedding.

With a father as a gym teacher who was always keeping us active, each of us developed some degree of athleticism. We had a floor mat in the living room on which we'd practice our gymnastics. I remember that blue and white mat regularly covered our green, 1970s-era carpet, which we affectionately referred to as "slime." We'd spend hours working on handstands, handsprings, round-offs, and cartwheels, always being careful to avoid the slime green carpet. When the weather was nice, we were constantly outside playing a game of whiffle ball, riding our bikes, or playing a game of tag. No matter what we were engaged in, my father ensured we were competing.

Needless to say, the annual school field day was a big event in our household. Elementary school field days included events from typical track and field meets—running, long jump, and hurdles—to things like the softball throw, tug-of-war, an obstacle course, and egg toss. Fourth grade was my first crack at elementary school field day, and Dad was going to make sure I was ready.

After school each day, he'd have me run around the cow pastures and hurdle the electric fences along the way. A couple nights each week, we'd go to the high school long jump pit and measure my distances. He even grabbed a few of the freshly laid eggs out of our hen house, and taught me the proper technique to catch an egg without breaking it for the egg toss.

As I went to school that June morning in 1988, the sun was shining brightly, and my classmates and I couldn't wait to get out to the cinder track to compete. It had been a dry spring, and the grass in the center of the track was crispy and brown. White clouds of dust from the cinders drifted through the air in the gentle early-summer breeze. I was dressed in my class colors, blue and white, and impatiently watched the seconds tick by as we went through the morning routine of recording attendance and reciting the pledge of allegiance. By the time our class walked down to the track with the three other fourth grade teams, my father was already standing there ready to cheer us on, stopwatch in hand.

My first event was the hundred-meter dash. All of those laps around the house, burning off energy, immediately paid dividends as I led the race from start to finish. My friend Bryan's mother was there with her thirty-five millimeter camera and took photos during each event. She walked up to me after the race and said, "I got a picture of you, but I don't think any other runners were in it because you were so far ahead!" Sure enough, when she got the picture developed the following week, it looked like I was running alone as I broke the tape.

Teachers stood on the hill overlooking the track with clipboards in hand, tallying points and ensuring students were where they needed to be. By the time the final event, the one-mile relay, was set to begin, we'd calculated that our class was in second place. My teacher, Mrs. Burlingame, excitedly whispered to me, "Based on points, if we finish at least second in this event, we will be the champions of the fourth grade." In the weeks leading up to field day, she had made it clear to our class that it had been a long time since one of her classes was the overall winner. The prize at stake was a blue and yellow fourth grade field day championship banner, along with bragging rights at the end-of-year picnic. We desperately wanted both.

As the last runner on our relay team, I eagerly stood by as my teammates handed the baton to one another and made their way around the track. As each runner completed their lap, we fell further and further behind. The dream of the field day championship banner hanging in Mrs. Burlingame's classroom was slipping away. Classmates were gathered around the track, and the distance growing between our team and the other teams left many of my friends hanging their heads. By the time I was ready to take the baton, it had been dropped twice by my teammates, and we were in a distant fourth place.

"Run 'til you die!" echoed across the field at Joseph Henry Elementary School as my father gave me an intensely competitive look. I quickly nodded in reply as I grabbed the baton and ran. I was one hundred fifty yards behind our closest competitor, and only four hundred yards to the finish.

My father has always had a coach's voice; the kind of voice that makes you stop in your tracks to give him your undivided attention; the kind of voice that makes you reconsider a bad choice, knowing you'll have to answer to that voice for your actions later. It wasn't that he was angry (at least not always) when he used his coaching voice, but when his words boomed across the playing field, track, or gymnasium, you listened. His words provided the recipient (and anyone else within a mile radius) a jolt of energy, motivation, and desire to excel to a level beyond that which most people are able to motivate themselves. His exclamations from the sideline have always been simple and to the point. If listened to carefully, his words provided all the advice ever needed, and at just the right time.

Run 'til you die! Looking back, I am sure most of the parents standing there, rooting for their children, thought the phrase bellowed by my father was a bit much for a ten year old running an event in a friendly, end-of-school-year celebration. However, at that moment, it was exactly what I needed to hear. I knew he meant, *"Give it everything you have and see what happens . . . no regrets, do your absolute best . . . it doesn't matter that you have half a lap to make up and only one lap to run. Never give up! Run fast, run hard, and don't save anything for a kick. Your kick starts right NOW!"*

At least as I reflect, I know that's what he meant, but his word selection at that moment was much more poignant. All I needed to hear the instant I received the baton was, "Run 'til you die!" The phrase reverberated to my soul. I might as well run as fast as I could, to see if I could catch anyone, or at least make it closer. Pacing didn't matter. What was important was giving it everything I had, for as long as I could.

All through elementary school, junior high, and even into high school, I was the smallest boy in our grade. I never let it stop me from wanting to compete in anything. One of my favorite phrases as I was growing up was, "It ain't the size of the dog in the fight. It's the size of the fight in the dog." Like most little guys, I liked to think I had more fight in me than anyone. I'd need every bit of that mentality to catch the runners ahead of me.

I rounded the first curve as fast as my little legs would take me. My head was down, my arms pumped like a locomotive as I kicked up dust with my KangaROOs sneakers. I squeezed the smooth, golden baton in my right hand with white knuckles. My breathing was labored as I sprinted around the track. I wasn't going to be sneaking up on anyone as I grunted and panted. I knew they could hear me coming as I struggled with everything I had to make up distance. With each stride, I gained ground and inched closer to the finish. I looked up as I barreled down the final straightaway, just in time to see the first-place team finish. One more gear, one final push to the line. I could taste blood in my mouth, caused by the intensity of my effort. My arms and legs felt like lead pipes as I lurched forward. The finish was just a few . . . steps . . . away . . .

I had started my painstaking lap one hundred fifty yards behind third place, one hundred seventy-five yards behind second, and two hundred yards behind first. By the time I finished my four hundred yards, completely exhausted, I crossed the finish line in second place! It was just enough to win field day for our class! Although it felt great to bring home the championship for Mrs. Burlingame, there was no doubt the greatest reward I received that day was the thumbs-up and cheering from my dad, as I ran with everything I had down the final straightaway. The simple lesson I learned, and have kept with me every single day since then, was to always give everything I have, and never, ever, *ever* give up!

TWO

Growing up in rural Upstate New York was perfect for a little boy. My great-grandparents owned some land in East Galway, and sold forty acres to my parents when they were newlyweds for five hundred dollars. My father then built our house with his own hands. He finished constructing our home as he worked as a teacher, and then made an effort to achieve his dream of living off the land. He planted vegetables, built a barn and a chicken coop, and started running fences to section off pastures.

Owning a small farm meant there was *always* work to do, and my father took care of everything. Although he taught full time, *and* coached soccer and baseball, *and* worked as a roofer during the summer, he made time to have a thriving garden every year, in addition to taking care of all of the animals. We consistently had a barn full of beef cattle, a coop full of laying hens, and two pigs in the barn across the road on my great-grand-parents' parcel of land.

As the only son, my dad frequently recruited me to help with whatever project he had going. My typical weekends as a boy were spent mending fences, clearing land, cutting firewood, getting hay from other (bigger) local farmers, going to Agway to get feed for the animals, or buying replacement parts for something that needed fixing. I was happy to do whatever was needed, as my father ingrained a strong work ethic in me from the start.

As I got older, I would help deliver calves when necessary. I helped hold cows in the stanchions when they needed to be given medicine. I learned lessons about the circle of life when Dad would butcher chickens and prepare them for the freezer, and when we would wrap the meat from our steer or pigs.

Being raised on a farm helped me to develop compassion. I took care of animals, and always had a pet dog, goat, bunny, or cat, in addition to the livestock. I used to name all our cattle, but decided not to make it a practice as I developed an appreciation for where our food came from, realizing we were eating "Archie" the bull for dinner. Years later, I would become a vegetarian.

The lessons learned were important in shaping me, but were sometimes painful to endure. One night, forever etched in my mind, was when Dad and I had to use rope and chain to pull out a breeched calf. We had spent hours trying to coax it along and make the mother comfortable. It was late in the evening and we couldn't get a vet to come to the house. We ended up calling a neighboring farmer to help us successfully remove the calf. The mother cow ended up with a prolapsed uterus, and I remember watching her try to bond with her baby while the calf made heart-aching little moos in response. I'd never felt so helpless.

Another memory that haunts me happened one day when I was about four years old and playing in the barn, barefoot in the hay. I stood talking to Archie and petting the curly hair above his eyes. He stuck his head through the stanchion and nuzzled as I patted his forehead. Despite being an enormous animal, I never feared him, but it was that day I developed a different fear. As I stood there visiting with Archie, a milk snake slithered through the hay right over my *bare foot!* I screamed and sprinted out of the barn. For years after that incident, anytime I saw a snake, my feet would freeze, I'd begin to sweat, and the flight response would kick in.

Despite the snake, virtually everything about growing up in rural America was fabulous. I loved being outside with my dad, listening to a ballgame or country music on the transistor radio, as we ran fence or cleaned up brush. We'd take a lunch break and roast hot dogs on a small fire as we burned the dead branches we'd cleared.

Time on the farm led to my first job selling farm-fresh eggs from our chickens. My mom stenciled a sign to put out by the road. The sign is still vivid in my mind's eye: a hand-painted nest filled with eggs, a red and white checkered edge, and the words, "Farm-Fresh Eggs $1." Since we lived on a main road, I quickly accumulated a long list of customers. My parents were kind enough to let me keep one hundred percent of the income, and never made me pay for feed or anything else the chickens needed. My duties were to collect and clean the eggs, feed the chickens, help clean the nests, and close the chicken coop at night so no raccoons, foxes, or weasels would take the hens.

Knowing those predators were out there at night helped me develop my running speed. Most nights, the sun had set by the time I finished my homework, which meant I had to get to the chicken coop fifty yards away in the dark of night, with wild animals lurking about! I'd seen the damage they could do to our chickens, as we'd lost several to attacks over the years. As a ten-year-old boy, I did *not* want to come face to face with a fox, raccoon, or coyote, but I also did *not* want them to impact my profits! So, I would sprint as fast as possible to the coop, make sure they were secure, and hurry back home. I did that night after night after night, running, leaving fear behind me . . . just like that snake in the barn!

I took my job as an egg salesman seriously and, growing up, I always knew my parents worked extremely hard to take care of us. My sisters and I always had everything we needed and nearly everything we wanted. I didn't realize that our family qualified for free/reduced lunches at school until a recent conversation with my father. My mind was blown. I simply could not process that when we were kids, our family's income was below the poverty line. We had decent clothes, presents on our birthdays, and what felt like a feast prepared by Mom for dinner every night.

While Dad took care of all the outside work, Mom took care of everything else. She kept us fed, bathed, and dressed; kept the house and laundry clean; drove us wherever we needed to be; and attended all of our parent-teacher conferences. Mom didn't work outside of the house on a regular basis when we were young, but she did pick up shifts at a local restaurant where she waited tables.

When my younger sister, Jyll, and I made it to middle school, Mom began working at an insurance agency across the street from the school. We loved having her there. She drove us to school each day before clocking in at work, and I am sure she liked being able to keep a distant eye on us to ensure I stayed out of trouble!

THREE

WE ATTENDED A SMALL, rural school with about one hundred students per grade. The elementary school, middle school, and high school were all connected by hallways. The proximity of everything made Galway Central School a close-knit, community-centered school throughout my time there in the 1980s and '90s.

Having everyone close together was great, but it meant I couldn't get away with anything without everyone knowing about it. I was the only one of the four Evans kids who ever got into trouble at school. Throughout my elementary school years, I was a handful for my teachers.

I was full of energy from the moment the sun rose each day, and while my parents or sisters could send me outside to run a few laps around the house to burn it off, at school, I had to save it for recess. Unfortunately, by recess, I had typically caused some type of trouble in the classroom by touching something, saying something, or being somewhere I was not supposed to be. Many days, my actions resulted in me having to stay inside for recess, leading to a vicious cycle of my inability to blow off steam.

In first grade, my teacher, Mrs. Hayes, and I rarely saw eye to eye. One of my most vivid childhood memories was during a handwriting exercise with Mrs. Hayes. She didn't approve of the way I held my pencil. I never had a great pencil grasp, and Mrs. Hayes insisted she was going to correct it. As I wrote phrases on the big, blue-lined paper, she walked up to me with a red marker in hand. I figured she was going to mark the paper and circle everything I'd done wrong. Instead, she took the marker and drew a fat, red line on my fourth and fifth fingers, and said she was going to cut those fingers off if I couldn't learn to hold a pencil without them. Of course, Mrs. Hayes was trying to teach me the proper grip and was joking about chopping off my digits, but as a six year old looking down at that red stripe on my fingers, all I could imagine was blood pouring out of them as she sliced them off. Needless to say, I was terrified. To this day, I don't hold a pencil the way she wanted me to.

Oftentimes as a first grader, I'd come home with a note for my mother from Mrs. Hayes reporting something like, "Shaun was a disruption in class today because . . ." Usually, those notes made it home to Mom but I do remember crinkling one up and leaving it in the ditch when I got off the bus one day. I don't know why I thought my mother wouldn't find out about it because, in a school like ours, she most likely knew about anything I did before I even got home.

I quickly learned that delivering the note to my parents was the better option. Trying to hide something, lying, or attempting to destroy evidence always led to harsher penalties. Luckily, none of the punishments I received at home were ever *truly* severe. It typically involved a conversation with my mother, another with my father when he got home from work, and then having to go to bed without watching TV. Though, every now and then, I *would* get a solid whack on the behind with a wooden spoon.

I can never remember any of my sisters being grounded when I was young, but I gave my parents the first opportunity to lay down stricter consequences. I was often sent to my room to "think." Any time there was an altercation with one of my sisters, I was typically the aggressor. I had a temper that I didn't control. I frequently went to my room in a rage, tears streaming down my face. One day, Jodie and I got into a nasty fight. She teased me, and I eventually lost my cool. It escalated into shouting, shoving, and punching until I was sent to my room. I threw things around for a while before I decided those walls couldn't hold me. It was then that I "escaped" out my window. When they noticed the noise of my tantrum had silenced, my parents went to check on me, with the intent to invite me to rejoin the rest of the family. Instead they found my room empty, and then looked out the window to find me two hundred yards away, dashing through the pasture like an Olympic sprinter, arms pumping and legs churning as I headed for my tree house.

By the time I was in second and third grade the notes and calls home from administration became less and less frequent. I connected well with my teachers and sincerely loved school. However, it was in third grade, on the bus, when I committed my biggest "crime" ever. Some of Jodie's friends rode the bus with us, and I thought it was pretty special they would talk to and sometimes even sit with me. One day, her friend, Matt, sat with me and gave me the idea to ask a second grader, Ryan, to bring me some spare change each day. Ryan and I were friends, and we'd sometimes get together to play in the sandpit by his house.

I thought about the plan Matt had presented and did some simple third-grade math. I figured, if I followed through each day and could convince Ryan to oblige, by the end of the school year I'd be rich!

The next day, I put the plan into action and Ryan was glad to cooperate. He didn't ask any questions. He was happy to grab a few quarters out of his change bin at home each day and give them to me when he boarded the bus. Matt then insisted I give him a cut of each day's money since it was his idea.

I gave Matt his money, and still had a quarter or so to bring home and put in my piggy bank each day. The plan went well for several weeks . . . until Ryan forgot to grab change one day and Matt said I couldn't let that happen. I would have to make sure he remembered . . . or else. *Or else?* Jodie's friends picked on me all the time, I didn't need any more of that, or worse . . . get pummeled by them. So, I took it upon myself to tell Ryan I was going to karate chop his arms if he didn't remember to bring the money. (I knew nothing about karate, but had recently seen *The Karate Kid*, and the action seemed violent and threatening enough.)

Sure enough, the next day, Ryan remembered. The plan went on for another month until one day, when Ryan got on the bus, I saw him hand a note to our driver. He then looked at me, shook his head, and mouthed the words, "I'm sorry." He and I had sat together every day for a couple months at that point. He'd give me the change, and then we would talk and play for the thirty-minute ride to school. But that morning was different. Ryan didn't sit with me. The bus driver asked him to sit somewhere else.

I could only imagine what the note he handed the bus driver said. I sat alone the entire ride to school and stared out the window. When the bus pulled into school, the bus driver, Mrs. Wolf, stood up and simply said, "Shaun, Ryan, I need you to step off the bus with me."

The other students on the bus, my sisters included, eyed me as I walked down the long aisle to the front. I could barely breathe. I knew what was coming when I stepped outside. Mrs. Wolf pulled the note Ryan had handed her out of her pocket and looked back and forth between the two of us.

She said, "Ryan's mom caught him taking some money out of her purse."

The words punched me in the gut. Ryan had told his mom what had been happening, and she hurriedly scribbled a note to the bus driver as Ryan waited to get on.

"I thought you guys were friends," Mrs. Wolf frowned. My stomach ached . . . Ryan was such a nice kid.

I responded with a huge lump in my throat, "We *are* friends."

Her response cut me deeper, "A friend wouldn't do that."

In the five minutes we had before students were to be dismissed from the bus, I told Mrs. Wolf the whole story: Matt's suggestion, how long we had been extorting the money, how sorry I was. I couldn't swallow. I was sure I was going to be sent to talk to the principal.

Mrs. Wolf looked at me and said, as if reading my mind, "I should send you in to the principal for this . . ." she continued, "but I am not going to. I know you guys are friends, and I want you to work this out."

What? Have I really dodged a bullet? The worst thing I had ever done in my life, and I wasn't getting sent to the principal!

Then, she dropped, "I *will* let you parents know."

I got back on the bus with my eyes to the floor as Mrs. Wolf lectured everyone about bullying, and made sure students knew that if they ever felt scared or threatened, they needed to see her.

I felt like I was going to throw up all day at school. *How did I become a bully?* I hated bullies! *How did I not see what I was doing to my friend was bullying?!*

I got home from school and waited for the shoe to drop. I hated seeing the disappointment in my mother's face. I had been doing so well with my behavior that school year. She told me I'd have to wait for Dad to get home to decide what the punishment would be. I fully expected to be the first child grounded in our family. I could deal with that. I deserved it.

My dad got home and introduced me to a punishment I hadn't even considered. He made me call Ryan and tell him I'd be right over with his money. I already disliked calling anyone over the phone, let alone to call a friend I bullied, knowing his mother would be the one to answer.

I made the call and, sure enough, was greeted by his mother's voice. I sheepishly apologized to her, told her my dad and I would be stopping over, and asked if I could talk to Ryan. She handed the phone to him and again, I apologized. He then apologized to me, which made me feel even worse. *How can he be so nice?* I was such a jerk, and he was saying he was sorry for telling his mom.

I gathered up all the money Ryan had given me that I'd secretly been stashing in my piggy bank. I put it in an envelope and dragged myself out to Dad's truck. I don't remember if my father said anything on the short drive to Ryan's house. All I could think about was knocking on the door and coming face to face with Ryan and his mom.

I reluctantly stepped out of the truck, and with Dad behind me, I sulked to Ryan's front door. I softly knocked, and he and his mom quickly opened it. I wasn't ready. I didn't know what to say. I handed him the envelope and said I was sorry one more time. His mom asked us to shake hands and said, "There . . . still buddies," with a friendly smile on her face.

I don't remember if my dad said anything to Ryan or his mom. I was numb. We returned home, and I went to my room. As much as I wanted to hop out the window and run to the tree house, I couldn't muster up the strength to do it, so instead I collapsed on my bed, put my head under the pillow, and cried.

FOUR

By the time middle school rolled around, I'd had my fill of teachers' notes sent home and getting in trouble at school. For the most part, I got through the later years of elementary school without too much trouble; my experience with Ryan had left a lasting impression.

As I entered seventh grade, my motivation centered on interscholastic athletics. I'd been playing three sports—soccer, basketball, and baseball—every year at the youth and recreational levels. However, junior high presented my first opportunities to compete against other schools and play with my friends on the same team.

I did well in classes and I always loved going to school, but scholastic sports gave me a whole new reason to be excited about getting out of bed every day. My parents loved it too, because it meant I'd stay after school for practice, burn off excess energy, and come home tired every night.

From the time I was three years old, my father had me kicking a soccer ball. As a soccer coach for a neighboring school, Burnt Hills-Ballston Lake, he introduced me to basic skills from the beginning. He and I would load into his truck every Saturday, and I'd play with the recreational program at Burnt Hills. Eventually, Galway would develop their own program where I'd play. So, when the fall of 1990 allowed me to play competitively for school as a seventh grader, I was ready. My friends Bryan, Jeff, and I would rush to the soccer field as soon as the two-thirty bell rang. We were always the first ones there and the last ones to leave. We'd beg our parents to let us kick around for five more minutes after practice.

Basketball in seventh grade was extra special because my father had applied to coach the team that year. Although I had been playing soccer my whole life, I'd only been playing basketball for two years, so I wasn't as sure of my abilities. I gave it everything I had on the first day of try-outs. With Dad making the decision about who would make the team, I felt good about my chances. However, when we got in the truck to go home after our first practice, I remember him saying, "You didn't look so great out there tonight. You better play harder tomorrow." I knew, at that moment, he wasn't going to cut me any slack.

I did earn a spot on the team and though we weren't the most talented players, we did win half of our games. I was amazed at the level of motivation Dad provided while teaching us skills, guiding us in team offense and coaching team defense. There was no doubt the common theme was "team," and he had us ready for every game.

As the years went by, I became involved in additional extracurricular activities including school government, band, choir, and drama club. As is the case in most small schools, the same students participated in everything. I loved it all and was glad to not be part of any one clique in high school. I didn't have many friends, but the few close friends I had were essential.

From the time I was born, my friend Bryan was by my side. Our oldest sisters were the same age and were already friends by the time he and I entered the world. We were friends before we were even in preschool. My friend Jeff moved to Galway when he was in third grade, and we became fast friends. Both Bryan and Jeff's families were second families to me and both were equally important in being the brothers I never had.

While Bryan was there for playdates and Lego building in our younger years, he was my confidant and co-captain throughout high school, as well as by my side in extracurriculars. While he played trombone in the school band, I played drums. We led our teams on the field and we worked together on projects in the classroom. Bryan lived close to school, so we'd go to his house after school on game days and concoct our favorite snacks, do homework, and talk about our goals on and off the field.

After junior high, Jeff and I had very few classes together and rarely even had lunch at the same time. As a result, we saved our time together for weekends and vacations. We slept in the old tree house, built zip lines over the pond, went sledding, rode bikes, and played soccer using our homemade goal in our front yard under the porch light until Mom called us in. Then we'd play video games until our eyes grew heavy and we'd fall asleep. We'd awaken the next morning to do it all over again. Every weekend, either Jeff was at my house or I was at his. With my three sisters and his four siblings, our parents were always happy to have one more child in the mix. We even went along with each other on family vacations; I joined his family for a trip to Cape Cod, and Jeff joined my family for a fishing trip in Ontario.

While Jeff, Bryan, and I didn't often hang out as a trio, one uniting factor for the three of us was athletics. One place we were all able to commiserate together was the basketball court. As freshman and sophomores playing junior varsity basketball, we took to the court each day driven to succeed. We'd always had success on the soccer field together, but when it came to basketball, success didn't come so easily.

For our entire freshman year, we played with intensity, discipline, and positive attitudes. We loved our coach, Mr. Maliszewski, and he constantly pushed us to get better. We improved throughout the year, but as the season ended in February, the statistics showed our record was 0–20. Zero wins in twenty games! Many of the defeats came in close contests; some were complete blowouts, but never did we give up.

We entered our sophomore year with optimism. We had a successful year on the soccer field, having won more games than we lost and qualifying for the postseason tournament. Yet, when the weather turned cold in Upstate New York and we traded our cleats in for high tops, our goal was simply to win a single game.

By the end of December, our record was 0–11, no wins as the season neared its conclusion. As the new year began, we practiced with extra fervor. We'd circled the game against Fort Ann on our schedules, figuring it might be our best (and only) chance at a win. They had a poor record as well (better than ours, but not by much). We lost a few close games leading up to our Fort Ann matchup, which actually bolstered our confidence. We were only losing by a basket or two. We were so close to breaking through, getting over the mental hurdle, and finally getting our first W.

The week of the Fort Ann game arrived, and we were ready! Unfortunately, I woke up with stabbing pains in my stomach on game day. I had no appetite, but forced myself to eat breakfast knowing we had a game that night. About five minutes later, I was vomiting with the worst stomach cramps I'd ever had. Other than the pain in my stomach, I felt somewhat okay. I didn't have a high fever, but I couldn't keep anything down. I tried to drink some water and it would immediately come back up. I'd feel good for about twenty minutes after my hurling sessions, but then, like clockwork, I'd get sick again. I watched the time as the morning progressed. The rule at school was students had to be present by 11:05 a.m. to be allowed to participate in after-school activities. I willed myself to get healthy as the minutes ticked by, but as the clock struck eleven, I was heaving over the toilet again. There was no way I was going to be able to play. In reality, there was never any way I was going to be able to play, but it didn't hit me until the clock made it official. I felt horrible, not because I was sick, but because I was the starting point guard and I was letting my team down in what could be our best chance to finally win a game. By the end of the day, I had thrown up twenty-seven times (a record for me that still stands to this day—and I never want to break it!), and missed the only day of school I would ever miss throughout my high school career.

The next day, the stomach pains disappeared, and I felt fine enough to go to school. I hadn't talked to my teammates after the game and was looking forward to hearing how close we were able to keep the score.

The first teammate I saw in the hall was Bryan, who had a big grin on his face. I thought to myself, *He must have had a big game and can't wait to tell me about how many points he scored.* But his smile was for the team. They had rallied together in my absence and *won.* A few guys had filled in to help our backup point guard and give him rest when he needed it. Jeff and Bryan both had highlight reel nights, which helped lead the team to our first win in thirty-five tries at junior varsity basketball.

It's funny, we talk about that game now, and Jeff and Bryan both swear I was there, passing them the ball, taking charges on defense, and leading the offense down the court. It's amazing how memory works. We have played hundreds of games together, so they can see me there with them on the court that day, in the position I always played. I am sure they carried me with them in their thoughts that night. But I will never forget where I was that winter day, the day the Galway Eagles junior varsity basketball team got its first win during my tenure. While I should have been there celebrating, I was home drinking Pedialyte and visiting the porcelain throne every thirty minutes, setting a personal vomiting record.

Of course, I made it back for the last few games of the season, and was thrilled at the fact the boys had conquered the demon and earned our first win, opening the floodgate for the rest of the year. However, when February ended, and after two years of junior varsity basketball, the Galway Golden Eagles' '92–'93 and '93–'94 seasons ended with a final record of 1–39.

FIVE

As basketball season came to a disappointing conclusion most years, track season gave me something to look forward to. It wasn't that I loved track, at least in the beginning. Track was more something I did to stay in shape for soccer and basketball. It was a way to keep active; something to fill my time after school. I wasn't keen on running around in circles and would get extremely nervous any time I had to race.

Yet, track always meant that spring was around the corner and we could go outside after being cooped up in a gym all winter long. In Upstate New York, the winters can stretch on forever, and cabin fever is a real thing. We spent the winters sledding on our back hill, making snow forts, and playing pond hockey—on days when the weather cooperated. On the days when it was thirty-below with wind chill at minus-fifty, we would stay inside by the fire, read books, do jigsaw puzzles, and play board games. We didn't watch much TV because the cable networks didn't run lines to our area until I was in high school. We had the three major networks with average reception. Occasionally, we would rent a video from the corner video store and watch a family movie, but most of the time I wanted to be outside.

So, when track season arrived, I knew the sunshine and spring weren't far behind. Track usually kicked off around the first of March, but there were years we couldn't run outside until April because the track, parking lots, and backroads where we would train were all still covered with snow. Our coach, Jim Thomas, did an incredible job making track practices fun. When we were stuck inside, we'd have "carpet races" around the gymnasium. One teammate would sit on a square of carpet, but it would be flipped so that the plush side faced the gym floor. The person on the rug would hold a jump rope, one end in each hand with the center of the rope around his teammate's waist. The runner sprinted around the gym, towing his teammate on the makeshift chariot, then switched places with his teammate halfway through the relay. We'd fly around the corners, polishing the gym floor, and there was nothing better than squeezing onto that carpet and cheering a teammate to victory.

Coach Thomas also set up scavenger hunts, where teams would be tethered together as they ran through the hallways looking for clues. He created obstacle courses, complete with cargo nets and climbing ropes, and hosted winner-take-all wrestling matches on the high jump mats.

While all of those events were a blast, there was nothing like the first semi-warm day when the snow had mostly melted away to reveal grass pushing its way to the sun. The smell of spring permeated the air as we ran around the school, splashing through puddles and sloshing through brown slush, happy to be breathing it in.

My freshman year of track was altered by one of those practices in early spring of 1993, when I noticed an incredibly sharp pain in my right foot during warm-ups. Thinking I had something pointy stuck in my sneaker, I took it off to inspect; no thorn, no splintered piece of wood, no rock … nothing. I then took off my slush-soaked sock to investigate further. I searched around with my hand, flipped it inside out, and again came up empty. I put my sock and sneaker back on and continued with practice. I cruised around for a while with no problem, thinking I had just missed whatever was in there and it must have fallen out. Then, a few steps later, the pain was back—a sharp, shooting pain that immediately forced me to limp to a walk.

As I stopped, the pain subsided. I couldn't for the life of me figure out what was happening. I hobbled through the rest of practice. When

I got home, I told my parents about the excruciating pain. Without any blood or visual evidence of injury, they quickly dismissed it as something like "growing pains." I forced myself through practice for the next few days, with some steps feeling fine and others feeling like my right foot was being pierced by a hot, metal toothpick.

I was completely confused. *Did I break my foot and not realize it? Why does it sometimes feel fine, and other times prevent me from taking a single step?*

My mom agreed to take me to the doctor, who—upon visual examination of my foot—couldn't find anything. X-rays of my foot looked perfectly normal. The doctor gave me some foam pads to put on the outside of my foot so that my sneaker wouldn't put pressure on the area that was sore.

I taped the C-shaped foam to my foot, put my sock over it, donned my running sneakers, and headed out to practice again. The first few steps felt perfect. Although I didn't know what was causing the pain, I strode along thinking to myself, *I can deal with this, a little bit of foam to make it comfortable—no big deal.* Just as that thought exited my mind, I landed on my right foot and the searing pain returned. It was so severe, I dropped to the ground and ripped off my shoe, convinced I would see a thumbtack jammed into my foot near my pinky toe. Again, nothing. *Is this all in my head?* I was sure my doctor, parents, and teammates all thought it was something psychosomatic. I dusted myself off, stood up, and mustered my way through another few days of track practice with no change. Every so often, I'd feel like I was cured, only to come crashing down when I landed on my right foot the "wrong" way.

I didn't know what to do. My mom called the doctor again. I was referred to a podiatrist, Dr. Jones. I was happy to have a specialist take a look. He immediately made me feel like he believed me, which was a welcome relief. I knew my parents were getting frustrated because, other than my complaints about the pain in my foot, there was no evidence of anything being wrong. Dr. Jones said he'd seen something like it before, and proceeded to ask me if we had any pets at home. I couldn't quite follow his logic, but I told him yes, we had a cat and a dog. He said that sometimes pet hair can get inside a shoe or sock and then jam its way under the skin, like a sliver, striking a nerve. He explained when that happens, there's no sign of where the hair entered. At first, I thought he was making it up just to humor me. There was no way the pain I was feeling was from a piece of hair. He insisted he'd seen it occur, and although the pain I was describing was more significant than most, it could be what was causing the discomfort. The doctor wanted to take X-rays to see if he could figure out where the hair was. Even though it wouldn't show up in the image, perhaps there would be some changes around where the pain was occurring that could give him a hint.

After the X-ray, Dr. Jones said he couldn't see anything. He turned to me and said he wasn't sure he wanted to cut into my foot. If he did, it would limit me from being able to run and could potentially make the situation worse. At that point, I couldn't consistently run without pain anyway. We sat there in silence and stared at the X-ray.

As we sat, I thought to myself, *There is no way I'll be able to play soccer or basketball with my foot like this. Will I ever be able to even walk, not knowing when the shooting pain will strike again?*

I remembered Dad's words as Mom and I left for the appointment that day: "It may be just something you have to live with." Without any of us knowing what was going on with my foot, maybe it was good advice, but I did *not* want searing pain every day. As my eyes started to well up with tears, Dr. Jones intently examined the X-ray.

He paused and leaned in closer. "What's this?" he asked, as if I would have an answer. "This could be something," he continued, as he pointed to a tiny speck of white at the base of my pinky toe. He pointed to a small spot that could have been a piece of dust on the film. "It doesn't look like what I have seen with pet hair, but it definitely could be . . . *something*."

I thought to myself, *That tiny dot is not causing me to drop to the floor when I run,* but I was desperate.

He continued, "We can do exploratory surgery, but there is no guarantee I can get it. There is no guarantee there is even anything there."

I looked at my mom and said, "Let's do it."

My mom sensed my increasing level of distress and scheduled the surgery for the first available appointment the following week. I'd never had surgery and was a little nervous. However, the procedure was simple. Dr. Jones would make a tiny incision on the outside of my foot to see if he could find whatever was causing my pain. I was optimistic.

I couldn't sleep the night before. I anxiously hoped Dr. Jones would find something—anything—to validate my pain. We arrived early, and Dr. Jones walked me back to the operating room. I sat on the table. He put up a curtain, blocking my leg from view, and injected a numbing agent into my right foot. My mom stood by patiently in the waiting room.

He made the incision and grabbed a pair of small forceps from his prep station. I prayed he would find something immediately, but that wasn't the case. I couldn't feel the surgical instruments as they poked and felt their way around my foot, but I could feel the blood as it dripped down to my heel. Dr. Jones reached for another tiny pair of tweezers. Although I couldn't see what he was doing, I could see his arms moving and his head lamp disappear as he leaned down for a closer look. *Please find something . . . please.* The moments ticked by.

"*Got it!*" he shouted as he placed a miniscule, blood-covered shard of glass on the table next to him. "You definitely weren't making this up. You'll be good to go in a few weeks. Let me stitch it up!"

He closed the incision and gave me crutches and a special shoe to wear on my right foot for the next two weeks. He put the tiny sliver of glass into a jar with rubbing alcohol and let me take it home as proof of my malady.

I went straight from the doctor to a track meet to cheer on my teammates and tell them what the doctor had found. To this day, I have no idea how that piece of glass ended up in my foot.

When my mom took me back to have the stitches taken out of my foot, she brought a huge plate of cookies for Dr. Jones. I couldn't thank him enough for his help, for being kind, persistent, and for simply believing me when I had started to doubt myself.

SIX

THE END OF FRESHMAN YEAR TRACK LEFT ME HUNGRY FOR MORE. My season had been shortened by my foot surgery, but I was able to come back and run the four hundred-meter hurdles in a few meets to end the season. Coach thought I could be a successful hurdler, and once the 1–39 stretch of JV basketball ended my sophomore winter sports season, I wanted to run!

My mother was not at all pleased with Coach Thomas' decision to have me jumping over barriers. She thought it was too dangerous. She had seen one too many kids catch their leg on the hurdle, crash to the ground, and come up bruised and battered. After the pain of glass in my foot freshman year, I was ecstatic just to be running. My goal sophomore year was to go from participating to being competitive. Track was primarily a means to keep me in shape for soccer and basketball, but while I was there, I gave it everything I had.

Renewed and energized after our dismal basketball season, my passion for track was elevated. Coach Thomas immediately recognized my intensity and drive. He named me team captain in a sport where I had only limited participation in the year prior. Regardless, Coach saw how hard I worked to get back as a freshman and saw that no one was going to out-work me in practice. Upperclassmen were equally impressed by my work ethic.

In Galway, we had a budget-friendly track surrounding our soccer field. While most other schools in our league had all-weather, rubberized tracks, we trained on stone dust and cinder. I didn't mind. It was the same track where I had outsprinted the competition in the hundred-meter dash, and almost completed an epic comeback in the 1,600-meter relay as a fourth grade field day participant. I had grown up during physical education classes at that track. I welcomed the feel of cinder under my track spikes and viewed it as a home-field advantage when we hosted meets.

I was fairly competitive on the track as a sophomore and junior. I was part of strong relay teams that were able to outrun most schools in our league. In the hurdles, I was first or second at dual meets and always finished in the top six at invitational events.

As junior year ended, I had become one of the top small school runners and had aspirations of breaking sixty seconds in the four-hundred-meter hurdles. By all-state high school standards, sixty seconds for a quarter mile with hurdles was nothing special, but for me, it was a barrier that needed to be broken. To me, it was as significant as Roger Bannister breaking the four-minute mile. I *needed* to get around the track in less than one minute.

Coach Thomas and I had worked out a plan for me to reach my goal in the final meet of the season. I came up just short, running 61.0 at the sectional meet, but proudly earned a patch as the third-place finisher. Coach had been a successful hurdler in high school, so I knew together we would reach my target the following season.

Unfortunately, Coach Thomas didn't return to Galway for my final year of high school. Changes in his job made him unable to commit to coaching. As a result, as a senior, I would have to achieve my goal with a completely new coach, Coach Russo.

Coach Russo was young, new to coaching, and came in with a college swimming background. Most of the team was not interested in his new training style. For the third straight year, I was named team captain and wanted to set an example for the newer athletes. I would do what Coach asked. Much of preseason training focused on core strengthening, abdominal exercises, plyometrics, breathing, and form work. We barely ran at all. I must admit, I was skeptical about what we were doing. We had been a successful track team in the past, but hadn't trained with those methods. Regardless, I stayed the course when some of my teammates did not. Some of the guys I'd been on the team with for four years practiced on their own. They didn't show up to team practice, and instead ran routes and drills we'd done with Coach Thomas. Despite my pleading for them to train with the team, they left, only to join us a week later when we started doing more typical training.

I enjoyed the new exercises Coach Russo brought that focused on flexibility and strength. He made me believe that those key ingredients would help me achieve my goal. As the season progressed, I felt stronger, faster, and more fit than ever.

While I was able to run farther and with better form, I had not yet cracked the sixty-second barrier. I was running 60.2, 60.3, 60.4, and even 60.1 on a regular basis, but could *not* get that last tenth of a second. I was winning most races, but, for the most part, my race wasn't against other athletes—it was against the clock. Less than a minute was all that mattered.

When I wasn't hurdling, I was part of extremely successful relay teams and set school records for the both 4x800 and 4x1 mile relays. The 4x1 mile relay was rarely contested at track meets, and I surprised myself as I clocked a 4:40 mile en route to our team victory. That race gave me a whole new level of confidence for the second half of the season. I had no idea I could sustain my speed that long. Although 4:40 isn't an especially fast mile time, for me, it was faster than I had ever gone and it was in an event I'd never even trained for.

The season progressed and my hurdle times hovered right at sixty. I ran 60.02 at the league meet and finished second. That night, in addition to the relays, Coach decided to put me in the two-mile race (eight laps around the track). I had never tried to run fast for eight consecutive laps. I had no idea how to pace myself, but Coach needed me to score some points for the team. I knew I had to finish in the top six to score so I made sixth place my goal. That would be a difficult feat in a field of twenty-four experienced runners.

I had butterflies in my stomach like never before. I had always started in blocks during the hurdles, or waited for a hand-off in the relays, but this race had a standing start. I tried not to fidget or jump before the gun. The last thing I wanted was a false start!

The starting gun fired, and I took off sprinting, leaving the entire field behind me for two hundred meters until I realized I started way too fast. I tried to reign in my adrenaline and settled in as all the "real" distance runners passed me. With two laps to go, I found myself in twelfth place. I was trying to hang on to the pack for dear life when I heard a voice in my head say, *Run 'til you die!*

I suddenly found one more gear and started to reel in the runners who had passed me. Eleventh, tenth, ninth, eighth . . . I was gaining ground and continued my kick into the final lap. Seventh, sixth was just ahead. Two hundred meters to go. My lungs burned. I noticed the familiar taste of blood in my mouth. My arms and legs felt dead. My heart cranked faster than a hummingbird's wings. I needed one final push . . . I rounded the final turn, going outside to get to sixth place, and sprinted with everything I had for the final one hundred meters. I passed one more career distance runner from our rival school to finish fifth, scoring two points for the Eagles. It was the hardest two points I ever earned!

The following week was the sectional meet, where all the regional schools of similar sizes raced. I would be running the hurdles as well as two relays and a bonus event. Coach had been so impressed by my two-mile performance, he entered me in the steeplechase: three thousand meters of running, with five thirty-six-inch barriers to jump during each lap around the track. One of the barriers also had a twelve-foot water pit to be cleared. The event was only included at sectionals and therefore would be a first for me. I had no opportunity to train for it but Coach thought that between my hurdling and my ability to run distance, I could fill out our three-man roster with the two solid distance runners he had already signed up for the event.

Coach knew my focus was the hurdles. He knew my goal, and that was where he wanted me to put my energy. I ran a preliminary race in the morning in order to qualify for the finals in the afternoon. I ran a solid first race and left nothing to doubt. I had won my heat and was seeded first, with the best time, for the finals.

I lined up in lane three for the hurdle finale. In my preliminary race, I had run a 60.2. I rested and hydrated afterwards and stepped into the starting blocks with nervous, excited energy coursing through my body. As I got down into the starting position, my feet gave me that feeling a snake was right behind me, about to crawl over my toes. Primal fear sank in as I knew this might be my best opportunity to break my sixty-second barrier.

The gun sounded, and my start was flawless. My strides were fluid and carried me to the first hurdle with perfect timing; no stutter stepping, I easily leaped over barrier one. My legs lunged forward as I cleared hurdle two. I didn't know, or care, where my competition was. All I saw was the hurdle in front of me, and I needed my timing and steps to be impeccable. As I came out of the first turn and into the backstretch, I was greeted by a wicked wind. The track we were running on sat at the bottom of a hill, which created a wind tunnel. We had run at that track many times, and I had experienced the wall of wind on the back stretch before. Although it slowed me for an instant, I would not let it deter me. I chopped through the blustery weather, leaned into it, and powered past the halfway mark. I cleared the hurdles effortlessly on the turn and came into the home stretch with intense determination. The Galway faithful were in the bleachers cheering. Many of my teammates' parents were there with stopwatches, timing me. They knew what my goal was, and they wanted to be the first to know if I had succeeded. Dad was standing at the finish line with his watch held high as I churned down the final straightaway.

Lead leg, trail leg, step, smooth! One more hurdle to go. Lead leg, trail leg, step, smooth! Sprint to the finish. Push, push, puuuuush!

I crossed the line with no one in sight on either side. I had won! Sectional champion! Hands on my knees, gasping for air, all I wanted to know was my time. I frantically looked for my father in the crowd. He gave me a quick thumbs-up. I ran over to a clearing in the crowd to look at his watch for myself . . . 59.89! I'd finally done it!

I walked to the end of the track to find my coach. I wanted to talk about the race and the headwind on the back stretch. We visited for a bit before I headed up to the team tent on top of the hill to rehydrate and rest before the relay finals and the steeplechase. Parents were buzzing about the great race and congratulating me on achieving my goal of "sub-sixty." A few teammates' fathers took out stopwatches to show me the times they had clocked: 59.81, 59.85, 59.74. I couldn't wait to see what the official time was. *Maybe it was even faster than my dad had clocked!* Although I still had races to run that day, my eyes started to focus on the state qualifier meet the following week. I had *finally* broken a minute . . . anything was possible. *Could I possibly qualify for the state meet?*

The hurdle results were posted a short time after our team won the 4x800 relay. I sprinted over to check the results. I couldn't believe my eyes! 60.00!

What?! I sought out the officials. They indicated they had three timers for each athlete. They explained how they take the average of the three times, and my average time amongst the officials was 59.95 . . . rules dictated they round to the nearest tenth of a second.

A short time later, I received my sectional champion patch for winning the event. I felt I had achieved my goal, but had I *really?* The newspaper the next day would show my time as 60.0, even though all timers had me under sixty seconds. I rejoined my team, but felt numb and slightly torn as I readied myself for the steeplechase.

SEVEN

As I toed the line for the steeplechase at sectionals, I didn't know what to think. I had won the hurdles, run a personal best, and for all intents and purposes, had finally broken the sixty-second barrier. Everyone there knew my time, but the record book would forever read, "Shaun Evans, Section 2 Champion, 400 IM Hurdles, 60.0." I knew I had the state qualifier meet the following week, and if I had run that fast into the wind, there was no doubt in my mind I could run even faster.

For the moment, I had to focus on running an event I had never run before; seven and a half laps with barriers to clear. I stood next to my two teammates, both with much more distance running experience than I had. They were younger than me, but I was ready to rely on their expertise, and I hoped to keep them close during the race.

Both teammates, Joel and Tommy, were part of our 4x800 relay team and we trained together daily. I could stay with them or outrun them for half a mile, but after that, their endurance would overtake me. They were both strong 1,600 and 3,200-meter runners. While I played soccer in the fall, they both ran cross country, honing their distance running abilities for moments like this. Once again, I was out of my element, and this time on the biggest stage: the sectional final.

I tucked in behind Joel and Tommy after the gun sounded. They were out front, setting the pace. Joel was the favorite to win the race and

Tom was a wild card for us. Coach had told us before the event that if we swept (took first, second, and third), we had a good chance of being crowned team sectional champions. Galway would have never dreamed about something like that in the years I had been running. *Overall team champions?! Wow! No pressure, Coach!*

The odds we'd sweep were long, but it was in the back of our minds and we figured, why not go for it? Joel led through the early laps, Tommy tucked in right behind, and I hung on in third. Joel set a comfortable pace that we could all maintain. There was a group of four or five other runners who were staying close, remaining sure not to lose contact with the three Eagles leading the charge. I figured they were just tucking in, letting us block the wind, and saving their energy for later laps. For the early laps, we cleared the barriers in stride, like we had choreographed it. It was obvious to the crowd we were training buddies. We cruised around the track, not talking but communicating with our breath, our foot slaps, and with the pumping of our arms.

After four and a half laps, we were still leading the way with only two other runners able to hang with Joel's pace. Tommy was starting to fade. I could hear his breathing become more and more labored. Joel started to pull away from the two of us. I shouted to Tommy, "Dig deep!" as I increased my pace and pulled ahead.

Joel quickly put a lot of distance between himself and everyone else, leaving no doubt about who was going to win. I surprised myself by hanging on to second, still feeling somewhat strong after a day of hard racing. *Just two laps to go in my senior year at sectionals.*

Tommy was struggling, but giving it everything he had to hold off the runner behind him in order to maintain third place. Joel gobbled up distance with every stride, clearing each barrier effortlessly. I was in awe as I saw him increase his lead from fifty, to one hundred, to two hundred meters so easily. I pushed with everything I had, leaving every ounce of energy on the track. I finished in a distant second place, proud of Joel, and proud of my run. We hugged and congratulated each other. He wasn't even breathing heavily by the time I came through the finish line. We both turned to see Tommy straining down the homestretch. He was just a few yards from the finish—his face grimacing, his arms and legs seizing—when another runner passed him. He fell across the line in fourth place. First, second, and fourth places for Galway! It was unheard of for a little school like ours to dominate any event like that, let alone in an event we couldn't even host at our home, cinder track. At the time, we had no barriers or water pit to practice the steeplechase, and the only time we saw the event was at sectionals.

We circled the track in a victory lap together, arm in arm, reliving the race as we smiled our way around the oval, lifting our arms in triumph, wondering if the points we scored would be enough for the team championship.

As we came back down the straightaway, we were greeted by cheers from our teammates and parents in the stands, all in awe of the race they had just seen us run. We approached the finish area and saw Coach Russo speaking with the officials, no doubt getting our official times for the results.

We continued to hug and hive five, but as soon as we made eye contact with Coach, we could tell he wasn't sharing in our jubilation. He had a concerned expression as he motioned for Joel to come over to meet with the officials. Tommy and I stood on the infield and wondered what the conversation could possibly be about. We couldn't even fathom a guess, but the discussion only lasted a few seconds when Joel stepped outside of the huddle. We could see the immediate change in his posture. His shoulders dropped as he slowly walked toward us.

He blurted out, "I was disqualified."

What?! He couldn't say any more. He jogged up the hill to gather his bag and head toward the bus. Coach came over to us and explained that the officials told him Joel had stepped over the white line too many times during the race. They said they'd told him to watch his feet on the turns.

I knew I'd stepped over the line a few times during the race. *Did the officials make a mistake?* I rushed over to the officials to ask, "Was it me who should have been disqualified?" They quickly re-huddled, checked their notes, and assured me it was Joel.

I got on the bus and offered Joel the first-place patch I'd been award-ed. He told me to keep it. I asked if he had heard the officials say anything to him during the race. He never heard them give a warning. He was locked in on the task at hand of circling the track and clearing barriers. He had crushed the rest of the field, with me being the closest competitor, half a lap behind. There was no way a few steps over the white line could give Joel the advantage he amassed over the rest of us. A hundred steps over the white line wouldn't have made the difference he won by, but rules were rules, and they wouldn't be bent.

The official results placed me in first and Tommy in third, and awarded sixteen points to Galway in the steeplechase (ten for first, six for third). Had Joel not been disqualified, we would have received twenty-two points (ten, eight for second, and four for fourth). The heartbreaker came when Coach announced the Galway boys track team had finished third overall. Any other year, that would have been an incredible accomplishment for our small team. However, when he read down the scores, we quickly realized it was an extremely tight finish at the top. The first-place team was only four points ahead of us, and second was only one point ahead. Had we gotten first or second place, we would have earned a team patch and plaque to hang in our school, but for third we received nothing. I painstakingly went home and crunched all the numbers. If Joel had officially won the steeplechase, pushing all other finishers back one place, we would have won the entire meet by one point. It was hard for me to swallow that reality, but I knew we had to get ready for state qualifiers the following week, and I wanted an official result below sixty seconds in the hurdles.

In addition to running the hurdles at state qualifiers, as the official sectional champion of the steeplechase, I would have to run in that state qualifier as well. The steeplechase and pentathlon state qualifier events would take place on Tuesday, with the rest of the events taking place two days later at a different venue. My friend Bryan attended the event with me. While I competed in the steeplechase, he would represent our school in the pentathlon.

The qualifying race started and I immediately knew I was *way* out of my league. I ran as hard as I could and pushed myself to my limit. Despite my efforts, I could not hang with the field. After one mile, I had dropped half a lap behind and was completely exhausted. I was running much faster than I had at the sectional meet the weekend prior, but was running against steeplechase specialists. They cleared the sloped water pit with ease, and as I fatigued, I landed in deeper and deeper water each lap. For the final several laps, I was landing in eight inches of water. My shoes were waterlogged. I finished in ninth place with a time thirty seconds faster than my "winning" time at sectionals. I was exhausted when I took off my shoes. I felt hot spots on the balls of my feet from running in drenched sneakers as fast as I could, for nearly two miles. When I took my right sneaker off, I realized the problem was much bigger—about the size of a half dollar, to be exact. As I peeled off my dripping wet track spikes, I noticed an enormous blood blister on the ball of my right foot.

Meanwhile, Bryan and I planned to go immediately from the state qualifiers to our spring soccer game that evening. I played for about five minutes before pulling myself out of the game. I took off my cleats to let my feet breathe a little. The bottom of my right sock was completely saturated in blood. The blister had burst. I sat and watched the rest of the game with my leg elevated and ice on my foot, cheering from the sideline while I thought about the hurdle state qualifier I'd be running in less than forty-eight hours.

I jogged the next day and tried to stretch my tight legs. I had used muscles I didn't know I had in the steeplechase. My hamstrings were sore, my quads were sore, my groin was sore, my arms were sore. I didn't realize how hard I'd pushed myself the night before.

I willed my body to heal on the day of the hurdle state qualifiers. I begged my foot to feel better, but as the gun sounded to start the race, I immediately knew I didn't have it. I qualified for the finals by running the preliminaries in sixty-one seconds, but I knew I didn't have enough left to break sixty. I gave it my all, aiming for a top three finish to qualify me for one more chance to run at the state meet. My body ached, my legs felt like lead, my hamstrings cramped . . . and I finished my high school athletic career in fourth with a time of 60.2.

PART TWO

"Excellence is the gradual result of always striving to do better."

- Pat Riley

EIGHT

As my senior year at Galway came to a close, my focus turned to the transition to college. I graduated tenth out of ninety-six in my class. I had applied to several schools throughout the Northeast with a vision of pursuing a career in physical therapy.

During our junior year of high school, Jeff had broken his right leg during the first soccer game of the season. The break was significant, and he was in a cast up to his hip for several weeks, and then up to his knee for several more. After the healing of the bone was complete, he had to go to physical therapy to strengthen his muscles, regain his motion, and improve his flexibility. It was grueling work for him, so I would often go to his sessions with him for support. While watching his rehabilitation, I decided that a career in health care, specifically physical therapy, was what I wanted.

My first choice of colleges was Ithaca College in Central New York. It was my father's alma mater, not too far from home, and I thought I might have an opportunity to be an athlete there. They also had a highly acclaimed physical therapy (PT) program. For me, the decision was easy. However, despite being a straight-A student; three-sport varsity athlete and captain; vice president of my high school class; participant in band, select choir, and drama clubs; active in my church youth group; and a peer mentor for SADD (Students Against Drunk Driving), my

47

acceptance to Ithaca had contingencies. While I was accepted to Ithaca, I was not accepted into the pre-PT program. I could go to the school, but there was no guarantee I'd be able to pursue a career in PT. I would have to take all the general classes, and then apply again. I'd only have the opportunity to enter the PT program if a spot was available.

My own disappointment aside, my father was dumbfounded. *Did his years at Ithaca not count for anything?* When he was at Ithaca, he had played soccer, was a resident assistant overseeing his dormitory, and had been an active member of the student body. In fact, some of his classmates at Ithaca worked at the university when I applied. We even had lunch with one of them who worked in the admissions department when we went on a college visit. Dad told me I should not feel any pressure to go to Ithaca. I should make my decision based on what I wanted to do. I had visited several other schools, spoken with several other college coaches, and ended up making the decision to go to a small school in Manchester, New Hampshire, called Notre Dame College (NDC). It was the best decision I ever made.

NDC was a small, Catholic college run by the Sisters of the Holy Cross. No one from Galway had ever gone there, which is just one of the reasons why I loved it. The college was started as an all-women's school with a concentration on educating teachers. The school became coed in the 1980s, and in the early 1990s, it became the first accredited school in the state of New Hampshire to offer a physical therapy program. Most of the students who attended Notre Dame College lived in the city or in neighboring communities, so they commuted to school, but there were also about two hundred residents who lived on campus. Coming from New York, I was one of those students. The unique thing about student housing at NDC was the fact that each residence was a converted, private home. Most of the "dorms" were actually old, four-story, Victorian houses with wraparound porches, multiple staircases, and high-peaked rooftops. They had been divided to accommodate twenty to thirty-five students.

NDC immediately felt like home, and my own space. Many of my high school classmates had stayed closer to home or gone to school with friends from Galway, but at Notre Dame, I could make my own way. Although being four hours from home without knowing anyone was intimidating, I was excited about the opportunity.

During the summer after high school graduation, all incoming college freshmen were invited to attend an orientation weekend at NDC. There, we would have the opportunity to stay on campus, get to know our way around, and meet other incoming students. It also provided me with the opportunity to meet my college soccer teammates. I had been given a partial scholarship to play for the varsity men's soccer team at the National Association of Intercollegiate Athletics (NAIA) Division II level. It was small-time college soccer ... but it was still college soccer, and I was thrilled to be able to continue playing.

Some of the first people I was introduced to at NDC were academic advisors, Sister Frances Lessard and Dr. Robert Michael. Sister Frances met with all students during orientation weekend. Dr. Michael was assigned to be my advisor once classes started in the fall. As I reviewed my weekend schedule, the first thing I noticed was the "Sister" before Sr. Frances' name. Although we went to church each Sunday, I was not Catholic. I had grown up in the Methodist church. Obviously, being a Christian, we had much in common with the Catholic Church, but one thing we did not have were nuns, and there were plenty of them at NDC! In my youthful naivety, I didn't know if Sr. Francis would want to discuss religion, or if she'd be praying or saying the rosary when I entered her office. As I turned the corner to Sr. Frances' desk, I fully expected her to be sitting in a traditional habit. Much to my surprise, the nun, who was in her mid-sixties, wore plain clothes and greeted me with a thunderous voice and enormous smile.

"Shaun Evans!?" she boomed.

I nodded.

"Right on time," she said. "I like that! I read through your file and am very impressed. We are glad to have you at Notre Dame."

Sr. Frances made me feel right at home; completely welcome and comfortable. She also delivered some great news. She informed me that since I'd taken calculus in high school for college credit, I wouldn't have to take the math placement exam that was scheduled for the weekend. I would also be exempt from taking math as a prerequisite. Therefore, I could take a lighter course load for my first semester as I adjusted to college life, and the demands of collegiate soccer. That sounded great to me! I would still have to take the English placement exam, but during the math exam time slot, I could take some time to meet with Dr. Michael and get to know him before classes were in session.

I left Sr. Frances's office with my preconceived notions about nuns being thrown out the window. Then, I heard a small voice from behind me. "Hello," it croaked in a tone reminiscent of Yoda.

I turned around and saw no one.

"Hi," the voice squawked. I looked straight down to see a four-foot nun, in full Catholic garb, peering up at me from behind her bifocals.

"Sister Jeannette Plante," she chirped.

"Oh . . . hi . . . Shaun Evans," I stammered, not sure if I should perform the sign of the cross or something.

"Welcome to NDC!" she said as she patted my arm and walked by.

"Thanks." I smiled. I instantly felt like I was in good hands. My mother would be thrilled by all the "mothers" I'd have looking out for me.

I wandered over to the library on that hot July day, and found Dr. Michael's office tucked away in a closet-sized room on the second floor. There were books stacked on shelves, on his desk, and piled on the extra chair he had in his office. *Paradise Lost,* Plato's *The Republic, The Canterbury Tales,* and countless Shakespeare works were some of the titles. A tall, thin man with glowing white hair sat hunched over his desk. He peered through his small, round glasses, and his lips moved quietly as he read an issue of *The New Yorker* magazine that lay open on his desk.

I knocked lightly. His head popped up and he smiled.

"Are you Shaun?" he questioned.

I smiled and nodded.

"Sister Frances told me you would be coming. Have a seat." He hurriedly moved the pile of books from his extra chair. "Sit, please, sit!" he beamed.

I obliged.

"What are you doing here?" he asked.

I was a bit taken aback. He had just told me that Sr. Frances let him know I was coming to see him. I am sure he could sense my confusion by my furrowed brow and quizzical expression.

"I mean, Notre Dame. What are you doing at Notre Dame?" he elaborated.

Oh . . . wow, I thought to myself. I had already been through the college interview and admissions process, but sure, I could talk to him about why I selected NDC and reiterate that I genuinely wanted to be there. I briefly spoke about what I admired about the PT program, the small school atmosphere, being able to play soccer, et cetera.

"That's all fantastic," he responded, "but Shaun, you don't belong here."

Again, he saw my perplexed look. *Am I being asked to leave?*

"Shaun, you scored over 1,400 on your SATs. Straight As all through school. I read your application. Excellent admission essay, all kinds of extracurricular activities, community service . . . you did it all. You could have gone anywhere. How did you end up at a little school in New Hampshire?"

I briefly explained my experience with Ithaca and my desire to start fresh, away from home.

He smiled. "Well, I guess I can understand that. You'll be in my advanced college English class this year," he continued.

I tilted my head to the side. "But I haven't even taken the placement—"

He interrupted, "I know, but after that, you'll be in my advanced college English class this year. Also, Sister Frances said you don't need to take a math prerequisite, so let's look at what you can replace that with for the fall semester. How about getting a psychology class out of the way? With the pre-PT course load, you automatically get a chemistry minor with your biology major, but a few more classes and you could be an English major too!" His smile radiated.

I politely smiled back. English was not my favorite subject in high school. For about ten minutes, I had thought about how nice my fall semester would be with only fifteen credits. Yet, Dr. Michael was encouraging me to fill my schedule and earn a double major!

He stood up and, as he towered over me, shook my hand and told me he looked forward to meeting with me again in August when I returned for soccer training camp. I thanked him for his time and turned to leave his office. He gently put his hand on my shoulders and looked at me with piercing, blue eyes as he said quietly, "I personally selected you to be one of my advisees. I want to make sure you're challenged enough academically."

I looked at the floor, not sure how to respond. I glanced up and managed a soft, "Thanks," with a smile.

He gave my shoulder a pat, said, "See you again soon," and sat back at his desk. He picked up his cop of *The New Yorker,* and continued the article he had been reading when I arrived.

I walked into the hallway and headed to the stairs with one thought on my mind: *Challenged enough?*

NINE

THE SUMMER OF 1996 FLEW BY. I was working five days per week, roofing with my father to earn some extra money for college. After spending ten hours hauling shingles, I trained to get ready for my first collegiate soccer season. We'd go straight from the roof to the school for two hours of pick-up soccer games, get home just before dark, eat dinner, take a shower, and repeat the routine the next day.

The summer was short, as I had to report to preseason soccer camp the second week of August. My parents and I loaded my belongings into the family van and we drove four hours east to Manchester, New Hampshire. Mom and Dad had been through the process several times before with Jen and Jodie. I'd always gone along for the ride in order to wish my sisters well. It felt strange to be the one getting dropped off, sent out into the world as an adult.

I was excited about the opportunities and adventures that college would bring, but was also nervous. I'd never been away from home for longer than a week at summer camp. I also was not a partier . . . at all. I'd never had a drink of alcohol and had no intention of starting due to some influential memories from my childhood.

One weekend, in fifth grade, I slept over at Bryan's house. We'd gone to a high school basketball game the night before, and then went to his house to watch movies. The next morning, my father came to pick me up. When Bryan and I walked out of his bedroom, my father and Bryan's mother, Julie, were solemnly talking. I overheard Bryan's mom say something about, ". . . he needed some stitches in his lower lip and hit his head pretty hard."

I immediately thought that they were talking about the basketball game the night before, because one of our players had cut his lip. I was still half asleep from our late night, but piped in.

"Who? Billy?" I asked, referring to the player who had been hit in the face at the game. Julie looked at my dad and said, "Oh, jeez."

I realized there was no way I could know what they were talking about.

Dad quickly responded, "No, grab your bag, and let's get going. I'll tell you in the truck."

I rushed to grab my stuff and when we got in the truck, he proceeded to tell me that my grandfather (my mother's dad) had been in an accident the night before.

"What happened?" I asked.

"Well, he'd been drinking too much . . . went off the road and hit a tree. Julie was on the ambulance that got the emergency call." (Bryan's parents both served on our town's volunteer ambulance corps.)

I wasn't surprised. I had always known that my grandfather drank too much. He lived across the road from us and frequently sat in his garage, drinking the day away. It wasn't the first accident he'd been in.

"Luckily, no other cars were involved, and no one was really hurt," Dad continued.

I'd always taken the "say no to drugs" campaign very seriously, and never had any interest in drinking. I was still in elementary school when the advisor of our school's Students Against Drunk Driving club recruited me to be a peer leader and mentor. I loved that group. We developed skits and programs to educate fellow students about the dangers of drugs, how to say no, and how to handle peer pressure. It didn't dawn on me until years later that I was selected because of the experiences I had with my grandfather.

Needless to say, by the time I got to college, I was well versed in saying no, avoiding drugs and alcohol, and not getting myself into situations I didn't want to be in.

In college, I wanted to focus on school, soccer, and making some new friends. I was worried that, as someone who didn't party, I might have a hard time with the latter. I didn't know if everyone would want to party, or if there would be others who would be happy hanging out and having a good time without the need for drugs or alcohol.

With my attention on studies and athletics, I had plenty to occupy my time. Soccer training kicked off with three practices a day to get us fit, and to give Coach an opportunity to assess our skills and abilities. There was no time for anything but soccer, eating, and sleeping for my first couple weeks on campus. We hung out as a team, but there was no time for partying. Classes got into full swing, and my college experience was underway. I loved college and quickly made a few close friends in my house, on the soccer team, and in classes.

One day, in mid-September, I was having lunch in the cafeteria when I noticed a sign for student government. I had been vice president of my class in high school. I wondered to myself if I would be able to take it to the college level. I filled out the application for president of the NDC freshman class, made some campaign posters to hang around campus, and worked on a campaign speech. A week later, I would deliver the speech to the entire freshman class, after which the class would vote for the candidate of their choice.

I looked at the other name on the ballot for president. It was the most popular young woman in our class. She lived on campus, and seemed to already know everyone when she arrived. Of course, it didn't hurt her chances that she was beautiful. She was also a pre-PT student and was a person who had attended parties every weekend since school had started. While I had made some close friends, I really didn't know that many people. I knew my chances of getting elected were slim, but I wanted to push the limits of my comfort zone. Several of my good friends gave me the boost and confidence I needed.

I knew I needed to stand out to my classmates when I delivered my campaign speech, so while other candidates wore everyday clothes, I dressed in the nicest clothes I had. I wore an American flag tie, blue blazer, and khaki pants. I can't remember the details of what I said in my speech, but I spoke for about five minutes about who I was; my experience as a class officer in high school; my willingness and ability to listen to concerns and ideas; my propensity for balancing classwork with extracurricular activities; and how I would represent our class to the best of my ability at student senate.

The speech must have resonated with my classmates. When the results were posted the next day, I saw that I had won the election by a comfortable margin! I was excited for the next challenge, which was to try to be a good leader to a large and diverse group of students. I became good friends with the other officers, and we immediately got to work planning our future at NDC. We developed new fundraising ideas, fun events, and community service projects, both on and off campus.

I continued to work hard in the classroom as well. I diligently studied every night, never missed class, and formed study groups with classmates. I'd get projects done when they were assigned rather than when they were due, to give me time to practice and perfect presentations.

I wanted to excel and midterms and finals can be an extremely stressful time in college. There was no doubt I was nervous about the "make or break" tests we'd be taking, but I aimed to thrive on the pressure. I used the anxiety to fuel my studying. I had taken out the maximum amount of student loans, was working to help pay tuition, and knew that my parents were supporting me financially any way they could. Even at the age of eighteen, I looked at my education as a huge investment of time and money, and I was not going to let it go to waste.

My consistent effort paid off when my first, official college grade report was delivered to me, just after Christmas. I slowly opened the envelope and quickly saw 4.0 at the bottom. I'd aced all my finals! That day, my goal became to keep the 4.0 streak going.

I don't remember ever telling anyone about my grades, but when I got back to school for spring semester, all my classmates seemed to know. In fact, after our first round of exams, several people started referring to me as "Mr. Valedictorian", with a resentful tone in their voices. I'd been on campus one semester, and was already a recipient of bitterness and sarcasm, simply because I studied hard. I didn't let it bother me. I had a goal and I was going to go for it.

I met with Dr. Michael regularly during second semester. He was always kind and I sincerely appreciated the mentorship that he offered. Although he was fifty years my senior, I never viewed Dr. Michael as a father (or grandfather) figure. As time passed, he smoothly transitioned from mentor, professor, and advisor to friend, and we both appreciated the uniqueness of our friendship.

Dr. Michael supported my decision to take organic chemistry the summer after my freshman year. Everyone had indicated that it was a difficult course, and I didn't want studying for it to compete with anything else. I finished freshman year with my 4.0 GPA intact. I applied and was accepted to become a resident assistant (RA) as a sophomore, and I asked the dean of students if I could be the summer RA for the students living on campus during the vacation. That would allow me to ease into overseeing a house, but also provide me with the opportunity to live on campus rent-free. I then applied for a job doing summer maintenance on campus, so that I could help pay for my summer class. As a student employee, I assisted in landscaping, painting, and cleaning the residences, as well as any other odd jobs around campus.

With all those pieces falling into place, I was ready to cram thirty-two weeks of organic chemistry into eight weeks of summer school! It was a grueling two months. I had to schedule ten-minute breaks in my day to use the bathroom and eat meals. There was little time for anything but school, work, and overseeing the house, but when the two four-week sessions were complete, my GPA remained at 4.0.

Amidst the chaos of that summer, I also decided to run my first half-marathon as stress relief. I registered to run it at the Empire State Games. The Games were like a mini-Olympics for New York State residents. I had run the four hundred-meter hurdles at the event after my junior and senior years of high school, but without a track to train on, I opted to sign up for the road race instead.

I squeezed in runs whenever I could while organic chemistry was in session and increased my training when the class ended in June. I returned home to train throughout July, and was ready for the race at the end of the month. I had built up to being able to run the 13.1 miles, but didn't know much about pacing, as I had never run a race longer than 3,200 meters.

On race day, I took a minute to reflect on the hectic summer as I stretched and warmed up. Up to that point, I had never put on a bib number. This would be my first road race ever, and it was a half-marathon amongst some of the best distance runners in New York! I looked around at the starting line and felt out of place. These men and women looked like they knew what they were doing. They all had fancy sunglasses, running shorts, and technical, moisture-wicking tank tops. I ran in one of my old running jerseys and a pair of soccer shorts.

The starting pistol fired, and I took off like a shot, leaving the competition behind. I clocked my first mile in 4:35! Adrenaline had carried me . . . and fast. The only other time I could remember running a sub-five-minute mile was on our 4x1 mile relay team in high school. All my soccer training and increased distance running was working.

Most of the course took place on a bike path, shielded from sunlight by the trees and removed from any traffic. It was an out-and-back course; run to the cone 6.55 miles away, turn around, and run back. I cruised along and was the first to approach the cone. At that point, a thought drifted into my mind, *Empire State gold medal, here I come.*

That dream quickly shattered, as my overly ambitious start caught up with me. My legs started cramping at mile seven. A duo of runners approached me from behind. They shouted to me, "Stick with us!"

That was a nice sentiment, and I would have loved to, but every step was an effort that I had not previously experienced while running. Muscles in my legs begged me to stop.

I struggled forward, embarrassed by my inexperience. I ran as hard as my body would allow and finished in one hour, nineteen minutes, just over six-minutes per mile and good enough for fifth place. Although I didn't get a medal, they awarded me a consolation Empire State Games warm-up suit, which I wore with pride.

I found my father after the race. He talked about pacing, and about how distance runners often start a little slower and increase their pace as the race progresses. Dad said that during the race, he had overheard some course volunteers asking, "Who was that young guy with the shaved head? He was flying!" They were referring to me and my first mile, which I ran like I was running a one-mile race. It was the only way I knew how to go in life and on the racecourse—full speed ahead for as long as possible.

"Run 'til you die!" echoed in my mind from years gone by.

TEN

JUNIOR YEAR OF COLLEGE, I was constantly on the go: studying, working on campus, helping to organize events and fundraisers as class president, and being a resident assistant. While I had worked hard and my 4.0 was still intact, junior year presented me with new challenges, both in the classroom and as an RA. Although the house I supervised had only a dozen—mostly freshmen—students, I had my hands full. Early in the school year, I returned home from a weekend trip for soccer to find holes in the walls, the house vending machine destroyed, and garbage and beer bottles everywhere. I spent the next several weeks at our campus community council as they tried to sort out the details of the weekend, and offered disciplinary measures to the offending students.

The needs of the freshmen in my house made it even more challenging for me to stay focused on classwork. Sophomore year, I'd spend late nights studying at the library, but during junior year, I needed to constantly be in the house. I wanted to be a positive presence and role model to the new students. I studied in my room with my door always open to my housemates. I scheduled game and movie nights three evenings per week in order to provide opportunities for them to bond, and over time, we developed a genuine camaraderie. While they may have learned from me or looked at me as their mentor, I learned even more from them and their varied backgrounds and family lives. I had residents from rural Vermont,

Bronx, and Hong Kong; residents who were African American, Hispanic, Chinese; residents who were Christian, Jewish, and atheist. The tiny house of twelve young men was frequently a time bomb waiting to explode with so many different viewpoints, lifestyles, habits, and preferences, all crammed into a small space, on a predominantly Caucasian Catholic campus in New Hampshire. Despite an extremely rough start, it ended as a great experience for us all.

In addition to having an oftentimes challenging house, junior year of college also offered the most rigorous classes. The pre-PT students understood the decisive classes were biochemistry, advanced physics, research statistics, and neuroscience. During our junior year, we had to take all of them. If a student didn't succeed in those classes, their chance of getting into the graduate PT program was gone. Therefore, my third year of college was my final year of undergraduate studies. The following year, I'd transition to physical therapy-based classes. As a result, in addition to all my science classes and core education classes, I had to complete all my elective requirements. My course load included Social and Political Philosophy, Native American Art and Culture, Music History, and a theology requirement. Furthermore, I had committed to earning psychology and English minors, so I was simultaneously taking a class about personality disorders and a Shakespeare class with Dr. Michael.

My brain was on overload. Switching from studying the inner workings of the brain in neuroscience, to studying and memorizing all the women in the Bible for Women in Christian Tradition left my head spinning, but I was more organized and committed than ever. I had to be! My academic goal remained intact and with all the challenges outside the classroom, I wanted to prove to myself that I could maintain it.

I knew it wouldn't be an easy task. Upperclassmen had said it was an enormous achievement if you could pull a B in neuroscience. Biochemistry and physics required endless memorization of formulas, and while I could do the math, neuroscience was something entirely new to me as we delved into the nervous system on microscopic levels. I put everything I had into my studying. I often remained awake long after the rest of my housemates had gone to bed so that I could focus, but still be present for them.

The focus remained ubiquitous. Most people spend their twenty-first birthdays celebrating with friends. I remember receiving a call from the dean of students (and my supervisor as an RA) on the night that I turned twenty-one. She fully expected I'd be headed to a bar to have a legal drink. She called to remind me to be careful and smart as I celebrated. I told her that I'd be sure to be safe, as I stayed in and studied for my biochemistry midterm exam the next day. I hadn't had a sip of alcohol up to that point, and felt there was no need to start. I was only two months away from completing a three-year streak with a perfect GPA.

Perhaps the greatest challenge, among my classes that year, was my philosophy class. Everyone knew that the professor was the most difficult grader at NDC. Dr. Michael had warned me that if I was serious about graduating with a 4.0, my essays, responses, and work would have to be pristine. There would be no wiggle room or grade inflation in philosophy. As a result, I had Dr. Michael read every single homework assignment before I handed them in. He never offered much more than a punctuation correction, but for that I was grateful. Although going into the final exam I had an A average, I knew that the final counted for such a high percentage of our grade that I would have to earn an A to maintain it.

Philosophy was my very last final before the end of the year. We had three hours scheduled to take the essay-based exam. My handwriting wasn't the best and, despite Mrs. Hayes' best efforts, I never learned to hold a pen or pencil correctly. I made sure to write as legibly as possible. My hand cramped terribly. As much as I wanted the test to end, I refused to shortcut my answers. After two hours, I was the only one left in the classroom, still feverishly writing my responses, including everything I could possibly remember about Machiavelli, Stalin, and Mao Tse-tung. I finished writing, reread my answers, and made edits. I used every minute of those three hours and I left feeling I'd done my best.

Since I stayed on campus each summer to work summer maintenance, I was there to check my school mailbox when the graded final exam was returned. I anxiously awaited the result and checked my mailbox daily after work. Finally, after two weeks, the sealed envelope arrived, and I couldn't bring myself to look inside. I went to Dr. Michael's office to open it with him. As I did, the first thing I noticed was there was no grade at the top. I hurriedly flipped through the pages I had meticulously written. No marks, no corrections, no suggestions . . . nothing. *Did the professor forget to grade it?*

I handed it to Dr. Michael. He looked it over, flipped each page, and skimmed the content, smiling as he went. He got to the last page, leaned in close, and beamed. He handed it back and pointed to a tiny letter and two-word phrase, penned in blue ink, at the conclusion of my essay.

It simply stated, in miniscule letters, "A. Well done."

ELEVEN

SENIOR YEAR AT COLLEGE WAS EXCELLENT. I was fully enthralled in my physical therapy classes and loved to be able to think about the practical application of all the studying I'd done. It was my final soccer season and after being a four-year starter, I was named to the all-conference team. I'd been playing well and though my skills weren't as good as some of my teammates, I was a solid defender and my ability to run made me valuable.

One Thursday, we traveled to Maine for an afternoon game. I was savoring every contest, knowing my competitive soccer career would soon be over. I gave everything I had in every game, not wanting to have any regrets when the season ended. That particular day was sunny and cool. Fluffy clouds scattered the sky, and colorful foliage adorned the trees surrounding the field. It was a beautiful autumn afternoon—perfect for playing soccer.

About twenty-five minutes into the game, we had a 1–0 lead, but the other team was pressuring us. As a defender, my role was to ensure the other team didn't score. We prided ourselves on the number of shutouts we attained, knowing if the other team didn't score, we couldn't lose.

A pass came from the far side of the field, in the air. An opposing player and I went up for the ball at the same time. As I went up to clear the ball with my head, he also went up, and our skulls collided. I fell to the ground and my head slammed against the turf. I quickly hopped up, slightly dazed, and had a difficult time determining which way to run. I saw that our team had the ball and I sprinted up the field. A few breaths later, as the other team gained possession, I suddenly realized I had no idea where I was. I wandered for a few steps and then sat down in our goal box. My teammates came over and asked what was going on. Per their recollection, the conversation went like this:

"Shaun, you alright?" Tony put his hand on my shoulder.

"Yeah, I think so . . . Are we winning?"

He could see in my eyes that something was off. "Yeah, do you know who we are playing?"

"No."

"Would it help if I told you we are in Maine?" he questioned.

"Maine . . . Maine . . . " I trailed off and Tony quickly signaled for Coach, who helped me to the sideline.

For the next twenty minutes, I asked what the score was every thirty seconds. An ambulance was called. I ended up in a nearby hospital, had a CT scan, and was diagnosed with a concussion and amnesia. One coach stayed with me until I could be released. After two hours, my memory started to return. The very first thing that popped into my mind was something we were reviewing in anatomy. I couldn't remember my girlfriend's name. I couldn't remember my phone number or address, but when the fogginess lifted, the first thing I recalled was the brachial plexus nerve complex I had been diligently studying. I had a vivid picture of it in my brain. I told the doctor who had been monitoring me, and he roared with laughter. He started asking me some questions, and soon felt comfortable sending me back to New Hampshire, as long as I had someone to watch over me that night.

I called my parents to tell them what happened, and by the time Coach and I got back to campus, they had coordinated for me to spend the night at Dr. Michael's house. He and his wife took me in without hesitation, made a bed for me, and made me feel perfectly at home. Dr. Michael woke me up every hour, per the concussion protocol prescribed by the doctor. I was then required to take a few days off from soccer before following up with a neurologist. The doctor at the hospital said he could give me a note to stay out of class for a week, if I wanted. He expressed I might feel dizzy, nauseous, and "hazy" for a while. I didn't take him up on the offer. I had an anatomy test to take the next day, and I didn't want to prolong the anticipation after all the studying I'd done!

As soccer season ended, I kept up with running because it helped me stay active, gave me time to think, and provided a break from books. There was a lot to think about and plan as the semester progressed. Each fall semester, our class held a fundraiser fruit sale. It had become popular throughout Manchester. We took orders at community events, church services, from family members, and on campus. We sold hundreds of boxes, raising money to donate to our sister school in Cap Haitian, Haiti, where several of our professors, including Dr. Michael, taught during the summers. We knew the few thousand dollars we sent down each year helped countless students receive a better education.

As class president, organizing the fundraiser was my responsibility and I was honored to do it. One of my tasks was to coordinate delivery of the fruit to campus. Due to the large size of the order, the fruit was delivered to our campus in a large tractor trailer. The delivery was made at the end of the semester, during finals, which allowed everyone to have fresh fruit for the holidays. I treasured the event; unloading the truck, sorting the fruit, labeling it, organizing it, and making calls to let everyone know it had arrived. It was fun for me and whoever helped. It was also a welcome reminder that the end of the semester was near.

When the fruit was delivered senior year, I had scheduled a time to meet the truck in front of the school. The driver was right on time, which was good because I had a kinesiology lab practical that afternoon. I ran to the street to talk to him and inform him where to unload. He was parked in the middle of Elm Street, so I didn't want him blocking traffic for long. I jumped up on his running board, spoke to him through his window, and directed him to the parking lot.

I hopped off the truck and sprinted toward the sidewalk so the driver could park.

Wham!

As I stepped in front of the truck, I was blindsided by a lady who was passing on the right. Since I was sprinting, both my legs were airborne when I took the impact of the Buick. As the car hit my right knee at forty miles per hour, I was flipped upside down. My head and shoulder smashed into the windshield and I toppled over the vehicle. I felt as if I was moving in slow motion. I lifted both arms to cover my head, not knowing what was happening, why I was in the air, or when, how, or where I was going to land. I crashed to the pavement headfirst, with my arms and top of my head taking most of the impact.

Screech!

She slammed on her brakes and stopped a few feet down the road.

I leapt up and dashed to the sidewalk, fearful I'd be hit by another vehicle. I immediately sat down on the cold concrete and felt my torso, arms, and legs. I fully expected to find bones protruding or blood spurting. Nothing. *Did that really just happen?*

I looked up at the truck driver, who stared back at me with his mouth agape and eyes wide. I stood up; nothing hurt. Behind me, the chief of campus security was running in my direction, shouting for someone to call 911. He quickly got to my side, put a coat around me, and told me to sit back down. People were convening from all directions. Lisa, the dean of students, was instantly there. She always seemed to be where she was needed. She was a huge Red Sox fan, and I was wearing my Yankee sweatshirt. She lightened the tension when she joked, "Good thing you didn't ruin your sweatshirt."

I laughed, still in disbelief.

The ambulance arrived a minute later. Paramedics checked my vital signs and looked at all my extremities to make sure I was moving okay. Still, nothing hurt. They asked if I wanted to go to the hospital, and all I could think about was my kinesiology lab practical at one o'clock that afternoon. I looked at my watch. It was noon.

"No, I am okay," I said.

They had me sign some papers to confirm I refused treatment. By then, the police had arrived and were questioning the truck driver and the woman who hit me. I could see she was extremely upset. Her body was visibly shaking, and she was frantically puffing on a cigarette. I walked over to her and told her I was all right. "Don't worry about it, I have a test to take. I'll be fine," I said as I gave her a hug.

I walked back to the group that had gathered. Lisa said she would take care of getting the fruit unloaded. I thanked her, gave her a hug, and told her I'd talk to her later. She encouraged me to go to the hospital to get examined, but I assured her I was okay.

I went back to my campus house, and the whole ordeal replayed in my mind. It all started to sink in. Shock and adrenaline passed and my body ached. I went back to my room to rest for a few minutes before my test. I decided to take a shower to warm up. I took off my jeans and realized they had holes in them from the impact of the car. My knee was starting to bruise. I took off my sweatshirt and noticed several areas of road rash on my arms, hands, and elbows. I climbed into the shower and instantaneously had an emotional release. Tears started flowing, and I sobbed. I felt like I had narrowly avoided death and was lucky to be alive. I stood in the shower until the tears washed away. I got dressed and walked across the street for my kinesiology final.

The professor overseeing the lab practical was a doctor. Of course, word had spread about my accident. By then, I was limping as the pain set in from head to toe. He could tell I was upset. He had me lay on the table as he examined me. He checked internal organs by feeling my abdomen, and checked for signs of concussion and neck injury. He said I was stable enough to take the test if I wanted, but he agreed that I should get examined at the hospital. I told him I'd complete the lab practical and then go to the hospital. He obliged and let me perform my test. The months of studying throughout the semester kicked in, and I earned a perfect score.

A classmate then took me to the hospital, where I underwent multiple X-rays and scans. Every test came back negative. I had no serious injuries. Everyone who witnessed the accident couldn't believe I walked away, let alone did so without any broken bones. I knew I was lucky that day. My kinesiology training told me that if my legs had been on the ground when I was struck by the car, the result would have been much different. The fact I was airborne in mid-stride may have saved me.

As the story spread and became more and more embellished, people around campus started calling me Superman. I'd shrug it off and smile, but inside I thought about how I'd been crying in the shower, feeling lucky to be alive.

TWELVE

SENIOR YEAR CULMINATED WITH A BLUR of events commemorating the passage of our college careers. As class president, I was invited to address the graduating class at commencement. In addition, after four years of grueling work, studying, and commitment to my goal, I was named valedictorian. My 4.0 GPA was still intact. I was tremendously honored, proud, and humbled to be the first student to deliver a speech as both valedictorian and class president.

My words that day centered on what our class had done to help others. I viewed all the community service we completed, all the donations we made to Haiti, and our commitment to helping others as our biggest accomplishments. I encouraged my classmates to take that service-oriented outlook with them after graduation, with the goal of letting the light of Notre Dame College shine on others, wherever they went. I then turned attention to the people who had supported us. I recognized faculty, staff, advisors, friends, and family for all the guidance, encouragement, and boosts they provided. The speech was well received by those in attendance, and I was glad I had reviewed it with Dr. Michael before the ceremony.

Even though my undergraduate phase of college was complete, being a graduate student in the physical therapy program allowed me the opportunity to spend two more years on campus. I could soak in student life for a bit longer. I continued to dedicate myself to academics. I also picked up jobs working at a local physical therapy clinic as an aide, and helping Dr. Michael teach English as a second language to refugees at the Manchester Resource Center. Both jobs kept me busy, but were a welcome respite from the demands of the classroom.

The true highlight of my time in graduate school, though, was meeting my eventual wife, Nichole. She was an undergraduate student, coming in as a freshman when I was in my fifth year of college. She was friends with my girlfriend at the time, and during Nichole's first day of orientation, she sprained her ankle. Knowing I was studying physical therapy, my girlfriend asked me to look at it, which I attempted to do, but Nichole wouldn't take off her shoes to let me get a closer look. She claimed her broken-in Vans were too stinky. We all laughed, and I gave her an ice pack for the swelling.

During the year, we hung out occasionally, but with busy schedules, Nichole having a boyfriend, and me having a girlfriend, we were not much more than acquaintances. Fortunately, Nichole and I were both part of a campus ministry group that went on a service trip, just before Christmas, to serve at St. Francis Inn, a soup kitchen in Philadelphia. I'd been on the trip annually as an undergrad, and was glad that the dean of students, Lisa, allowed me to continue to participate as a graduate student. The service trip provided clarity after an arduous semester and right before the holidays. It served as a reminder of the true meaning and spirit of giving. While it was rewarding to help and give to others, I always knew that the viewpoint the trip provided me with was the real gift. I recognized on those annual visits that people are on this planet to help others. Through that service, I found a sense of purpose, compassion, and joy that I hadn't felt before.

It was Nichole's first trip with us and since she knew me a little, I was happy to sit next to her on the van ride from New Hampshire to Pennsylvania. After a demanding semester, we finally had a chance to visit. While the other students slept to pass the six-hour drive, we shared stories. We arrived at the soup kitchen after driving through parts of the city that were covered with trash and graffiti. Broken glass and drug needles lined the streets and sidewalks. People without homes looked for places they could stay warm. The main road was symbolically hidden from the sun by the elevated train tracks that ran above. Nichole and I exited the van and entered the main building just in time to help serve and prepare breakfast. We traveled through the night to avoid traffic, so upon arrival, it was time to get right to work. Despite the lack of sleep, we worked with enthusiasm.

Nichole and I served side by side. We met some of the guests and learned their stories. People with AIDS, drug addicts, alcoholics, prostitutes living and working on the streets, and families fallen on hard times were just some of the people we helped. No one was turned away. As long as they weren't actively doing or selling drugs or being violent, they were welcome at St. Francis. We were there to help them get a hot meal, find warm clothes, and celebrate Christmas.

We worked all day, sorting donations, arranging clothes and toys, serving meals, and delivering furniture or food throughout the Kensington area of Philadelphia. After serving, we reflected on our day as we sat around the table of the guest house where we were staying. It was emotionally and physically exhausting, yet incredibly fulfilling. We sat together and sometimes cried about the stories we'd heard, or about the things we'd witnessed.

Each day, we would thrive on each other's energy, and I loved the fact that Nichole completed every menial, and sometimes disgusting, task with a smile. For example, no one really wanted to clean the public bathrooms, but I was always willing to volunteer. I was there to do whatever they needed. When asked who would clean bathrooms the first night, Nichole immediately volunteered as well. Together, we scrubbed toilets and cleaned urine and fecal matter from the floor, walls, and ceiling! Rubber gloves up to our elbows and smiles on our faces, we laughed and reveled in how blessed we truly were.

The days went by quickly, and soon we were on our way back to New Hampshire, back to our cushy lives, and back to getting ready for Christmas with our families. We were tired on the ride home, and after talking for an hour, Nichole dozed off with her head resting on my shoulder.

When we arrived back to campus, Nichole and I realized we hadn't purchased Christmas gifts for our significant others. I walked her to her residence in the December darkness, and we made plans to get together to go shopping at the mall the next day. After being surrounded by poverty and despair for a week, neither of us was excited about going out and buying material things, but, together, we went and helped each other pick gifts. After the holiday break, Nichole and I saw each other infrequently. We both had busy class schedules and were preoccupied with our own respective love lives.

At the end of my fifth year, I was set to return to New York for the first time since leaving for college. I had scheduled an extra clinical affiliation during the summer. I had a strong interest in pediatric PT and was able to find a clinic near home that focused on pediatric therapy. My second affiliation of the summer centered on sports rehabilitation. It was a stimulating time in my life, but also exceptionally stressful. I had confidence in my therapy skills in the lab setting at school, but I questioned how those skills would translate to real patients, as opposed to my lab partners.

I'd be in New York with my parents and sisters, which would be good, but I'd be away from the place I had called home for five years, and a girlfriend I'd been dating for three years. It would be a long summer, but I believed our relationship would endure.

My schedule was chaotic. I worked at the pediatric clinic during the day, and then bussed tables at a local restaurant at night. Despite being overwhelmed with obligations and clinical paperwork, I wrote my girlfriend letters every day and sent packages to let her know I was thinking of her. I believed that although I couldn't be there physically, by writing, we'd still feel connected. As the weeks went by, I found that any time we talked on the phone, our conversations were fleeting. She seemed to have other places she wanted to be. While I wrote her regularly, I never received letters back. It was a huge change. Up to that point, she had been equally committed to our relationship. After three weeks of feeling like she wasn't invested, I asked her what was going on . . . I received silence. I asked if she wanted to end our relationship. It seemed she was waiting for me to suggest the idea. She said she thought it best if we take a break.

I was crushed. I was at a point in my life where I was thinking about life beyond college. Things like getting married, having a family, and settling down somewhere had started to enter my mind. Although she and I were not at that point yet, I felt there was potential. We had been together for three years. I was gone for three weeks, and she'd had enough.

I couldn't eat, couldn't sleep, and constantly wondered what I did wrong. To cope, I put all my focus on my clinical practice. I worked all day, worked at the restaurant at night, and read therapy research articles in my free time. Part of my master's thesis was to develop a case study and research related diagnoses, therapeutic interventions, and techniques. I would then present my findings to classmates and a college research board. My purpose every day became to find my case study and make it the best research thesis possible.

Research wasn't enough. I couldn't get my mind off my failed relationship. I felt as though the one consistent thing in my life had changed. With all the unknowns of the upcoming year—like finding a job and deciding where to go after college—I needed something to look forward to. I needed a constant to turn to, outside of my studies, outside of my family, outside of my work. I needed to focus on something *I* wanted.

It was then that I turned back to running and I went all in. I hadn't run a race since the half marathon in 1997. It was 2001, and the only running I'd done was training for soccer and then only occasional running to clear my head. In the months prior to my clinical rotations, I had probably run only a handful of times. Once clinic work started, I hadn't found a moment to do any exercise.

But I was lost, floundering, and needed *something*. I needed a goal outside of school. I wasn't sleeping much anyway, so I started running early in the morning. Then, I jogged during the hour between my time at the clinic and work at the restaurant. I ran whenever I could find a moment, and decided to set my sights big. I signed up for my first marathon.

THIRTEEN

I RETURNED TO COLLEGE IN LATE AUGUST FOR MY FINAL YEAR of graduate school. My fall semester would be spent doing my final clinical affiliations at local hospitals, while also spending any free moments training for my first 26.2-mile race that November. I selected a fall race because I wanted enough time to train, but didn't want to wait until the following spring. September and October would also be less busy, as my final affiliation didn't begin until Halloween. I chose the Philadelphia Marathon; a city I was familiar with from our trips to St. Francis, and a race that had positive reviews from previous participants.

Late August was a fabulous time to train in New Hampshire, as the weather transitioned to autumn. The changing season also meant new students were arriving on campus, and as a graduate assistant, I served on the orientation committee for incoming freshmen. It was during orientation that Nichole and I reunited after my challenging summer in New York. She'd spent her summer working at a YMCA camp and was glad to be back at school, excited to get much-needed respite from the pre-adolescent campers.

Nichole and I boarded a school van together, as we took the new students to partake in team building activities off campus. On the drive, we discussed our summers. She and her boyfriend had also parted ways in June. Neither of us were interested in pursuing a relationship, but we both needed a friend. We hung out a few times in August, amongst the frenzy of orientation, before I went home for Labor Day weekend to celebrate my mother's fiftieth birthday. It was good for me to be home for a few days, but it was a quick trip and I was back on campus after the holiday, with the semester in full swing.

When I arrived at NDC, I had more time to train for the race. While working on my research, I chose to work less hours at my job as a physical therapy aide. I knew that I needed to increase my long-run mileage. I was comfortable running distances of ten or eleven miles during the summer, but knew I'd need to double that distance and then survive another few miles to successfully complete a marathon.

I used the Saturday morning after Labor Day to test my endurance. While the rest of the house slept in, to then roll out of bed at noon to make it to brunch, I was on the road at sunrise, logging a sixteen-miler. I set out at an optimistic pace. In the back of my mind, I had a goal of qualifying for the Boston Marathon. To do that, I'd need to run a three-hour, ten-minute marathon (about 7:15 per mile) in Philadelphia. I knew I could run that pace, but could I sustain it for 26.2 miles?

It was not an easy task for me to escalate my mileage to sixteen. I struggled with staying hydrated. I struggled with pacing. I limped home. I was dehydrated, barely able to walk, and then I collapsed into bed, wondering how I would ever run ten miles *farther* than I'd run that day. I hobbled around for the next two days.

I was *still* sore when I woke up on Tuesday. I had slept in after staying up late to work on my research. I groggily turned on the morning news to see a live broadcast from New York City. Smoke was pouring out of the World Trade Center. The broadcasters speculated about an errant plane that flew off course. I was still watching when a second plane hit the adjacent tower. It quickly became evident that the first collision was not an accident, and that our country was being attacked.

I didn't know what to do. Like many other Americans that day, I felt helpless. I called my mother and we watched the broadcast, not believing what was unfolding before our eyes. We were on the phone as more hijacked planes crashed into the Pentagon and in Pennsylvania. We didn't say much. We just watched with the phones held to our ears. After I hung up, I didn't know where to go. *Will more planes crash? What other places are being targeted? Are my friends in New York City okay?*

I couldn't get ahold of friends who lived in Manhattan, which further increased my stress level. I knew that most of my local friends were in class and unavailable. I couldn't sit in my room and watch the television coverage all morning. I decided to go for a run. My legs ached from my long Saturday run, but adrenaline from stress and fear coursed through me. I patriotically threw on bright red shorts, a white T-shirt, and navy blue running sneakers, then I bolted out the door, headed for the hills. My legs loosened quickly. I ran without direction or a plan. I simply ran: by the river, through the city blocks, past parks, and to a nearby ski mountain. I ran to the summit, trying to gain perspective. From the top, I could see most of the city. I turned from one side to the other, wondering what was going on in the houses, schools, hospitals, and streets below. *What's everyone thinking about the events this morning?* I sat and listened to my breath for several minutes. When I realized I wasn't going to find any resolution or answer to why our nation was under siege, I stood up, inhaled deeply, and sprinted down the hill, back to my room.

When I arrived, my phone was ringing. I could hear it from the hall outside my door. I was exhausted, the adrenaline had worn off, but when I heard the phone ringing, I got another jolt. *Will it be bad news on the other end? What have I missed while I was running?*

I snatched the phone and uttered a rushed, "Hello?!"

"Oh, thank god you're okay!" I immediately recognized Nichole's sweet voice, the concern evident in her words. She explained that she had been trying to call and was worried when I hadn't answered earlier. She knew that I'd gone home to New York the weekend before, but didn't know I'd made it back to New Hampshire. She wasn't sure where I lived in New York, and when she heard about the attacks, she immediately thought of me. I was glad to hear from her.

Everyone on campus was rattled. As details emerged, we found out the flights had originated from Boston, just forty-five minutes south of our school. I invited Nichole to come over, since neither of us wanted to sit in our rooms alone all afternoon. When she got to my house, she gave me a big hug—a hug I will never forget. It was a hug of pure concern, caring, and joy that I was safe. As she embraced me, everything felt a little better. We walked around the city, sat by the Merrimack River, and talked. Why did the attacks happen? What could we do? What would happen next? Of course, there were no answers, and the conversation drifted to getting to know each other; like where I lived in New York, how I grew up on a farm far removed from the city, and how Nichole had lost her father at age sixteen. As the youngest of four sisters, she'd spent the past few years moving around Manchester with her mother. I learned the anniversary of her father's passing was a few days away. To honor him, she and her sisters planned to get tattoos later that week. As we talked, we decided to make plans to get together that weekend to go bowling and watch some movies. There was no hint or suggestion from either of us at romantic interest. We looked at each other as friends, and that was what we needed.

As the week went by, we hung out every day before our scheduled date. She took me to a place at an old railroad bridge where she liked to think. We walked around campus. We had lunch together in the cafeteria. From an outsider's perspective, I am sure we looked like more than friends, but neither of us saw it happening.

That Saturday, Nichole and her sisters got their tattoos before she came over for our bowling date. She apologized for being later than she'd expected, but I was simply happy to see her. At the bowling alley, Nichole slipped and fell as she approached the lane for her first turn. She shyly looked up, completely embarrassed. I offered a helping hand and we laughed. As she stood up, she said, "I fall . . . a lot. Thanks!" We bowled and joked about how bad we both were. Later, we went back to my room to watch movies. She gave me another perfect hug when we said goodnight, and we made plans to get together again soon.

I started to wonder if I'd been fooling myself into thinking we were just friends. *Does she feel the same way?* I loved spending every free minute with Nichole, and every time my phone rang, I hoped it was her. I noticed I didn't want to let go when we hugged. *Does she squeeze everyone she hugs so tightly?*

The next time we saw each other, I knew I wasn't alone in my feelings when I reached to hold her hand and she didn't pull away. I then leaned in to give her a kiss, and she kissed me back. We declared our feelings for each other and were both ecstatic that our friendship had evolved into more.

A week later, I asked Nichole if she wanted to join me at a Yankees game, since games had then resumed following 9/11. She was excited to go to New York for the weekend. First, we went to my parents' house and I took Nichole on a walk around the forty acres I called home. I showed her the chickens, the barns, the treehouse, the sledding hill, and the pond where Jeff and I made ziplines. After living in or near a large city all her life, Nichole loved the fresh air, the stars at night, and said she felt right at home. We had a great weekend, enjoyed the game, and celebrated the patriotism on display in New York City.

Nichole had the opportunity to meet a few of my family members that weekend. She and my sister Jen got along well, and my parents were warm and welcoming. Conversely, I hadn't met any of Nichole's family. On our late evening drive back to college, I asked her if she thought her father would have liked me. At the exact moment I asked the question, the headlights of my car went out. I quickly pulled over in the pitch-black darkness. Before I could get out of the car, the lights were working again. We looked at each other and couldn't help but laugh.

After a brief pause, she said with a smile, "He was a *huge* Red Sox fan!"

FOURTEEN

IN OCTOBER, MY RUNNING INTENSITY INCREASED. I became smarter about hydration and nutrition. After long days of research, working, and running, I spent the last few minutes each day studying the marathon training program I'd been following. I had built my long run up to a solid twenty miles by the end of the month, and with just three weeks until race day, I felt ready. I informed Nichole and my family that my goal was to meet the Boston Marathon qualifying standard. After all my training runs, I felt like it was actually possible. I ran my final twenty-mile run in two hours and twenty minutes. All I would have to do to qualify was run that pace and then run the final 6.2 miles in fifty minutes. To me, that seemed doable; however, I knew those last few miles would be the unknown. I'd heard about runners "hitting a wall" late in a marathon. I had experienced some of that exhaustion and fatigue in some of my training runs. My hope was that my body was ready. I tried to be smart as I backed off my training in the final few weeks in order to fuel, hydrate, stay loose, and save energy for race day.

Nichole and her mother drove me to the airport to catch my flight to Philadelphia Friday night. Airport security had changed quite a bit after the terrorist attacks in September, and I was naturally nervous. I was cautious about flying, but it would be much faster, and I wouldn't have to worry about driving back after the marathon.

The flight was uneventful and quick. My mother and sisters had driven down to meet me at the airport. We spent Friday and Saturday at a friend's house and went to the race expo. I felt overwhelmed by all the high-tech running gear: from sunglasses to socks, shorts, and moisture-wicking tops. I had never seen so much running merchandise or so many runners in one place.

I hadn't run a race since the half-marathon four years earlier, and this was *much* bigger. This race included *thousands* of runners. I felt underprepared as I saw the other runners' gear. My mother sensed my uneasiness and purchased some running sunglasses and new shorts for me. Race morning was forecasted to be cool, so she also bought a bright, orange winter hat so family and friends would be able to spot me in the crowd of runners.

Full of anticipation, I didn't sleep much the night before the race. I had spoken with Nichole briefly. I told her I'd be thinking of her during the race and wished she could be there. She let me know she'd be thinking of me and cheering from afar. She wished me luck, and we said good night. The last thing I did before I went to bed that night was write Nichole's initials, "NDW," on my shoelaces, so I could look at them whenever I needed a little pick-me-up over the course of 26.2 miles.

When I awoke early on Sunday, November 18, 2001, the morning was chilly, and the stars were still shining. The race started at seven o'clock, and we had a forty-minute drive from our friend's house to the Philadelphia Art Museum where the race would begin. While my mom, sisters, and our friends got ready, I stepped outside to breathe in the morning air, focusing on the goal at hand: qualifying for Boston. I looked up at the sky and saw a shooting star, just as dawn was breaking. *Is it a sign?* I felt confident as I sat in the car as we drove into Philly. We found a parking spot just across the Schuylkill River and began our walk to the excitement of the starting line.

As we crossed the bridge, there was a flurry of activity. There were police cars and officers, an ambulance, and other emergency personnel. I thought that perhaps in the wake of 9/11, they were honoring first responders prior to the race.

As we got closer, I realized that wasn't the case. Just below the bridge, on that cool November morning, the body of a man had been found floating in the river. Word was quickly traveling through the crowd that it was a homeless man, who had apparently drowned overnight. My thoughts immediately turned to the guests I had met at St. Francis. *Could it be a man I met at the soup kitchen? Had I broken bread, visited with, and maybe even learned the story of this unknown man?*

I made my way to the start line with a heavy heart. I was about to begin a race with over four thousand runners, while that man had died alone. I tried to regain my focus. We had arrived early enough to allow me to jog, stretch, and concentrate on the goal at hand. What had started as "needing something to look forward to" a few months prior, had turned into a full-fledged attempt to qualify for Boston—in my very first marathon. I knew I'd trained diligently, my body was ready, and I'd give it everything I had.

I lined up at the start and nosed my way up to the front. When the starting gun fired, I took off at a near sprint to avoid tangling with other runners. I felt comfortable. I felt strong. My breathing was good, my legs felt loose, and my stride was easy. I was in cruise control. I chugged along for several miles. I glanced at my sneakers periodically to catch a glimpse of NDW on my laces, knowing that Nichole was thinking of me. I blew her a kiss as each mile marker passed.

By the time I got to mile ten, I looked around to realize I was surrounded by men with single-digit bib numbers, denoting their elite-runner status. I also noticed they were only wearing running singlets and really short shorts. I was wearing running tights with shorts over the top, two shirts, a hat, gloves, and a bib number with four digits.

Perhaps I started too fast . . . again! We were clipping along at a sub-six-minute pace. We had run the first ten miles in less than an hour. It felt fast, but not uncomfortable. I had trained hard and put in a lot of six-minute miles. I figured I could keep cruising.

As the miles passed, I quickly determined I was not able to keep up with them. My mile times increased. I ran some 6:20s, then 6:40s. *No big deal*, I thought. *I have time to spare and am still well under Boston pace.*

I backed off, trying to run smarter, but soon after, the hammer came crashing down in the form of the "wall" I'd heard so much about. At mile eighteen, my legs cramped. I focused on my breathing, hydrating, and putting one foot in front of the other. I desperately tried to keep running, but by mile twenty I was walking . . . barely. Each step was an effort as my muscles resisted what my mind asked them to do. By mile twenty-one, the leg cramps permeated through every muscle from the bottom of my feet to my hips. When I stepped forward, my thigh would seize. When I pushed off, my hamstrings and hip flexors stiffened.

I could not run a single step. I hobbled for six miles, constantly looking at my watch. As the seconds ticked by, my hopes of a Boston qualifying time slipped away. I willed myself forward, and as I approached the finish line, I broke into a jog for the last quarter mile, being sure to run across the finish line.

My finishing time was three hours and fourteen minutes—four minutes shy of qualifying. I knew that had I run smarter, not started so fast, and paced myself, I would have finished much better, with not nearly as much pain, and most likely a faster time. *I walked six miles and had been so close.*

As I crossed the finish line and reunited with my family, the first person I saw was . . . Nichole?! *What? Was I delirious?* My face was caked with salt from sweating. My eyes burned from the combination of sweat and sunscreen that had been dripping in them all day. It couldn't be Nichole . . . but as I got closer, she started to run toward me. She wrapped her arms around me, despite my sweat-soaked running clothes, and said, "I tried to get here sooner. I wanted to see you before the race! But I made it for the finish!"

She and her friends had come down on Friday. When we talked the night before the race, she had actually called from her friend's house, not wanting to let on that she was already nearby. It was a great surprise, and I needed her hug. I was happy I finished my first marathon, but felt so close to a much bigger goal. I understood that many people would run marathons for years before qualifying for Boston, if they were ever able to qualify at all. I had trained, given it my all, and had been so close. Although I was somewhat disappointed, I knew right away the Philadelphia Marathon in 2001 would not be my last. At the same time, my legs were in no rush to run again anytime soon.

I had lunch with Nichole before saying goodbye, as she left for the six-hour drive to New Hampshire. Meanwhile, I flew back to Manchester, trying not to move my legs on the plane, thankful it was only an hour-long flight and not a six-hour drive. Nichole's mother was at the airport to pick me up. She told me she was proud of me, and I'm sure she was, but I could also see by her expression that she thought I was a little crazy for putting my body through what I had.

Nichole arrived a few hours later and brought me some ice bags and Gatorade. I thanked her again for coming to the race and for driving all that way just to see me for a few minutes. She said she had done it because she was proud and knew how hard I'd worked to train for a marathon while finishing grad school. I drifted to sleep that night, feeling good about my day, but also knowing it was just the beginning. As my legs periodically cramped under the weight of my sheets, I knew I would not rest until I qualified for Boston.

FIFTEEN

WITH MY FIRST MARATHON BEHIND ME, I recognized how difficult it was to run 26.2 miles. While I could cover eighteen or twenty, or even twenty-two miles pretty well, those last few fuel-depleted miles presented a significant obstacle for me.

I had learned a lot from my first attempt, and I used that knowledge as I strove for the celebrated Boston Marathon. After Thanksgiving, I returned to school and searched for marathons somewhat close to home and stumbled upon the Buffalo Marathon. The race was scheduled for the Sunday of Memorial Day weekend, just a few weeks after I'd receive my master's degree. It was settled. I had a target race, and I needed to start training again. Finding time to run was difficult because my graduate studies and course load had increased. I had to finalize my thesis *and* I took on a graduate assistantship, helping to teach pediatric therapy to the fifth-year graduate students. The pediatric professor was also a therapist at Boston Children's Hospital, so I was afforded the opportunity for bonus clinical work at the prestigious facility. It was a remarkable experience for me, but it also took a great deal of my time.

School, work, and training were not the only obstacles on campus. Shortly after Thanksgiving, Notre Dame College announced that it would be closing its doors at the end of the school year due to financial problems. While I would be graduating, all undergraduate students and fifth-year

PT students would be forced to transfer. One of those undergraduates was Nichole, in her second year of the education program. It was a difficult time for many of my friends and all the faculty members who were driven to find new positions.

As if that weren't enough for our small school to cope with, just after the start of the New Year, Sr. Jeannette Plante, the nun who had greeted me with a friendly "Yoda-like" hello when I arrived at NDC, was struck and killed by a vehicle as she was walking to a school concert. It happened in the same exact location where I was hit by a car two years prior. That event shook our campus to its core. The year had started with September 11, 2001; school had announced an unexpected closing in November; and in January 2002, we lost Sr. Jeannette, who was one of the beacons of light and hope on campus.

While faculty, staff, and students mourned and scrambled to figure out their future, I sought to give campus some sense of normalcy. The school newspaper, *DeNotre*, hadn't been published for several months. Most of the college clubs ceased operations after the announcement of the school closing. I thought that having the publication return for one final issue was important. Subsequently, I asked the deans' permission to take on the role of editor with no staff, no contributing writers, and no budget. It was a formidable task with just a couple of months left in the school year, but I was given approval. I recruited a few friends to take pictures, write stories, and conduct interviews with me. We gathered enough money from donors to have one thousand copies printed. It was a simple and subtle salute to all that NDC had meant to me for my college career. With so much out of my control, and so many changes across campus, I felt I had to do *something*. I had never done anything like it before, but I was proud of the completed product. It was well received throughout the community, with the final piece in the paper being something I penned titled, "The Spirit of Notre Dame College." It was a reminder to everyone to spread the mission of NDC far and wide, and to let our light, and the light of our tiny campus at the north end of Elm Street, burn brightly as we went our separate ways.

I spent my training runs during my final few months at Notre Dame thinking, reflecting, dreaming, and wondering. I thought about my research project, my final classes in health care administration, and my clinical work. I reflected on my six years on campus, and all I'd learned inside and outside the classroom. I reflected on Nichole, our relationship, and how it evolved from acquaintance, to friend, to partner. Things were going great for us. We spent as much time together as our schedules permitted. We cherished being together. *But what will happen when Nichole transfers to a new school and I search for a job?* I was offered a position at a new pediatric therapy practice in New York, and Nichole still had two years of school to finish before she could think about joining me. Two years was a long time to be apart. We were both deeply committed to each other, but we'd been together a relatively short time and I recalled the demise of my previous relationship when I'd left for a summer. I thought about Nichole a lot as I ran.

In addition to everything else that our school had been through, Nichole lost one of her high school friends to cancer in March of 2002. While she was devastated, she continued to excel in the classroom and remained upbeat. As I ran, I drew strength from her, from our relationship, from the unconditional support she gave me in everything I did. I daydreamed about our future. I visualized her giving me one of her famous hugs as I crossed the finish line in Buffalo.

Training was my outlet and my stress relief. I ran when I could. I ran as fast or slow as I felt like running—ensuring I ran adequate distances, but not worrying about how long it took. In fact, my training was interrupted twice in the final few months. Once, when I had food poisoning that kept me from running for seven days, and again when I had the flu, which laid me up for another couple of weeks. When I did train, I ran early in the morning so that running wouldn't interfere with meetings, classes, *DeNotre,* or quality time with Choley (Nichole's nickname as the semester progressed).

Meanwhile, Nichole secured a transfer to Southern New Hampshire University, a mile down the road from Notre Dame College. She got an off-campus apartment, and I was set to return home where I'd live with my parents, take the physical therapy licensing exam, and start my career as a pediatric physical therapist.

Our trip to Buffalo for the marathon would be our last getaway together before I moved back to New York. We decided to make a long weekend out of it and reserved a place in Niagara Falls to spend the night after the race.

Marathon morning, I was relaxed and elated to have Choley by my side. This time, unlike the Philadelphia marathon, I knew she was there, and we planned a few spots where she'd be able to see me as I ran. My one goal that day was to run the entire distance—to not have to walk at all. That meant I needed to pace myself. I started at a much more conservative speed than my five-minute miles in Philly. I wanted to have something left for the homestretch. I kept a close eye on my watch, knowing I needed to reign myself in or suffer the consequences later. I peeked at my wrist at each mile marker and tried to keep each mile split just below seven minutes. I remained consistent, only speeding up when Choley could be heard cheering, "Go, Shauni!"

On those miles, my adrenaline would carry me far beyond the reaches of her voice, and I dropped much closer to a six-minute pace.

I passed mile twenty feeling strong, but I waited for my legs to cramp and fail. At mile marker twenty-two, I maintained a steady pace. Mile twenty-three brought a twinge in my right hip. I took some deep breaths, increased my stride length a fraction, and the cramps faded. By mile twenty-four, my confidence was growing. I knew I wouldn't see Choley until the finish, but my goal of running the entire 26.2 miles nonstop was within reach. I floated along, looking forward to her hug.

Better Together

I could see her jumping up and down as I turned the corner for the final hundred meters. I accelerated as my eyes caught a glimpse of the finish clock. I sprinted through the line with a finishing time of 2:54—twenty minutes faster than I'd run six months earlier, and a Boston qualifier! I knew my training wasn't perfect and believed I could run faster, but as they placed the finisher's medal around my neck and notified me that I'd won my age group, I ended the day feeling proud, strong, and accomplished. The finish-line squeeze from my biggest supporter had never felt so good, and together, as we embraced, we cried tears of joy.

93

SIXTEEN

AFTER THE BUFFALO MARATHON AND OUR GETAWAY to Niagara Falls, Choley returned to New Hampshire and I passed my board exams and began my career as a pediatric physical therapist. I enjoyed work and was thankful it kept my mind off missing my girlfriend, who now resided four hours away. After spending time together nearly every day for nine months, it was an adjustment for us both.

As soon as Choley knew she was transferring to Southern New Hampshire University, she immediately enrolled in summer classes. Her goal was to finish school as quickly as possible. She'd chosen NDC because she loved the small school atmosphere. She wanted the ability to get involved and make a difference on campus and through service projects like the one at St. Francis Inn. Everyone knew each other and felt like family at NDC. Prior to school closing, Choley had been named "Emerging Leader" at a spring awards ceremony. When she was forced to transfer, she felt robbed of her college experience. While I am confident she could have thrived in student leadership at SNHU, her way of coping with the loss of NDC was to get her remaining semesters completed expeditiously so she could begin her teaching career and join me in New York.

While Nichole focused on her studies, my goal for running was to get ready for the Boston Marathon and return to the Buffalo Marathon five weeks later. I often got miles in by running four miles to the nearest post office to send Nichole a slightly sweaty letter. Through the winter, I would stay late at work to run on the treadmill. I felt confident when it was time to run from Hopkinton to Boston on Patriots' Day.

As a young boy, my father and I frequently went to Boston on Patriots' Day. We'd visit with one of Dad's college friends who lived outside the city, and then ride the T to Fenway Park. We'd arrive in time for the traditional early-start Red Sox game. After exiting the game, we watched crowds of marathoners run by the stadium, en route to the famous finish on Boylston Street.

The year 2003 would be my first opportunity to run the historic marathon course, and roughly follow Paul Revere's trail as he warned his comrades the British were coming. My sister Jodie helped to make the event an extra special occasion by getting Choley and me a room at the Ritz Carlton. Given our limited budget, it was by far the nicest hotel either of us had stayed in, and it was a great place for us to relax during the weekend leading up to Marathon Monday.

Naturally, sleep was short the night before the race, and I boarded a bus at 4:30 a.m. that took me to the Athletes' Village at Hopkinton High School. The race start time was noon, so we were there in plenty of time for me to get excited about the race. I soaked in every step as I made my way out of Hopkinton with over twenty thousand runners. I thought the miles lined with spectators, signs, and true party atmosphere were passing too quickly. Caught up in the excitement and the downhill start, I had started too fast and struggled through the Newton Hills, including "Heartbreak Hill," as I neared the finish. Overall, I was satisfied with my finishing time of 3 hours and 2 minutes, and knew I'd be running the Buffalo Marathon the following month.

I had taken some extra time off from work after the race so I could go to New Hampshire with Choley. My legs were sore as we got in her car. She drove as I looked out the window and reflected on the fact that I had just finished the hallowed Boston Marathon. She looked over at me and beamed, delighted with my accomplishment. She lifted her hand and gently tapped me on the leg to let me know how proud she was. As her hand patted my thigh, I screamed as my leg went into spasm and extended, kicking the bottom of the dashboard. Nichole quickly pulled the car over and apologized profusely for the next five minutes. We laughed for the remainder of the ride, with me holding my hands up, jokingly guarding against any errant love taps.

Five weeks later, Choley was by my side again as we headed to Buffalo. Jyll and my friend, Blake, also met us there. Blake would ride his bike during the race, supplying me with water and encouragement whenever he could. Jyll would be there to keep Nichole company and cheer on her big brother. All their support was welcomed and appreciated.

My goal for the race was to improve on my time from the previous year. I succeeded, breaking two hours and fifty minutes and finishing eleventh overall. It was then, just five weeks after running the Boston Marathon and running even faster in Buffalo, that I realized perhaps I had a propensity for distance running—and for recovering quickly! Of course, I was working hard, but felt I hadn't reached anywhere near my full potential.

It was challenging to say goodbye to Choley after each visit, especially when the visit was on a marathon weekend. Those weekends, I was focused on running; spent Saturday resting, fueling, hydrating, and then spent Sunday running and recovering. We had made a deal with each other that if I broke 2:50 in Buffalo, she'd stay an extra few days before her next round of summer classes. There's no doubt Choley was my extra incentive to run 2:49 that day.

As she returned to New Hampshire, we made plans to get together a month later at St. Francis Inn for our first summer volunteering experience in Philly. There, we met some friends from NDC and served at the soup kitchen—in warm weather, for a change. We spent the week sorting cans, serving meals, organizing clothes at the thrift store, collecting donations from local grocery stores and pantries, and touring downtown at night.

We adored spending time in Philadelphia because it was where our friendship had blossomed during our trips to St. Francis. We had become familiar with the shops and restaurants on South Street, the historic areas around the Liberty Bell, and the love surrounding St. Francis. It was like home, and we were glad to be back. As the week went on, Nichole's allergies spiked, and she ended up with a bad case of laryngitis. She was feeling okay, but couldn't speak. As a result, she was left gesturing as we translated for her interactions with guests at the soup kitchen. We didn't let her lack of voice dampen our moods at all.

At the end of the week, we said our goodbyes at St. Francis and went to downtown Philly for one more night in *our* city before departing. We walked from our hotel to the Museum of Art, the site of the start and finish of my first marathon where Nichole had surprised me almost eighteen months earlier. There was a music festival in the park at the base of the museum steps, and the late-June weather was ideal. The smell of seasonal flowers infused the humid air. We didn't talk much, since Nichole couldn't really speak, but we were happy walking near the Schuylkill River hand in hand, soaking in the upbeat music. It was a picturesque summer night.

Unbeknownst to *anyone* else, all week long, I had kept a diamond ring safety-pinned in my pocket. It was my intention to propose to Nichole that weekend. As we walked away from the music to a slightly less active area, I pulled a necklace out of my other pocket. I'd handcrafted a silver heart with the date etched into it: "6-28-03." As we walked around that evening, I'd been rehearsing the moment in my mind.

I gazed at Nichole and affirmed, "It's a special weekend for us."

Choley nodded, not knowing what was coming. Every weekend together was special to us, and this weekend was even more special because it was in Philadelphia. She thought the necklace was the gift in celebration of our weekend. As she looked at the date etched into the heart, I quietly knelt and professed my enduring love for her and my dreams of us growing old and raising a family together. As long as we were together, everything would be spectacular. I presented her with the ring I'd been tightly holding in my pocket. When she saw the ring, she cried happily and squeaked a barely perceptible "yes" as she nodded frantically, confirming her joy. She then gave me one of my favorite Choley hugs—the squeezes that have melted my heart since the first time she had embraced me. The top of her head supported my chin as her love, warmth, caring, and kindness permeated to my soul.

We spent the night celebrating with some Ben and Jerry's ice cream, to soothe her throat from the laryngitis, and woke up the next morning to call our mothers, who were both ecstatic. I would be the first child to be married in my family, and Nichole would be the final child to be married in hers.

Before the official planning could begin, we had an obligation to fulfill. At the end of the week, we'd volunteered to help some friends, Mark and Beth, as they took their four children to Sesame Place, a water park out-side of Philadelphia. The two older children, Aiden and Madeline, were four and three, respectively, while the twins, Brady and Dawson, were six months old. Choley and I loved their family and adored kids in general, so we were happy to help by caring for the twins, or riding rides with the preschoolers. We met them after our morning phone calls home, and we let them know the good news. Mark and Beth gave pause to having us help them and said we should celebrate instead. Nichole and I had never even thought about backing out. We knew we wanted to be parents together someday. We were both focused on family and insisted there was no better way for us to celebrate than by spending time together, helping with the little ones. The weekend at Sesame Place only solidified our commitment to each other, as we cherished our time taking Maddy and Aiden to see Elmo, Ernie, and Cookie Monster; going on rides; playing in the water; and feeding, entertaining, and soothing the twins.

Once again, Nichole returned to New Hampshire, and I headed back to New York. We had been in our relationship for nearly two years, and more than half of that time was spent with 180 miles between us. Despite being apart, and frequently missing each other with aching hearts, we never felt closer or more confident in our commitment to one another, knowing we would soon be married.

SEVENTEEN

Nichole worked ceaselessly at Southern New Hampshire University. She doubled up on classes each semester and was able to complete all of her student teaching in the fall of 2003. She graduated a semester early and moved to New York the day after Christmas, which allowed us to be together to plan our wedding.

Choley found a long-term substitute teaching position as soon as the Christmas break ended. After eighteen months of nonstop classes, she was used to being busy. While she was happy to be teaching, she wanted to make sure she was earning enough to help pay for our apartment expenses and our wedding. She picked up evening hours three nights per week, covering the front desk at the local YMCA. On weekends, she worked at the mall. I was working twelve-hour days and often staying longer to finish paperwork and squeeze in a few miles on the treadmill. We didn't see each other much, but we were thrilled to be in the same zip code for the first time in two and a half years.

The spring went by in a blur as we prepared for our wedding. Choley and I went to Manchester for her graduation ceremony, drove back to New York, and then the following week drove to Buffalo for the Buffalo Marathon. Immediately after the race, we drove to Canandaigua to attend my friend Bryan's wedding. We went home for one week before Nichole departed for New Hampshire to finalize last-minute details for *our* wedding. We'd settled on a spot in Wolfeboro, New Hampshire on Lake Winnipesaukee for the ceremony. It would be an hour's drive for most of Nichole's friends and family, and a five-hour drive from New York, but we loved the location. One of Choley's sisters lived in the area, which provided Nichole with a place to stay, complete preparations, and get ready in the week leading up to our big day: June 12, 2004.

The morning of our wedding was picture-perfect. I spent the night before in the hotel with my groomsmen. Nichole spent the night at her sister's house. When we woke, the sun was peeking over the mountains surrounding the lake, reflecting its rays in orange and yellow across the water. I was awake before my friends, so I slipped out the hotel door, put on my running sneakers, and went for my final run as a single man.

I ran on the gravel road near the edge of the lake, soaking in the scenery, the early summer air, and the trees newly in bloom. I savored the morning and felt completely blessed. My senses were heightened as the adrenaline of the day took effect. As I traversed the hills, I admired the cabins and homes surrounding the lake. Each footstep offered me a reminder of the marathon I'd run two weeks prior. My legs hadn't fully recovered, and I had blisters on the ends of my toes, but it didn't matter. The sunshine on my face and the fresh air in my lungs were exactly what I needed as I jogged out some wedding-day jitters. I returned to the hotel just after eight o'clock, sweaty and panting, but completely content, knowing my bride would soon be meeting me at the end of the aisle where we'd be saying, "I do." As my friends stumbled out of bed, I walked to the shoreline, took off my sneakers and socks, and dove into the cool water; a chilly, soul-cleansing swim in the lake as I prepared to enter my new life with Nichole.

The morning zipped by with last-minute wedding preparations. The next thing I remember, I was standing on the balcony of the hotel honeymoon suite, watching guests arrive for our outdoor ceremony. My boyhood friend, Jeff, was there for me. I watched as he escorted his parents and several other guests to their seats. My college roommate, Wesley, was not only a groomsman, but also played piano as guests arrived. An incredible musician, he also played an original piece during our ceremony. Blake was there in support as he would be for so many future marathons.

My sister, Jyll, served as my best "man." When contemplating who to choose to bear witness on my wedding day, there was no one more appropriate than my little sister. We'd always been close. She was my biggest supporter growing up and throughout our early adulthood. I was honored to have her next to me.

As guests arrived, the moment became real. College friends, professors, deans, and advisors from NDC—including Dr. Michael and his wife— were all in attendance. There were friends of our parents, friends from high school, friends from work, and Nichole's student teaching friends. There was family on Nichole's side I had not yet met. All were coming together to celebrate our day with us.

I stepped into the bathroom one last time before I walked downstairs for the ceremony. I looked at my reflection in the mirror. I saw myself dressed in a tuxedo, ready for the day that Nichole and I had been anticipating for so long. I was overcome with joy and memories. All the moments in my life, Nichole's life, and our time together that had led to that day flashed through my mind.

I felt indelibly blessed. As Nichole emerged from behind a white fence and walked on the lawn toward the gazebo where we would say our vows, I was overwhelmed by the vision of her. I began to cry the happiest tears of my life. She radiated. I was certain that my world revolved around her as she walked down the aisle. When she saw I was crying, she too began to cry tears of joy. I pulled a tissue out of my pocket and quickly blotted her cheeks.

The ceremony was perfect, performed by a friend of Nichole's family, with readings by my two older sisters. Nichole was escorted down the aisle and given away by her nephew, Eli. Madeline and Aiden Tooker were our flower girl and ring bearer. The weather was unblemished, with the sun shining on the lake below. We celebrated all day, from the noon ceremony until the wee hours of the morning, surrounded by friends and family.

We drove back to New York the next day, never having felt so tired in our lives. The exhaustion from the emotional highs, combined with the lack of sleep in the days leading up to our wedding day, caught up with us. We were so tired we could barely function. We slept most of the day before departing for our honeymoon in Punta Cana the next day.

Our honeymoon was the biggest vacation either Nichole or I had ever taken. We stayed at an all-inclusive resort and enjoyed every second of it. We swam, scuba dived, kayaked, learned to windsurf, danced, did water aerobics, read books, ate great food, and spent uninterrupted time together. The only time we were apart was when I would go for a morning jog on the shoreline. As I soaked in the ocean breeze, Nichole sunbathed on the beach. I'd pause to give her a quick kiss each time I passed.

After a ten-day honeymoon, we returned to our apartment as a married couple. My mother and sisters, who had been taking care of our cat, Bubbles, had redecorated for us, purchased new furniture for us, and straightened up everything we didn't have a chance to clean after our wedding. While we had a glorious honeymoon, it was good to be home . . . together.

Nichole shifted her sights to finding a teaching job, and I went back to work and focused on marathon training for a race that fall. When September arrived, Nichole had secured a long-term substitute teaching position, and I had gotten into the best running shape of my life. I was scheduled to run the Clarence DeMar Marathon in Keene, New Hampshire on September 26, 2004.

On September 23, I arose to get the newspaper before work. Nichole had already left to go to school. I was dressed in my pajama pants and, with it being an unseasonably warm morning, I left my shirt off. My intent was to grab the paper from the paper box, come back in, and read it for a half hour before going to work.

I grabbed the paper, but when I got back to the apartment door, it had jammed behind me. It had happened before—the key wouldn't work, and I had to find another way in. Each time, I'd shimmy up a pillar, climb up on the metal roof outside our second-story window, open it from the outside, and enter our apartment. Then, I'd walk back downstairs to unjam the door from the inside. I'd performed that routine a half dozen times in the year and a half I'd lived there.

However, that particular morning, the dew was heavy, and the metal roof was slippery. I attempted to climb it once and quickly realized there was no way I could get a grip. There was no one around to help, so I grabbed a ladder that was stowed in the basement stairwell. I figured that would help me to get up high enough so I wouldn't have to pull myself up and over the overhang of the roof. I set up the stepladder and climbed to the top. I placed my hands on the green, metal roof and began to push myself up. My hands slipped, the ladder fell and, in an instant, I was on the ground. Luckily, I'd been able to keep my bearings and landed on my feet. I walked over to retrieve the step ladder that was now laying on the pavement, ready for another try, when I felt something running down the right side of my body. My first thought was that the roof must have been more wet than I thought and the dew was trickling down my side. That thought immediately turned to panic when I looked down at the right side of my chest and saw a gaping wound.

When I'd fallen, my chest, right next to my armpit, had been sliced by a ridge in the metal roofing. The gash was about three inches long, and had cut through the fat and my pectoral muscle. The scientific part of my brain was analyzing the tissue, while the survival part of my brain was desperate for first aid. I then recognized, not only was I bleeding from my chest, I was also bleeding from my chin, realizing I'd hit it on the roof as I fell. I couldn't find anything to pack or cover the wounds with, so I pushed on my chest with my left hand as my right arm dropped to my side. Blood steadily dripped out of the underside of my chin. I walked to the street and looked for someone to call for help. I signaled to several cars that looked at me in terror and kept driving. I can only assume that they thought I'd been in a knife fight. I was walking around with no shirt, in my pajama pants, torso covered in blood, and I had recently shaved my head for the upcoming marathon that weekend. I can't fault anyone for not helping.

Finally, I was able to get a kind man to stop when I lifted my left hand off my chest to expose the gushing laceration. The good Samaritan pulled into the parking lot and called 911. He knew I was going into shock from the blood loss. He handed me some napkins and invited me to sit in his car until the EMTs got there. All I can recall is trying to prevent getting blood on his car's upholstery.

The ambulance arrived, with an old high school classmate serving as the paramedic. I explained what happened as she packed the wound and rushed me to the emergency room. They hurried me to the back and set me on a table to wait for the doctor. Still in shock, the first thing I uttered to the doctor when he arrived was, "I have a marathon on Sunday. Do you think I can run?"

EIGHTEEN

THE DOCTOR BARELY HAD A CHANCE to enter the room when I asked him if he thought I could run the race that weekend.

His initial response was, "Let me take a look first," followed immediately by, "Would it matter if I said you couldn't run? I have a feeling you wouldn't listen to me anyway."

The doctor knew me for less than ten seconds and, of course, he was right. If I felt able to run, I was going to try.

The doctor examined me, "Your legs weren't involved so there's no problem there, but you'll be pumping that arm when you run. I don't want the wound to reopen. I am going to use the heaviest gauge stitches we have. They're what I use on boxers, so they should hold."

When he was done, I ended up with thirteen internal stitches to secure the muscle, twenty-two external "heavy gauge" stitches that extended from my collarbone to my armpit, and five stitches in my chin.

"Your biggest issue will be the blood you lost," the doctor said. "No telling exactly how much, not enough for a transfusion that's for sure, but you'll need your red blood cells Sunday. That'll be the key. If you're feeling faint, dizzy, or weak during the race, you should call it quits."

I nodded my understanding, glad that neither Nichole nor my mother was there to hear the doctor's advice.

"I'll put you on an antibiotic. Make sure you're up to date on your tetanus shot, and change the bandage daily. We'll see you in two weeks to take the stitches out. Good luck!"

"I really appreciate your help," I said as he exited the room. I sat a while longer, making calls to work and my mother, not wanting to bother Nichole at her new job. I felt foolish for falling and injuring myself, but all I could think about was running on Sunday and how much I needed a nap.

I went to my parents' house to rest and called Nichole, asking her to meet me there. When she arrived, I showed her the wound, which was covered with a clear bandage to keep it clean and dry. She helped me change the dressing for the first time.

She and my mother agreed. "There is *no* way you are running on Sunday," they said, as if they had been rehearsing it. I tried to look strong for them, but I was pale and exhausted. I knew it wasn't the time for an argument; I nodded off to sleep.

When I awoke, I researched what foods could boost red blood cell production and discovered some articles about raw spinach. I stepped outside to jog around the house. I felt like I was going to pass out after one lap. I collapsed on the couch, drank a glass of water, and fell asleep again. I ate a big spinach salad for dinner and tried to stick with my typical pre-race routine. I muddled through work on Friday, trying to hydrate and stretch my legs, though I didn't feel like running at all. After much discussion, I convinced Nichole that we should go to Keene after work that day. I told her we could hang out and watch the race, even if I couldn't run. But deep down I knew there was no way we were going to Keene for me to spectate. Although I wasn't feeling much like running 26.2 miles, I hoped an overnight recovery would occur.

We went to the race expo, where I sought out the race director. I explained my situation to him and inquired about runner support on the course. I asked for locations of aid stations and requested that he give my bib number to volunteers and medical staff on the route. My thought was, if I needed to drop out, help wouldn't be too far away. It was a relatively small race with a few hundred runners. The race director was happy to relay my message to volunteers and said he would personally keep an eye on me.

We checked into the hotel and found Jyll and Blake, who had driven in to offer support. I reviewed my plan for race day with them. Blake would ride his bike and meet up with me when possible, and Jyll and Nichole would have a vehicle nearby. My intention was to start the race, make it to mile ten, see how my body felt, and then make a decision about continuing. Mile ten would be our rendezvous point.

Race morning, I was as white as a ghost—no overnight recovery by any means. I'd been diligent about my nutrition and hydration, but my body didn't have enough time to restock all the blood I'd lost. I felt defeated as I got out of bed. Nichole made one final plea for me to not run. She realized it was pointless as I donned my running gear, placed some energy gel packets in my running shorts, and headed to the car, insisting we should drive to the start line. I could feel Nichole and Jyll rolling their eyes when I turned to head out the door. Blake gave me a look, as if to say, *You do not need to do this today. There will be more marathons!*

Everyone was quiet as we got in the car for the fifteen-minute drive to the starting line. I fell asleep on the ride; not a great sign for me to be able to finish the race. Typically, race mornings were full of nervous energy and excitement, and reviewing checklists to make sure I had everything. That morning, all I wanted to do was sleep, but I felt like I needed to at least *try*. I'd trained so hard and had been focusing on being able to sustain my speed for longer and longer distances. I hoped to set a new personal best. Though that goal looked highly unlikely, I felt I had to give it a shot after all the time, dedication, and sweat I'd invested. I took a few more sips of Gatorade, ate a bagel, and checked my bandage. Nichole changed it one last time before the race, and we hoped the sweat wouldn't make it peel off.

I walked to the starting area with my crew, reviewing the plan and ensuring that everyone knew where the ten-mile marker was. If I needed to drop out of the race sooner, Blake would find me, reach out to Nichole and Jyll, and locate race volunteers. As I walked away from them and lined up for the national anthem, I secretly hoped I could *make it* to ten miles. *I'll use this as a training run,* I thought. *I have the Philadelphia Marathon scheduled in a few weeks.*

The gun fired and I took off with the pack of runners in a daze. I simply trotted and plodded along, trying to find a rhythm in my steps. I tried not to think about the accident a few days prior. I hydrated at the first water stop when typically I would just stride by and thank the volunteers for being there. That day, I was more thankful than ever. I took a gulp of ice-cold water, then splashed the rest of it on my face. *Snap out of it,* I thought. *Wake up! You can do this!*

By mile five, I was running a little better, focused on trying to take in the beautiful scenery and enjoy the "training" run. The leaves were changing colors to stunning oranges, yellows, and reds. Every once in a while, I watched a leaf as it fell and drifted to the ground ahead of me, wondering if it would land before I passed. Normally, during a race, I would never have thought about my surroundings. I would have been concentrating on my stride, my breathing, and my pace. I'd be taking inventory of my body—feeling for twinges that might signal a problem if I didn't alter my stride or stay hydrated. I'd know exactly what place I was in, and exactly what my split times per mile were.

On that fall morning, I just ran, and as I ran, I started to feel a little stronger. My heart was pumping, and the color returned to my face. By the time I got to mile ten, I was feeling decent. By no means did I feel one hundred percent, but when I saw Blake, Jyll, and Nichole, I gave them a thumbs-up, indicating I'd keep going. The girls headed back to the finishing area to find Nichole's family, but Blake stayed nearby. He planned to check in with me every few miles.

I took a carbohydrate gel pack out of my shorts pocket after mile ten. I hydrated at each aide station, alternating water and Gatorade, and would dump a cup of ice water on my head. I started to feel more alert as the miles ticked by, but had no idea how many runners were ahead of me. I guessed I was somewhere in the top twenty-five.

Blake was waiting for me at the halfway point, mile 13.1. "You're in tenth!" he shouted.

I was stunned. I had been oblivious to the race going on around me. For the first half hour, I was just trying to survive. After that, I attempted to enjoy the day and the miles I *was* able to complete. Yet, there I was in tenth place, starting to feel better. I decided to increase my pace to see if I could stay in the top ten.

As I pressed on, I felt healthier. I actually passed a couple of runners and was in seventh place when I got to mile seventeen. It was then that the combination of constant sweat and nonstop arm swinging forced the bandage to peel away from my skin. The stitches on my chest were rubbing into my shirt as the bandage rolled halfway down the wound. It was uncomfortable. As the stitches rubbed, they pulled on the tender skin and muscle. I tried to secure the bandage while running by pushing on it with my left hand, hoping it would stick. *No luck.* I was way too sweaty for that. I attempted to run without swinging my right arm. It was awkward and my back spasmed. *That won't work either.* I didn't want to stop, for fear that if I did, I wouldn't start again. I opted to take off my shirt to avoid the stitches getting caught in the fabric. After mile nineteen, I used my shirt to clean up the blood that was dripping between the stitches, and tossed it to Blake as he waited at the roadside. He stuffed the sweaty, bloody shirt in his bike bag without a second glance and rode to catch up to me.

"How you feelin'?" he asked.

"Good . . . six to go, I'm gonna make it!" I panted as we passed mile twenty. I'd worked my way up to fifth place and continued to feel strong. I could see a group of three runners ahead of me. They were my target. They would pull me through the last few miles. *No cramps, no blisters, legs feel good, stride is the best it's been all day.*

I looked up and noticed I was slowly gaining on the pack. My goal was to not lose sight of them, but they were getting closer! I could hardly believe it. At mile twenty-two, I was only a few yards behind. I increased my speed briefly to join them, and ran stride for stride with their group. We didn't talk. I could tell they were all running on fumes. Although the bleeding had stopped, I wondered what they thought about all the stitches in my chest.

A half mile later, I left the small group behind as I ran stronger, and they couldn't match my pace.

"Go get 'em!" one of them shouted as I pulled away. I gave a thumbs-up with my left hand and pressed forward.

Just after mile twenty-three, I saw the leader, the one person who was still ahead of me. I started the race hoping to endure the first ten miles. With less than three miles to go, the race leader was in my sights—in the distance, but visible. Again, I just wanted to keep him in my view, but I realized I was quickly closing the space between us.

"He just started walking!" I shouted to Blake, who had pulled up beside me.

"Go get him!" he said. "You good?"

I nodded.

"See you at the finish!" he said, and he pedaled ahead to meet Jyll and Nichole.

"I'll be there as fast as I can!" I responded.

I knew I had enough distance left to take the lead. I just had to maintain my pace. The runner ahead quickly started running again. *Just keep running,* I thought to myself.

I continued to gain ground and by mile twenty-four, I pulled even with him. I could see he was struggling. I said, "Hang tough, stay with me, we're almost there."

He nodded and was able to stay by my side for a half mile before uttering, "It's yours, go get it!"

I smiled a thank you, told him, "Good race," and headed for the finish line.

At mile twenty-five, I accelerated, knowing I had to hang on for one more mile. With four hundred meters to go, I caught a glimpse of Nichole, my sister, and Blake jumping in the distance. I started bawling in disbelief of the events of the day. I sprinted through the finish line with my arms raised, breaking the tape of the finish line with a time of two hours, forty-four minutes. I immediately found Nichole to give her a hug, and I cried into her shoulder.

The race director congratulated me, shook my hand, and said, "So you thought you'd need medical assistance on the course, huh?" as he laughed. With my shirt off, he could see the stitches and the damage I'd done. Several interviews with local newspapers followed as the story of my injury trickled through the crowd.

Once I finished retelling my roller-coaster journey of the weekend, I quickly reunited with Nichole, Jyll, and Blake, and thanked them for their incredible support. When Nichole and I got home, I was physically and emotionally drained. I slept more heavily than ever, and beyond my wildest dreams, as a marathon champion!

NINETEEN

Things were going well as the calendar turned to 2005. My parents had sectioned off six acres of their land and given the plot to Choley and me as a wedding gift. We excitedly started making plans to build a house in an old pasture where I used to play as a kid.

We looked forward to the challenge of designing our home on the family land. We worked with architects to draft the house, keeping in mind our future family. There were a lot of aspects we didn't have a clue about, but my father was there to guide us. In addition, the grandparents of our flower girl and ring bearer had recently started a contracting company. They were willing to build our house for us at cost, allowing us to move much more quickly through the process. The trade-off was that they'd be trialing different crews, and it might take a little longer. We were fine with that. We were eager to make the next big leap in our life together: a new home.

We knew we wanted children, at least two, so we came up with a floor plan that would allow our family to grow. Our plan was to be in our new home and settled before starting our family. However, life doesn't always go as planned. Just before our one-year anniversary and a week before the Buffalo Marathon, we were surprised to find out Choley was pregnant!

Although it wasn't expected, we were euphoric when Nichole took the home pregnancy test and discovered it to be positive. We immediately made an appointment with her OBGYN to confirm the results. We went to the appointment excited to make the news official.

When the doctor walked into the room, she announced to us that Nichole was indeed newly pregnant. By the look on the doctor's face, she was worried Nichole and I would be upset. She was quiet and reserved with a look of sympathy. Nichole and I looked like teenagers, so perhaps she thought we weren't ready to start our family, but we were ecstatic, as were our mothers when we delivered the news to them. For Nichole's mom, her baby was having a baby! For my mom, her only son would be providing her first grandchild! Nichole and I were preparing to be parents!

Our lives were as busy as ever: both of us working full time and pursuing advanced college degrees; doctor's appointments for Nichole; designing and building a house; all while I trained for marathons.

We drove to Buffalo for the annual marathon with extra joy in our hearts and an extra spring in my step. It showed on the course, too. Every stride, I'd repeat to myself our unborn baby's name. Nichole and I had already selected names for a boy and a girl. If it was a boy, he would be Shamus; if it was a girl, she would be Veda. For some reason we were convinced that we were having a girl, so for the duration of the marathon, my mantra was, *For Veda and Choley*. I repeated it over and over as I covered the 26.2 miles of the familiar course. I cruised through the finish line with another personal best. Just six weeks after another Boston Marathon, but bolstered by a baby in utero, I ran the race in two hours and thirty-eight minutes; my first sub-2:40 marathon!

I used that result as an automatic qualifying time for the New York City Marathon. While most people enter the NYC Marathon through a lottery, or charity team, my qualifying time guaranteed my entry for the race in November, and that became my focus for training.

Meanwhile, our house was growing, and so was Choley. Her prenatal ultrasounds all checked out great. The baby was on schedule, and we loved watching on the sonogram machine as he/she moved arms and legs and did flips. Neither Nichole nor I wanted to find out the sex of the baby. We wanted it to be a surprise on the baby's due date in January.

In September, Nichole and I went to one of her regular check-ups. The doctors saw something on the ultrasound and wanted to get another view. There was nothing wrong with the baby, but Nichole was diagnosed with placenta previa, which meant the placenta was blocking the birth canal. If it didn't move prior to delivery, it could result in various problems for Choley or the baby. It was devastating to hear as a new husband and pending father. From the time we'd found out Nichole was pregnant, I took my fathering role seriously, and felt like a dad right away.

As soon as we got back from the appointment, I researched placenta previa and was distraught by the potential complications listed, which included death of the baby and mother! Of course, I overlooked the fact that most times when it is found early in pregnancy, it resolves on its own. I was frantic about it for several days while Nichole remained calm. I should have been the one soothing her, but she was the one helping me relax.

Sure enough, a few appointments later, the placenta had moved where it needed to be for a safe labor and delivery. I felt like a fool for getting so worked up about it, but couldn't imagine life without Nichole or the baby, who I already loved with all my heart. At night, I sang to Nichole's belly, and sometimes talked and visited with the baby while Choley slept or did schoolwork. Nichole had all day, every day with the baby, and I wanted to make sure I was doing my part to help her, and to bond as well.

Helping Nichole most often meant going on a craving-run to our local barbecue spot, five minutes away from our apartment. Prior to getting pregnant with baby Evans, Nichole had been a vegetarian for eleven years, but the baby wanted barbecue! Whatever Nichole needed, I was happy to oblige. From foot rubs and back massages, to beef briskets and pulled pork sandwiches, I was there.

The first weekend in November, we drove to New York for the marathon. My mom came to the race to accompany Nichole, as she became more and more pregnant every day! My friend Jerusha lived in the city, and would help them navigate the course via subway so they could see me at several spots without too much walking—a welcome relief for Choley.

The race held extra meaning because I'd dedicated it to a longtime patient at our clinic who had succumbed to a brain tumor. I wore a race shirt with her photo on it and ran in her memory. The race itself was a challenge. Although I was a seeded runner, I ended up starting back in the crowd of thirty thousand. I spent the first several miles weaving my way through runners. By the time I found some breathing room, my legs were already fatiguing. When I finally reached Central Park, I had to walk. It was the first time I'd walked in a race since my first marathon. I felt dejected. *I'm letting our patient's family down.* As that thought entered my mind, I turned into Central Park and started to climb a hill. At the top of the hill, I spotted our patient's parents jumping up and down, leading the surrounding crowd in chants of, "Go, Shaun, go!" I immediately started weeping on the course and began running to give everyone hugs. The boost they provided was all I needed to propel me through the final miles. It wasn't my fastest race, but it was an unforgettable experience, full of emotion.

I was relieved to get to Nichole and my mother after the race. They'd had an adventure of their own, traversing the city via subways and shortcuts with Jerusha. Nichole was exhausted too, and we were happy to get home, relax in bed, and feel baby Evans kicking, running their own little race in Mommy's tummy.

Ten days after the marathon, Nichole was getting ready for school and noticed red spots on her chest. We weren't sure why, but she was breaking out in a rash. She called her doctor and got an appointment the next day. By the time she got to the doctor's office, it was evident the rash was spreading quickly. When we first noticed the spots, there were only a handful. At the doctor's office, there were more than twenty. The doctor took one look and exclaimed, "You have chicken pox!"

Apparently, Nichole never had chicken pox as a child but didn't think twice about it. While we were in the city for the marathon, Choley must have come into contact with someone with the virus amongst the millions in the city. The doctor predicted the spots wouldn't get much worse, and unfortunately there wasn't much else we could do. She also indicated that we were lucky Nichole contracted them when she did, because it wasn't too early or too late in the pregnancy, and would not harm the baby.

To Nichole's dismay, the doctor was wrong about the spots not getting worse. The next day, she woke up covered from head to toe. A day later, there wasn't anywhere on her body that wasn't plastered with pustules, including inside her throat and on her eyelids. Nichole's case was the most complete body covering possible, and since she was pregnant, she couldn't take any medication. All she could do was soak in the tub, take oatmeal baths, and play games with baby Evans in utero. She'd dangle a dripping washcloth over her abdomen, protruding from the water, and the dripping water would make the baby move. It was a way for her to pass the time and bond with the little one, as she endured the itchiness and discomfort of chicken pox while being seven months pregnant. Perhaps it was good she was pregnant, as the baby gave her something positive to focus on, rather than on how uncomfortable and painful the time was.

By early December, she felt much better, and we decided that we'd take one more trip to Philadelphia to serve at the St. Francis Inn soup kitchen before Christmas. We had continued the tradition with friends from NDC and looked forward to our time helping others. Our plan was to go the weekend before Christmas and stay for a few days.

Sadly, we never made it. On December 15, 2005, when Nichole was on her way to school, her car was sideswiped. A seventeen year old, who'd had her driver's license for only a week, drove through a stop sign and T-boned Nichole's tiny Toyota Tercel. The airbags deployed directly into baby Evans. Her car was totaled. Choley was shaken, but all she could think about was the baby. She held her breath as she waited for the baby to show some sign of life, but the baby didn't move. She immediately told emergency personnel to get her to the hospital. They took her via ambulance, and as they pulled into the emergency room entrance, Nichole finally felt a kick from the baby. Sobs of relief ensued, but she was also beginning to have contractions because the trauma to her body sent her into premature labor. She was only thirty-five weeks pregnant and the doctors wanted to hold off on delivery.

Nichole was unable to contact me because I was with a patient. She called my parents and told my father what had happened. He yelled for my mom, who then hopped in her car and raced to Saratoga to be with Nichole. I arrived a short time later when I got the message Nichole had been in an accident. I didn't breathe the entire drive to the hospital. It wasn't far from where I worked, but every red light took an eternity. I needed to see Nichole, hear her voice, and put my hand on her stomach. I ran into her room and she smiled. They had been giving her IV fluids, but Nichole wanted to get to her doctor, who was at a hospital twenty miles away. I signed her out of the hospital to be transferred to Glens Falls, to the maternity ward (also known as the snuggery) where we planned to deliver baby Evans. If the baby was coming early, that's where we wanted to be. The contractions were occurring inconsistently, so the doctor cleared us to drive ourselves.

I sped up the Northway, and we were comforted to be with Nichole's doctor. Choley was immediately given medication to halt the contractions, and was told they wanted to do some ultrasounds of the baby to ensure everything was stable. We were happy to hear that they would be taking a look. We had felt the baby move, but more images would ease our minds.

The contractions subsided with the medication, and the pictures showed baby Evans was doing great. There was no injury whatsoever. Nichole and her body had done an incredible job of protecting our child, and for that I couldn't have been more grateful. She'd been the perfect mother from the day she found out she was pregnant, and no car accident or chicken pox or placenta previa ever rattled her.

With Nichole attached to several monitors, we snuggled in the hospital bed that night. Choley rested her head on my chest, and I rested my hand on her stomach as we drifted to sleep. Together, the three of us got some much-needed rest.

TWENTY

CHRISTMAS WAS BOTH EXCITING AND EMOTIONAL FOR US. Many of the gifts we opened were for the baby. Nichole's due date was less than a month after the holiday, so baby preparations were in full swing. Our house was also progressing, with an anticipated completion date that was also in January. We regularly took pictures of Choley standing in front of our house as it was being built. It was fun to watch our home and the baby bump grow in unison.

Nichole continued to teach throughout her pregnancy, and intended to work as long as she was able. In addition to finalizing details for the house, preparing for the baby, and the hectic holiday season, we needed to go car shopping to replace Nichole's totaled vehicle. We borrowed a car from a friend for a week while paperwork, insurance settlements, and financing were finalized. We picked up the new family friendly SUV on January 9. Nichole drove it to school on the tenth, but was feeling physically uncomfortable. Her due date was less than two weeks away. She went into school and sat at her desk, unable to find a position she could tolerate.

Upon seeing her that morning, a colleague said, "Nichole, you need to go home! You are in labor!"

Choley replied, "I don't think so, I am not having any contractions, and my water hasn't broken . . . I still have to go to my breastfeeding class tonight!"

Her coworkers convinced her to take a half-day by reminding her that she didn't want her water to break at school. As the day progressed, periodic contractions began, but they were far apart and inconsistent. Nichole spent the afternoon with my mother, purchasing light fixtures for our new home and getting a manicure to distract from any pain and discomfort she was experiencing.

Choley met me at the apartment when I finished work and told me she was in labor, but she still wanted to go to the breastfeeding class. I consented, feeling she knew her body best. We arrived at class with several other couples and introduced ourselves.

As the other couples went through their introductions, Choley squeezed my hand tightly. "The contractions are getting stronger," she whispered. The instructor of the class could sense our distress (okay, my distress) and asked if everything was okay.

"I am in labor," Choley smiled. "But we really wanted to take this class, and this is the only one we could make." The previous class we signed up for had been when Nichole was in the hospital after the car accident. Before that, she had chicken pox!

"Well, stay as long as you like, but don't try to cut it too close. If you have problems nursing, there are lactation consultants who can help after you deliver."

We understood, but we decided to stay for a few more minutes. However, we quickly realized we couldn't focus on anything that was being taught, and excused ourselves at the first break. Everyone wished us well, and we went back to the apartment to grab our bag, which had been packed and ready to go for weeks, complete with the baby's first outfit: orange and yellow velour polka dots. It was soft, warm, and tiny! It would be great for a boy or girl. The car seat was installed in my car. We were ready.

I drove to Glens Falls with Choley reclined in her seat. We checked into the hospital at ten o'clock and waited. Nichole and I had been to several hypnobirthing classes. She'd wanted to have a natural childbirth without medications. Hypnobirthing centered on breathing techniques and relaxation, picturing colors, and meditating. It was a little non-traditional for both of us, but we enjoyed the classes, and it worked for Nichole. We'd practiced the relaxation techniques and phrases I'd repeat to help Nichole achieve a meditative state.

The strategy worked well for several hours, but the delivery process wasn't moving as quickly as we had hoped. Nichole experienced lots of pain in her back. We used a yoga ball to find comfortable positions for her. She spent a lot of time on the ball in the shower, with me spraying her lower back with the massaging showerhead. We had a routine we worked through for hours: relaxation, meditation, breathing, resting in bed, resting on the ball, in and out of the shower. I wished there was more I could do, but I helped in any way I could. It was the wee hours of the morning and the doctors were happy to leave us to our routine, checking in only to track Nichole and the baby's vital signs.

Finally, at seven o'clock in the morning, after laboring all night, a midwife checked Nichole's amount of dilation and said something about breaking her water. A nurse answered that Nichole didn't want any intervention. Nichole quickly interjected, "I just didn't want *medications*. If breaking my water will speed things up, let's do it! I didn't know that was an option, or I would have had it done hours ago!"

We laughed. I was amazed at how relaxed Nichole was. I knew her body was hurting, but she knew the result would be worth it.

After the midwife broke Nichole's water, labor progressed rapidly. Contractions increased dramatically, which simultaneously increased Nichole's discomfort. Forty minutes later, she was encouraged to start pushing. A nurse arrived and asked if it was okay for some nursing students to come in to watch the delivery. In the middle of pushing, Nichole nodded her head. I stood by her side, helping as I could: ice chips, massages, hand-holding, whispering mantras . . . but my scientific mind watched everything. I could see the baby's head emerging, but couldn't figure out exactly what

I was looking at. I saw all kinds of wavy lines on the top of the skull . . . *Is that brain I am seeing?*

A few minutes later, with an audience of nurses, students, midwives and doctors, I was cutting the cord as we welcomed our baby to the world. Those wavy lines on the skull were a *full* head of hair on our *son's* head. Shamus Neal Evans was born at 8:07 a.m. on January 11, 2006. He weighed eight pounds, five ounces, and was twenty-one inches long, with big, blue eyes. He was perfect and we were all in love. Tears of joy streamed down my cheeks as I held him for the first time.

I was so proud of Nichole as I laid Shamus on her chest. She had gone without sleep and endured the pain, but never once complained. There was no doubt in my mind that despite being just five feet, three inches tall and the sweetest human being on earth, she was the toughest, strongest, and most determined person I knew.

After an extremely eventful pregnancy, Shamus was born without complications. His hands and feet were a little blue, but his newborn Apgar score was normal. He was breathing, crying, and pooping . . . all the important stuff. He was taken to the NICU for a few minutes to determine if he needed supplemental oxygen. He didn't need it, and although the nurses offered to watch him so we could get some rest, the only place we wanted him was with us.

I hopped in as dad, finally able to do something useful. I changed his first diapers, and helped give him bottles because he had difficulty nursing from Nichole. We celebrated as he took his first gulps. I assisted the nurses as he got his first bath. As we washed his hair, it quickly became apparent that he was a little blondie, just like Nichole. I'd never seen a baby with so much blond hair! All the baby hair I had seen had been dark, and sometimes it would lighten as the child got older, but Shamus was blond from day one, and his hair naturally drifted into a fluffy little mohawk. We were so in love and couldn't wait to share the news. My parents and sisters came to see and hold him. Nichole and I beamed.

As the long day ended and Nichole finally drifted to sleep, I took Shamus out of his crib and laid down with him on a pull-out chair next to her bed. I sang to him for the first time *out* of the womb, and he snuggled into my chest. There was no better feeling than gently kissing our son's velvety hair and holding him close. We cuddled for hours as I listened to him hum the sweetest little hum to me with every exhalation. I was consumed by love for our family, and our world was forever changed.

TWENTY-ONE

WE SPENT OUR FEW DAYS IN THE HOSPITAL SOAKING IN FAMILY TIME, not wanting to be more than a few feet from our new baby, Shamus. The sun was shining when we buckled him into his car seat as we prepared for our first drive as a family. We were filled with excitement as we drove him home on an unusually warm January day. We arrived at our apartment and settled into our new routine. Story time, feedings, naps, diaper changes, baths, playtime, and snuggles were our life and we loved it.

As usual, it was an extremely busy time in our lives. We were preparing to move into our new home, which was nearing completion. We anticipated our certificate of occupancy in February. While we acclimated to our new role as parents, I was completing my doctoral degree. Fortunately, my classes were online, and the majority of my credits were research-based. Since I was working in a pediatric clinic, my research focused on pediatric patients, specifically methods of reducing high muscle tone and spasticity in children with cerebral palsy. Shamus sat next to me in his bouncy, vibrating chair that we nicknamed "The Rump Shaker" while I did my research, took my online tests, studied diagnostic imaging, and while Nichole tried to get a little sleep. I loved having him by my side, with his big, blues eyes looking up at me. We took breaks to snuggle, sing, and read stories. Eventually, we'd doze off on the couch together after late-night feedings, which allowed me a few winks before work the next morning.

At the time, I worked in a clinic downstairs from our apartment. For the first few weeks until we moved, I was able to run upstairs between patients and visit with Nichole and Shamus. During the brief visits, I played with Shamus on his baby mat and, as a new dad/pediatric physical therapist in the midst of doctoral research, studied his movements. One day while we played, when Shamus was two weeks old, he suddenly rolled from his belly to his back. At first, we celebrated. *He's rolling and he's only two weeks old—how precocious!*

I wanted him to repeat the movement, so I turned him back to his tummy. Sure enough, he rolled again! It wasn't a fluke! As I watched the movement more closely, though, I saw that he wasn't rolling naturally or purposefully. He was extending his spine into a backwards C-curve, a position referred to as opisthotonos.

I started observing Shamus much more closely. He'd been having difficulty nursing from Nichole, but had been taking a bottle well. He was gaining weight, slept, pooped, and peed as much as babies should, but I tuned into his movements. I noticed he held his hands in little fists with his thumbs tucked into his fingers. I noticed he startled excessively when there was a loud sound or a bright light. While I knew that some startle was normal, Shamus would shake, hyperextend his body, involuntarily thrust his extremities, and cry. I noticed when we gave him a bath and I'd wash his feet, they would thump like a rabbit's foot, pulsing up and down uncontrollably. I knew this was something called ankle clonus. I put all the pieces together and realized that all the signs and symptoms pointed to some type of neurological differences in Shamus's body.

I immediately talked to Choley about it, and at Shamus's next well-baby check-up, we brought my concerns to the pediatrician. I described everything in detail to the doctor, who did a thorough examination of Shamus and duplicated all the symptoms.

Afterwards, the physician said, "Shaun, I think you're just being a paranoid dad who knows a little too much." He continued, "Everything

Better Together

you're saying is accurate, but Shamus isn't even a month old. It's normal for some reflexes to take a little while to integrate. He'll outgrow this."

We felt more at ease as we brought Shamus back to the apartment. I had to admit, I'd only seen a handful of babies under the age of one month, and probably hadn't studied them as closely as my own son. I felt silly for bringing my concerns to the doctor.

As Valentine's Day approached, Choley and I recruited family and friends to help us move into our new home. We rented a U-Haul in a mid-February snowstorm and spent Saturday shuttling our belongings. Our new home felt enormous to the three of us. We didn't know what to do with all the space. We were content with the three of us in one bedroom, with Shamus close by in his bassinet.

We adjusted to our new home quickly, filling it with memories right away—family dancing in the kitchen, Shamus playing with our cat Bubbles on the living room floor, and bath time in the sink. We loved every minute. Adjusting to a twenty-minute work commute was a bigger challenge. I left the house at six in the morning, and wouldn't get home until eight in the evening. Luckily, I only went to the clinic four days per week, but it was a change to not have Choley and Shamus upstairs. I never saw Shamus awake on days when I worked, except for middle-of-the-night feedings I volunteered for, to give Nichole some rest and give me some quality time with my little man.

The new schedule lasted about a month until I lost my job. Nichole had just resumed teaching after her six-week maternity leave, and I was scrambling to get my resumé together while trying to complete my doctorate. I found a job starting at the end of April. I used the month off from work to finish my research and spend time with Shamus. I'd put him in a front pack and carry him around the property, showing him where I grew up, looking at the fish in my parents' pond, and visiting with them next door. They'd watch Shamus while I ran a few miles, but I couldn't wait to get back to play with him, feed him, and simply be "Dad." I loved

131

being a stay-at-home dad, and it was a great month for Shamus and me to be together. I knew it couldn't last forever, as I had to help pay for the mortgage we had just taken on, but I savored every minute. While I played with Shamus, I noticed that nothing had changed with his development. He hadn't yet outgrown some of the things the doctor thought he would. However, I trusted the pediatrician and believed Shamus would eventually progress, so I tried not to fret and cherished our playtime together.

Just prior to starting my new job as a homecare physical therapist, I was set to run another Boston Marathon. When Nichole had become pregnant with Shamus, my mom said I might have to decrease my running and training to focus on family. At the time, I wondered if that would be true. I figured I'd keep training, as long as it didn't interfere with our family. Conversely, I hoped my running could be part of our family routine. In fact, the whole family would come to Boston to support me, including three-month-old Shamus. The marathon happened to coincide with Easter weekend. We celebrated Easter morning in a hotel room, and Easter dinner carb-loading at an Italian restaurant. Choley carried Shamus around the city in the front pack as they cheered, and there was no better sight at the finish line than Nichole and Shamus waiting for me at the family reunion area.

After the Boston Marathon, we made our annual trip to Buffalo for the marathon, this time with our baby boy! While the year prior, I spent the race thinking of the baby that was to be, in 2006 I had him there with me. The Buffalo Marathon is a much smaller race in number of participants and spectators when compared to something as massive as the Boston Marathon. I loved the opportunity to spot Nichole and Shamus in the crowd, and to see them in several spots around the city as I ran. Together, they propelled me to another personal best, two hours and thirty-six minutes, just six weeks after Boston. We celebrated by taking Shamus to Niagara Falls. He loved the soothing sound of the rushing water.

That year for Father's Day, Nichole and Shamus bought me a jogging stroller, further cementing the idea that running would be part of our family life. As soon as Shamus was old enough to ride, we'd run together. After a few short runs, we increased our distance, and before we knew it, he joined me for my weekend-long run each Saturday. He slept for most of the eighteen to twenty-two miles, but woke up if I breathed hard or slowed down as we climbed a hill. He'd doze off again on the descent. I'd sing to him, talk to him, and dream with him about someday running in the Olympic trials. As my marathon times got faster, the reality of meeting the qualifying standard became more tangible. My new work schedule allowed me to train more, and there was no one I'd rather train with than Shamus. He pulled me through the countryside, with his little jogging stroller leading the way as I held on tight.

We had a great time training that summer as I prepared for yet another marathon: the Wineglass Marathon in Corning, New York. Shamus provided purpose and meaning to my runs. When he wasn't with me in his jogging stroller, I'd run faster to get home, not wanting to miss anything. I held myself to certain mileage standards, but tried to shave minutes off, knowing every minute faster was an added minute home with my family. When he *was* with me, we toured the backroads and hills of our small town, two hours at a time. He slept most of the time, but I was happy to have him with me. Unfortunately, he still wasn't making progress in his motor development. He wasn't attempting to crawl, get on his knees, or pull to stand. He did love tummy time and playing with us. He was interested in his surroundings. He had the best belly laughs and was able to use sign language before he had words. We could tell he was bright and engaged, but his muscles and nerves didn't work like most.

At every pediatrician appointment, Nichole and I vocalized our concerns, but were constantly reassured by Shamus's doctors that he would catch up in his delayed areas. I was starting to have doubts, but they continued saying, "Just give it some time. Every child is different. Everything looks great, he is thriving."

At his nine-month check-up, just before the Wineglass Marathon, the doctors finally agreed. If he didn't make progress by the time he turned one year old, we could get an early intervention evaluation to see if Shamus qualified for some help. While we were relieved the pediatricians were recognizing the developmental delays, we also realized that perhaps Shamus did indeed have some type of neurological impairment.

Of course, Nichole, as a special education teacher, and I, as a physical therapist, had been implementing our own "early intervention" since Shamus was born. As much as we wanted to be Shamus's mom and dad, it was impossible for us to turn off our professional knowledge. Nevertheless, we hoped that our instincts had been wrong and he would outgrow his differences.

Nichole had been feeling guilty, wondering if the chicken pox, car accident, or anything during her pregnancy could've led to Shamus's delays. In addition, Nichole was diagnosed with cerebral palsy when she was five years old. She was diagnosed because she was clumsy and fell a lot at school. Her doctors noticed she had increased spasticity in one of her legs, and her hips were inflexible. She started physical therapy, and though it went well, she was advised by her doctors to not participate in sports. She was also told she wouldn't be able to naturally deliver a child, and it might be difficult for her to have children at all. We were aware of the warnings when Nichole became pregnant, and she was proud to have proven her childhood doctors wrong, yet she worried her mild cerebral palsy had something to do with Shamus having delayed motor skills. Furthermore, her sister's daughter, our niece Paxton, was diagnosed with spastic quadriplegic cerebral palsy. Nichole feared there was something "wrong" with her family's genes. I assured her that all those things were beyond our control. She'd been a great mother from the time we discovered she was pregnant. She did everything right and was amazing the day she gave birth, bringing Shamus safely into the world.

There was nothing we could do but wait to see how the next few months progressed. In the meantime, Nichole and I left Shamus for the first time as we headed to Corning for the Wineglass Marathon. "Keika" (my mom) and "Grandpa" were overjoyed to have him for the night. We felt a little lost without Shamus in the back seat as we drove. Ninety percent of our conversation in the car revolved around Shamus and how much we loved him, and how we just wanted everything to be okay.

On race morning, Nichole kissed me good luck, reminding me she planned to drive the whole course that started in Bath, New York and ran one way to Corning. It comforted me knowing she would be nearby for the duration. I didn't feel nervous, and had never been more focused as I walked to the starting line. I toed the line with just under a thousand runners, with only one thought consuming my mind, *Run for Shamus and run faster than ever!*

In a bargaining moment, I thought to myself, *If I win this race, everything will be all right.*

The gun sounded. I took off like a shot out of a cannon, never looking back. I sailed through the miles, blowing kisses to Nichole as she passed. I thought about Shamus every single step, wanting to transfer the strength, endurance, balance, and stability of my legs to his. I ran solo from start to finish, leading the entire way, winning the race, and setting a new personal best of two hours and thirty-five minutes.

Nichole and I stayed just long enough for me to complete some interviews, collect my award, and stretch my legs before hopping in the car to get home to Shamus.

TWENTY-TWO

As THE WEEKS WENT BY, it became evident that Shay wasn't progressing with his mobility or motor skills. He wasn't pulling to stand or attempting to crawl. He could sit, unsupported, if we helped him into the position, but we had to surround him with pillows because if something startled him, he would topple. Of course, we wanted him to progress with his development, and we wanted him to be able to walk and play like other kids. At the same time, we loved being parents and treated him as we would any child. We read, played, scheduled playdates, and helped him to be mobile when required. We watched him study his environment and explore ways to get to what he wanted. We celebrated small progress, but we knew that he had physical limitations.

With his pediatricians in agreement, Shamus started early intervention services when he was twelve months old. He showed enough motor delay to qualify for physical and occupational therapy. He did excellent on the cognitive components, scoring above his age in all areas. The scores simply validated what Nichole and I already knew; Shamus was intelligent, but his body had restrictions. We still didn't know the cause, but knew it presented like cerebral palsy, so the pediatrician referred us to a neurologist.

The neurologist concluded that Shamus did, indeed, have a form of cerebral palsy. We told the specialist about the complications during pregnancy, but he assured us the car accident and chicken pox hadn't caused Shamus's diagnosis. With no birth trauma and an unremarkable labor and delivery, the neurologist questioned if it was familial spastic paraplegia. In other words, since Nichole had a mild form of cerebral palsy and her niece had a more significant version, perhaps there *was* a genetic component. We opted to not put Shamus through any genetic testing, as we were informed additional testing wouldn't alter treatment.

Shortly before our neurologist appointment, Nichole had become pregnant with our second child. We were euphoric for Shamus to be a big brother, but we kept it quiet from our families for the first month. We were concerned that if there *was* a genetic component to Shamus's spasticity, the new baby might be equally or more significantly impacted. Regardless, we opted for no special testing in utero. We were going to love the new baby just as we loved Shamus, and any testing wasn't going to change how we proceeded with the pregnancy.

We delivered the news about Shamus's diagnosis to our parents. No one was surprised, but all secretly hoped our inclinations had been wrong. We hoped there was a simple explanation and quick treatment, so Shamus could develop like his peers. Prior to Shay's neurological assessment, I remember talking to my father and telling him I thought Shamus had a form of cerebral palsy. I explained the signs and symptoms I had seen, and my father replied, "This is the only time in my life I've wanted you to be wrong."

We all wanted Shamus to have every opportunity, and we wouldn't let any physical limitations impede that. Nichole and I could have been despondent and spent time denying or grieving. It would've been an appropriate response. Instead, we moved forward. We had spent Shamus's entire life knowing he wasn't developing like other kids. It didn't stop us from loving him, nurturing him, and teaching him. The fact that he now had a diagnosis didn't change anything.

Without ever discussing it, Nichole and I decided that whatever Shamus wanted to try, we would make happen. We knew we'd have to adapt, modify, and accommodate to allow his participation, but we were willing to do whatever it took to make sure his childhood was fulfilling. While Shamus continued to grow, it became more and more obvious how bright and engaged he was. Although he was behind in his motor milestones, he developed language early. While other kids his age explored the world with their bodies, Shamus was busy exploring with his mind. Like all kids, he was a little sponge for knowledge, and it was wonderful for us to see his progress. He was excited about becoming a big brother; as much as he could understand what that meant. As Nichole's belly grew, he understood his baby brother or sister was inside. When Nichole would feed Shamus in his high chair, we would often catch him giving the baby a high-five or a kiss through her stomach as she stood next to him. We felt proud of the little boy we were raising.

At the same time, Nichole's pregnancy advanced. When we first told our families, we weren't greeted with the type of fanfare or excitement we expected. They responded with mild happiness and a fair amount of worry. Questions ensued about the potential for the new baby to have cerebral palsy. Nichole and I knew that there was nothing we could do if that were the case.

We understood that our family meant well and were concerned that we would be overwhelmed. Nichole and I persisted in caring for Shamus and doing our best to keep Nichole healthy, safe, and protected. After everything she'd been through during her first pregnancy, we wanted the second to be smooth sailing.

Alas, it wasn't that easy. Physically, Nichole was well, but not having a lot of support and feeling guilt about her genetics put her under more stress. As the months passed, our marriage became strained. It was difficult for me to understand her feelings of guilt, and I didn't know how to support her. I began working late to avoid arguments at home. When I was home, I spent most of my time focusing on Shamus, rather than Nichole. I felt I was doing my part by giving her some respite from caring for Shamus since her growing body made that difficult, but what she really needed was my love and support.

Fortunately, I figured that out as summer wore on. Thanks to our professional backgrounds, we knew that parents of children with disabilities often end up separated. We weren't going to let that happen to us. After two months of high stress and mild depression for Nichole, we focused on family and made time for the two of us again. I realized I felt equally guilty, but had never been able to vocalize it. I was a physical therapist, specializing in pediatrics, and wasn't able to change Shamus's development. While we were focused on moving forward, there were moments we couldn't help but blame ourselves as the new baby developed in utero.

Have we made any mistakes with Shamus? We knew we hadn't . . . *Should we be doing something different this time?* Just acknowledging our fears, finding support in one another, and getting so much joy from Shamus's smile and laughter each day propelled us to being ready for any challenges we might encounter.

The due date for baby number two was October fourth. Before Nichole had become pregnant, I'd registered to run the Rochester Marathon in mid-September. When we discovered the baby would be due in early October, I questioned whether I should participate. Nichole knew how my training had focused on peaking for that race and she *insisted* that I run.

It had been an extremely hot summer. I couldn't imagine what Nichole had to endure daily—eight months pregnant in the heat and humidity of August.

As mid-September got closer, Nichole regularly uttered the phrase, "Okay, baby, you can come out any time now." Every time she said it, I thought, *Should I really run in Rochester? I appreciate her support, but perhaps I should stay home and be the loving husband and father I need to be. It would not be worth missing the birth of our second child.*

Labor Day weekend came and went (the holiday, *not* the birth/delivery kind of labor day!). We discussed the marathon at length and Nichole continued to insist that I run. I agreed I'd go if there were no signs of early labor. I decided to drive out late Saturday afternoon, just in time to pick up my race packet, sleep at Blake's parents' house in Rochester, and drive back immediately following the marathon. Nichole made plans for her mother to visit for the weekend, in case anything happened during my eighteen-hour absence.

On September 15, 2007, I reluctantly left home. I hugged and kissed Nichole, her mother, and Shamus goodbye. They wished me luck and assured me everything would be fine. Nichole's parting words were, "I was in labor a *long* time with Shamus. If anything starts, we'll call, and you can come back."

That was not how I wanted things to happen. I didn't want to miss a moment. I wanted to be there through the entire labor. We'd worked together so well during Shamus's birth. I wanted to continue to be a team.

Before leaving, I got down on my knees and whispered to Choley's stomach, pleading, "Okay, baby, Daddy is going to go run a race. I'll run it fast and be back quick. You need to make sure you stay in there until I get home! I love you and I'll be back in a flash!" I gave her belly, Nichole, and Shamus one more kiss before I hopped into my car and drove to Rochester.

TWENTY-THREE

As I drove to Rochester, I had serious second thoughts. While Nichole was almost three weeks from her due date, Shamus had been eleven days early when he was born. I wouldn't forgive myself if I missed the birth of our second child. Additionally, it was the first marathon I'd be running without Nichole in attendance. Even when I didn't know she was in Philadelphia, she'd been there, and had been there every race since. Not only would Nichole not be there, but no one would be there. Even Blake's parents were out of town. They'd left me a key so I'd have a place to stay, but I was on my own. Thankfully, I had trained relentlessly, felt prepared, and knew I was getting closer to running under two hours and thirty minutes. My goal for the race was to run fast, stay safe, and get home as quickly as possible to my very pregnant wife.

More than once on the three-and-a-half-hour drive to Rochester, I thought about turning around and heading home to be with my family. Yet, I pressed on. I called immediately upon my arrival to check in. Nichole promised me she was doing well. I told her to call if anything changed overnight and I'd be there in three hours. She reassured me she'd be fine and wished me luck. Needless to say, I barely slept the night before the race. I looked at my cell phone every fifteen minutes to make sure I hadn't missed a call. All I could think about was running fast and getting home, feeling guilty I wasn't there.

Early the next morning, I drove to the shuttle bus that would take me to the starting line. Being alone was a whole new challenge for me. I didn't have anyone to hand my warmups or car keys to. I tucked my key into my running shorts and brought disposable sweatpants. I also knew it meant I'd be driving myself home with sore legs, a very tired body, and an exhausted mind after having run on minimal sleep. I blocked that all out of my mind and focused on the task at hand: running fast.

I was sponsored by Saucony at the time and was proud to wear their apparel. I saw a few other Saucony-sponsored athletes at the start line. We gave each other good-luck nods as we warmed up. No one had any idea about the struggle going on inside me, wanting to be home with my family two hundred miles away. Make that 226.2 miles away, with the first 26.2 miles being on foot through the city of Rochester. My mind was preoccupied, but the race was imminent, and the sooner we started, the sooner I could be there for my wife, son, and baby.

The gun fired and we strode into the cool September morning. I had shed my race warm-up and placed it in the donation pile of clothes prior to the race, but I wished I'd kept a layer for the first few steps. Luckily, as runners jostled about and the sun rose over the horizon, I quickly heated up. In the first five miles, a pack of several runners and myself distanced ourselves from the rest of the field. By mile ten, it became clear it was going to be a three-person race. I was running strong and there were two other runners by my side. The three of us ran in stride, none taking the lead, no one blocking the wind—just three guys cruising along through the streets and bike paths of Rochester, as if we were old buddies out for a jog.

As each mile passed, I blew three kisses back home. One for Nichole, one for Shamus, and one for the baby. There was absolutely no way for Nichole to contact me during the race, so I simply hoped and prayed she was sleeping in and enjoying a relaxing morning. I locked in on the mission of getting to the finish line as quickly as possible.

Despite looking strong, one of the runners dropped off at mile fifteen, which left me and just one other. He and I exchanged small talk and enjoyed having each other to keep up our pace. I learned that his name was Dave and we talked briefly about our families, our training, and what food we craved at the finish. Dave was the only one in the race, or Rochester for that matter, who knew I had a wife at home who was over eight months pregnant. A committed father and marathon runner himself, he empathized with my situation.

As the third runner dropped off, Dave and I swapped surprised glances, and realized the race was going to come down to the two of us. As we fatigued, our pleasantries simplified to phrases like, "stick with it" and "hang close," any time either one of us started to fall behind. I soon became aware I was the one who couldn't hold the pace we'd maintained for twenty-two miles.

Dave pulled away and I wished him well. My legs couldn't respond. I watched as he steadily increased the distance between us. When I was halfway through mile twenty-three, I could no longer see him. My goal became to not get caught by anyone behind me. After plodding along for several strides, my attention turned back to my family at home. Nichole had always been so supportive. Shamus had joined me for dozens of long training runs over the summer. I had a baby on the way that I desperately wanted to get back to. I couldn't give in to the fatigue. I'd put in too much time to coast to the finish. I was on pace for another personal best and I didn't want to sacrifice that in the final miles. I found another gear and started turning my legs over faster. My stride shortened, but my quicker step-rate increased my speed. I focused on that cadence and charged forward. By the time I was halfway through mile twenty-four, I could see Dave again. From what I could see in the distance, he looked strong, but I was gaining ground. I put my head down, gritted my teeth, and gave it everything I had for the last mile. I arrived at the finish twenty seconds after Dave, who was surprised to see me finishing so close behind him. My time was a new personal best as I crossed the line in 2 hours, 31 minutes.

I congratulated Dave, collected my second-place award, and quickly ambled to my car on sore legs. My sweaty hands fumbled with my phone to dial Nichole. I was in a hurry to both check on her and share the good news about the race. She promptly answered and said she was doing fine. She was uncomfortable as the baby kicked, pushed, and turned in her petite frame, but she wasn't in labor.

I raced home, anxious to see Nichole and Shamus. The lack of sleep, hard training, and changing fall weather were catching up with me. By the time I got home, I was sore, exhausted, and had horrible head congestion. Nichole, her mother, and Shamus were at a clambake enjoying an overabundance of food. When I got back, I met them there. I was elated that she hadn't gone into labor, although as I saw her stretched out on a lawn chair in the hot sun, I could tell she was ready to have that baby!

I hadn't showered or cleaned up after the race, but Choley gave me a congratulatory hug nonetheless, and Shamus gave me a beaming smile, happy to have his daddy home. We spent the afternoon relaxing in the late summer heat and didn't arrive home until the sun was setting. Neither Nichole nor I could wait to lay our heads on the pillow and get some much-needed sleep after a long, taxing weekend. As we laid down, we briefly talked about the baby and how he/she would be here before we knew it. The pregnancy had been so much different than Nichole's pregnancy with Shamus—the way she carried the baby, the food she craved (mashed potatoes and tonic water for baby number two). Once again, we were both convinced we were having a girl, but also excited to be surprised. Before drifting off to sleep, I whispered a big thank you to Nichole's belly, so glad the baby hadn't entered the world without me.

Our sleep was short-lived when Nichole woke up a few hours later, saying she was having contractions. She said it wasn't an emergency, so we opted not to wake up her mother, who was still staying with us. We laid in bed a while longer, resting briefly and then waking to more contractions. At seven o'clock that morning, we decided we'd let everyone know the baby was coming. First, we went to Shamus's room to let him know we were headed to the hospital.

Nichole's mother heard us stirring and came downstairs. She took over watching Shamus as Nichole and I headed to the snuggery. The weather had turned dramatically overnight. While it had been hot and humid the day before, the morning of September 17 was in the thirties. Fall had suddenly arrived. Nichole didn't mind. To her, it was great to feel refrigerated after boiling for the previous few months. She headed out the door in a T-shirt, sandals, and sweats while I bundled up and grabbed our baby bag.

When Nichole delivered Shamus, she hadn't been allowed to consume anything except ice chips while she was in labor, and she hadn't eaten before going to the hospital. Enduring labor on an empty stomach wasn't a mistake she'd make twice! On our way to the hospital, we stopped at our favorite café where Nichole devoured a chili and cheese omelet. Fueled and ready to go, we drove to the hospital, both of us devoid of sleep from the previous few days. Neither of us was comfortable—me on sore marathon legs, and Nichole ready to deliver a baby!

We checked in and went to our private room. We quickly settled into our hypnobirthing routine, and Nichole was doing great. We knew what to expect, and she wanted to do it the same way. This time, she knew to ask for the doctor to break her water if needed, but it wasn't time for that yet. Choley focused on relaxing and letting her body do what it needed to do.

She meditated through one of her contractions when our midwife burst into the room to check on us.

At warp speed, she barked, "Hey sweetie, how are you doing? Is this baby coming? Do you need anything? Let me know what I can do. I know you're doing the hypnobirthing thing so just relax, and get in the zone!"

Choley and I were caught off guard. This was the one midwife we had hoped wouldn't be there. She was sweet, caring, and kind, but her overzealous personality did not fit the relaxation Nichole was trying to achieve.

The midwife continued, "We have some leftover lasagna from Olive

Garden in the break room. Shaun, do you want some? I know you ran a race yesterday. You must be exhausted. Don't you wanna sit down? Sit, get some lasagna."

We hadn't answered one of the thirty questions she'd fired at us, and I didn't want to leave Nichole's side. Yes, I was tired, but so was Nichole, and her task was a million times harder than any marathon. No, I didn't want to sit down, I wanted to be with Nichole. Before I knew it, the midwife was grabbing my arm and escorting me to the break room, putting a piece of day-old lasagna in front of me, and pushing me into the chair to sit and eat.

"Take your time," she exclaimed. "It'll be a while. This baby is not coming yet. Nichole is in good hands. Get your fill of lasagna, get some rest, and come back later."

Wait, what?! I could barely process a word that was coming out of her mouth. One minute I was helping Choley relax, the next I was being bullied by a five-foot-tall midwife who needed a break from caffeine!

I took an obligatory bite of lasagna to be polite, cleaned up the dishes, and went to rescue my wife. When I got back to the room, the midwife was stroking Nichole's hair and shouting at her, "Relax, breathe!" She looked up at me. "You're back already? Go rest, I've got her!"

Choley's desperate expression said, "*Help me!*"

"I'm good," I said. "I really want to be here. You can check on the other patients and we'll let you know when Nichole is ready."

The midwife reluctantly left, and Choley and I looked at each other with eyes wide in disbelief over what we'd just witnessed. Then, we started laughing. We knew the midwife meant well and was excited to help, but Nichole and I were much too laid back for her exuberant style.

We settled in over the next hour and got back into our rhythm. Eventually, Nichole did need to have her water broken, and only had to push for a few minutes before we were holding our baby in our arms. I relished the opportunity to thank our newborn in person for waiting until I got home. What a good little *boy!* We were eager to tell Shamus the news! Simon Blake Evans was born at 2:34 p.m. on September 17, 2007, with chubby, little cheeks and bright, blue eyes, just like his big brother.

TWENTY-FOUR

SHAMUS WAS IN LOVE WITH SIMON FROM DAY ONE. He gave his little brother a big hug and kiss in the hospital when he met him and wanted to be by his side nonstop.

As Simon met his motor milestones, Nichole and I were able to release the breaths that we had been holding. We'd been watching him closely for any signs of neurological differences. Occasionally, we would see similarities to Shamus in his movements, but there was never anything that truly alarmed us. Simon began crawling and at the same time, Shamus began to belly crawl. While Shamus was motivated by Simon's movement, Simon had a fabulous role model for behavior. Shamus was an angel, and his limited mobility and reliance on others established a great deal of patience in him. While most kids their ages would appropriately tire of a toy within a few minutes, our two boys could sit and play with toys for hours. They were content being together. Shamus would talk in full sentences, and Simon would listen and smile. They quickly became best buddies.

When Simon started taking his first steps, Shamus had just gotten his first walker. We celebrated their walking together. When we took them out, people would often say, "Aw, look at the twins!"

Shamus would quickly correct them, "We're twenty months apart."

He'd heard Nichole and I repeat the phrase countless times to anyone who inquired about our little towhead "twins."

Simon also quickly became involved in Shamus's and my running routine. As soon as he was old enough to ride along, he'd hop in the double stroller Nichole bought for us. We gave Nichole an hour to herself as we had some "boy time," exploring the roads near home. Shamus loved showing his little brother the ropes.

Time zipped by, as it does with two toddlers in the house. I continued to work full time, train hard when I could, and race four marathons per year. Nichole stayed at home with the boys for a year and a half before returning to work in a preschool. Shamus and Nichole started at the new preschool together and both adjusted well. Shamus had made great progress. He was soon able to pull himself to standing, walk short distances with his walker, and had improved his sitting balance. Meanwhile, Simon started daycare. At eighteen months old, he was too young to attend school with Mom and Shamus. I dropped Simon off four days per week when I worked, and had him home with me one day per week. It was a transitional time for our family as the boys grew, but everyone adapted. Shamus did well in school, and it was good for him to be around a diverse group of children. Nichole did a phenomenal job teaching the little ones in the three-year-old classroom—a big change from the middle school students she previously taught. She was excellent at balancing being a caregiver and a teacher to her students, and she was glad to have Shamus in the classroom next-door. Simon had a few bumps, bruises, and occasional bite marks from daycare, but he loved going.

The routine continued, and eventually Simon joined Nichole and Shamus at preschool three days each week. By 2010, everything was clicking for my running career. I was running over a hundred miles each week, cramming in miles whenever I could. I ran those miles every six days, giving myself Fridays off to recover from the pounding and to prepare for my Saturday long runs. While I was laser-focused on running, family remained my number-one priority.

I was fortunate to have every Thursday off from my daily work routine, so I spent those days with Simon. We'd start our day with cereal and an episode of *Curious George* before we headed to the library for story time. He'd sit on my lap as we listened to stories read by the librarian. After selecting a book to bring home, we'd stop at a local bakery to grab a snack while we watched construction vehicles work across the street. We then returned home for our weekly run.

When the weather didn't allow us to run outside together, Simon played in our basement playroom while I ran. He would sit in a purple, plastic kiddie pool filled with toys while I hammered out nine or ten miles. We'd relax the afternoon away, reading on the couch and dozing together as we anticipated Mommy and Shamus's arrival.

When the weather was nice, Simon would join me in his baby jogging chair, and we'd tackle our favorite fifteen-mile route. The route took us past his former daycare provider's house. We waved hello as we zoomed down the hill. We then climbed another road and took in the view of the valley below, before running past a sheep farm and babbling creeks. Most days, Simon would be asleep by the time we got home. I would unbundle him from his layers, place him in his bed, and let him finish his nap while I stretched and showered.

One of those Thursday afternoon runs remains vivid in my memory. It was blustery and slightly chilly in late March. Simon and I decided to brave the elements. I covered him in blankets to shield him from the wind. He led the way, giggling as we ran up a steep hill into the breeze. The jogging chair canopy caught the wind like a sail. I'd never forget how difficult it was to push him that day—running up the incline, into a stiff wind. Despite the difficulty and my legs screaming for mercy, it was exceptionally satisfying to see his eyes light up through the blankets, hoods, hats, and scarves covering his tiny face and pudgy cheeks.

Two weeks after that run, we went as a family to Queens, New York, so I could run a half-marathon the Saturday before Easter. The race started and ended at Flushing Meadows Park. On Friday, we scouted the area so

Nichole would have an idea of where I'd be running and where she and the boys could play. The park was beautiful, and the weather cooperated fully. I was in the lead group throughout the race and pulled ahead with five miles to go. I never looked back, and ended up covering the 13.1 miles in one hour, nine minutes—another personal best. As I accepted my winner's trophy, Shamus joined me for the victory photo before we spent the afternoon playing on the playground. It was a picture-perfect weekend.

My running confidence was enhanced by the fact I'd broken two hours, thirty minutes in a marathon the previous spring by running 2:26 in Burlington. Having run sub-1:10 in the half-marathon in Queens, I began to believe I really *could* run sub-2:20 in the marathon and achieve my goal of qualifying for the Olympic Marathon Trials.

The half-marathon served as a tune-up for my spring marathon that year. I was selected as an elite athlete at the 2010 Cleveland Marathon and viewed the race as my chance to push for sub-2:20. Sunday, May 16, 2010 was marked on my calendar. Every training run with the boys, every hill workout, speed workout, treadmill run, long run, and rest day was planned with that date in mind.

I'd be making the trip solo. Nichole would be home with the boys but, as always, they'd be with me in spirit every single step of the 26.2 miles. As I entered my three-week taper in preparation for race day, I felt more ready and confident than ever. Unfortunately, in the final week before the race, I developed a nasty cold and sinus infection. I'd experienced head congestion previously, as I let my body rest prior to a big race, so I wasn't overly worried as I boarded my flight from Albany to Cleveland. I arrived a few days prior to the race so I'd have plenty of time to rest, hydrate, and fuel my body. I was provided with a *huge* hotel room, which just made me miss Nichole and the boys more. I had a kitchenette in my room, so I grabbed groceries to make myself dinner each night. I ate alone at the table in my hotel room and thought about nothing except the race and my family. My head cold worsened, but I continued to push fluids and decided to take some cold and sinus medicine three days before the race.

It was at that point when I started to stress. I read through the race manual and saw winners could be subject to post-race drug testing. I felt fairly confident I could win, so I logged in to the USA Track and Field (USATF) website to see what medications were banned. Sure enough, the cold and sinus medication I'd taken was listed because it contained phenylephrine. I immediately called USATF to speak with someone to tell them my situation. They confirmed the medicine was a banned substance, but since it was still a few days before the race, they advised me to stop taking it. The phenylephrine would most likely be gone from my system by the time of the race. I took their advice and continued to drink lots of water as I got ready to line up Sunday morning. (To note, a few years later, phenylephrine was removed from the banned list.)

Saturday morning, I woke up and wasn't feeling quite as confident. I spent most of the day lying in bed with a hot washcloth on my face, trying to relieve the sinus pressure. In addition, I was missing home, feeling like I deserted Nichole by leaving her on her own with the boys. As the day progressed, I tried to remain focused on my goal, sub-2:20, and tried to ignore the fact my head felt like it was going to explode, no matter how much fluid was running out of my eyes and nose! I picked up my bib number from the race expo and took a short jog around Cleveland to see the city, the Rock and Roll Hall of Fame, the baseball and football stadiums, and Lake Erie. When I got back to my room, I had a message on my phone from Nichole and the boys. The message is still saved to this day; Nichole saying hi, then turning it over to the boys. "Hi, Daddy! Love you! Good luck in youw wace! Miss you! Bye."

I called the family to say good night and send my love. Nichole reiterated that they believed in me. My confidence was reignited. The love of my family gave me some much-needed wind in my sails. I woke up early Sunday morning and jogged out the stiffness from my legs. My head was congested, my body ached, and I couldn't breathe through my nose. Regardless, I honestly believed May 16, 2010 was the day I would break 2:20.

As I stepped up to the starting line and removed my cap for the national anthem, I thought back to the thousands of training miles, to the 2:26 I'd run one year prior, and to how easy 1:09 had felt at the half-marathon. *All I have to do is run back-to-back 1:09s.*

My adrenaline was firing and my heart was pumping. As the gun sounded, I ran with the lead pack. I tried to tuck in and let the other guys lead the way. The wind was picking up considerably and I didn't feel like I could fight it alone all day. I could tell the others were feeling it, too. I thought back to the windy run with Simon, his baby jogger acting like a sail pushing against me. *If I could push through that, I can push myself through a little wind, no problem.*

I hung with the lead group through twenty miles, but realized my goal of 2:20 had slipped away. I wasn't sure if I could hang on for the win or not. My lungs usually didn't bother me while I ran, but that day I felt like I couldn't get a deep breath. I'd tried to be diligent about taking fluids frequently during the race, but I still felt my muscles cramping from dehydration. I plugged along as one runner and then another pulled ahead. I finished third, with my strength sapped by the wind and chest congestion. I finished in 2:32 with the winner crossing the line in 2:27. It would have taken a mighty effort for any of us to cross the line in less than 2:20 that day, even if I had been one hundred percent healthy. I wasn't disappointed. I had given it my everything. I finished on the podium and ran a respectable race.

I called home to report the results. Nichole, as always, was incredibly supportive. Upon arriving home that evening, I turned my sights to my next marathon. Up to that point, I'd run two to four competitive marathons each year. I decided to back off and not run any more marathons in 2010, and instead set my sites on going sub-2:20 in 2011.

My training amped up as soon as I recovered from the race in Cleveland. I was not discouraged by the result of that Sunday in May. It only made my desire to achieve my goal stronger.

I'd already read every training book I could get my hands on, so I read them again. I scoured through old training logs, looking for patterns and areas I could improve. I became absorbed with optimizing my nutrition. I stretched and practiced yoga. I had a routine of core-strengthening exercises I would do every single night before bed. I worked on my breathing and used a mountain air generator to simulate altitude training.

I focused on speed and being able to maintain that speed for longer and longer times. I ran hills. I ran two to three times each day. Anytime I was on the treadmill in our basement, I was running at its maximum speed: twelve miles per hour. I'd run that pace until I couldn't run anymore. I was excited that summer when we took the boys on vacation to the Jersey Shore because the hotel we stayed at had a treadmill that could go up to fourteen miles per hour (4:17 per mile). While the boys and Nichole rested from our day at the boardwalk and the beach, I went to the gym to squeeze in as many treadmill miles as possible before relaxing in the pool with the family. I felt better, stronger, and faster than ever.

Every weekend, I'd push Shamus and Simon together in their double jogger. Saturday mornings, we'd let Mommy sleep in as we ran through the morning fog, singing preschool songs for fifteen to twenty miles. The runs became interval training as we stopped periodically for stretch, snack, and potty breaks. We rolled through the countryside. We ran up and down hills as fast as my legs could take us. We ran by farms, streams, fields, lakes, trees, and houses. Everything was an adventure as we'd wave to gardeners, count animals, play "I spy," and visit until I was the only one talking and the boys were resting their heads on one another, dreaming the morning away. As they dreamed, I dreamed. My resolve was unparalleled, and my dream . . . the Olympic trials!

TWENTY-FIVE

Unfortunately, my relentless training took a hit as I developed pain in my hips that wouldn't resolve. I plodded through 2011, trying to force my body to be well enough to achieve my goal of qualifying for Olympic trials, but it wasn't meant to be that year. I gave it everything I had and trained through a lot of pain. I'd seen several orthopedic specialists and was diagnosed with an abdominal hernia and femoral acetabular impingement (FAI) in both of my hips, as well as labral tears in my hip joint capsules. X-rays also revealed bone spurs in my hips. At least I knew I was not imagining the pain I was experiencing.

The highlights of my training were running long runs with Shamus and Simon on Saturday mornings. They kept me distracted from any discomfort I was feeling and encouraged me to keep going. I was informed that there were a few surgeons who could perform arthroscopic surgeries to repair FAI, but the best way to treat the diagnosis was activity modification. In other words, stop running! I wanted to continue competing. Discontinuing my training didn't seem like a viable option. Not only was running my preferred method of exercise and stress relief, it had become a huge part of our family life. Between training runs with the boys, traveling to races, and the running community we'd become a part of, I was not ready to say goodbye. I made that clear to every new doctor I saw, and my first question was always, "Will I be able to return to running?" My ultimate goal of qualifying for the Olympic Trials remained intact, and after coming so close in 2009, I believed it was within reach.

I tried some conservative treatments in the second half of 2011 after I ran a time of 2:34 in the Green Bay Marathon. I attempted all kinds of stretches and exercises. I iced my hips, used electric stimulation, ultrasound, infrared therapy, and hot packs. I took baths in Epsom salts, used arnica cream, had massages, and attended several sessions of acupuncture. You name it, I tried it over the course of several months. While some of the treatments gave me temporary relief, I eventually needed to receive cortisone injections in each hip. The injections provided minimal relief, and confirmed that the best option was to have surgery. I had difficulty finding a local surgeon who would do it. One of the doctors I consulted with was trained in the surgical technique, and I had fully intended on having him complete the procedure.

When I called to schedule, I was greeted by a receptionist who responded, "He no longer works here. We don't know where he is. If you have any contact with him, let us know."

For several weeks, I tried to track him down with no luck. Before disappearing, the doctor had given me the name of one of his colleagues in Boston, who was also trained in the surgical procedure. I called and scheduled a consultation with him. He did X-rays and MRIs, which confirmed the diagnosis and recommended the surgery. I worked with my insurance company for several weeks, but since he was not in New York, the surgery would not be covered. After several more weeks, my health insurance directed me to one surgeon in Albany who could perform the procedure. He was relatively new, so there were minimal reviews on him, but I was out of options. The pain in my hips wasn't only limiting my running, it was also limiting my ability to play with the boys, transfer Shamus, and even complete simple tasks like getting in and out of the car.

I consulted the new doctor and told him my running goals and concerns as he patiently listened. He felt confident in the procedure, though offered no guarantees. I knew I needed to have both hips repaired, and the surgeon thought it best to perform two separate surgeries, recommending I fully recover from the first before proceeding with the second. He spent a great deal of time reviewing the procedure, describing the arthroscopic technique, the recovery process, and therapy protocol. He understood I was a physical therapist, and I appreciated all the details he provided.

Since it looked like 2012 would be spent recovering, I decided to schedule additional surgeries as well. I met with a surgeon to repair my sports hernia, and since Nichole and I decided if we were going to have more children, we'd adopt, I also scheduled a vasectomy.

The easiest surgery to schedule was the vasectomy. I had the surgery in February and was back on the roads jogging through the late winter and early spring. I didn't run every day and usually only ran a few miles due to the pain in my hips. If I didn't run too fast, or up too many hills, I could enjoy the miles. On those days, it made me question my decision to proceed with the hip surgeries but I was quickly reminded I needed to do *something* when I'd squat to get on the floor with the boys and had a difficult time getting up.

My first hip surgery was scheduled for the Thursday before Memorial Day. My sister Jen had the day off from work and volunteered to take me so Nichole could be at school and care for Shamus and Simon. I was nervous. I'd never had a "real" surgery. In fact, the only procedures I'd had were the glass being removed from my foot in high school, the vasectomy a few months earlier, and my wisdom teeth being removed in college. I reacted poorly to the sedative when I had my wisdom teeth out, complete with nausea and vomiting. I was anxious about how my body would react to the anesthesia and the epidural I'd be given for my hip surgery.

After the pre-surgical preparation, the anesthesiologist came in and set down a huge syringe on the table near my hospital bed. He said, "Don't worry, this isn't for you."

I knew that it *was* for me, as I heard him say the same thing to several other patients that morning. I wasn't sure if he thought he was putting people at ease, or if he thought he was being funny. Either way, I knew I'd be receiving the injection, and soon after I wouldn't be able to feel my legs. Following the epidural, I was given medicine in my IV to make me sleep, as well as anti-nausea medication. I was then wheeled away to surgery.

The next thing I knew, I was waking up as the doctors and nurses finished the procedure. They spoke about the weather and were surprised when I joined the conversation through my oxygen mask. They acknowledged I was awake, told me they were almost done, and shortly after took me to recovery.

I was only there for a few minutes when a nurse asked me to move my toes, to see if the epidural was wearing off. I was ecstatic when they wiggled. Then, she asked me to raise my leg. No such luck. I lifted with all my might—nothing. Not being able to move my leg was scary, but the nurse advised me it could take some time for sensation and movement to return. I pushed myself, straining to move my leg. Finally, after an hour in recovery, I felt the post-surgical pain creeping in. I struggled again and determinedly lifted my leg.

Recovery had begun!

The surgeon talked to my sister while I was in recovery. He indicated he had to do a lot more bone work than he'd anticipated. The labrum was easy to repair with a few stitches, but the bone spurs required quite a bit of grinding. He told her he didn't know if running the number of miles I wanted to run would be possible.

Jen relayed the information to me when we got home and I responded by laying on the couch and crying. I couldn't imagine having undergone surgery and not being able to run. I was frustrated, but when I woke up the next morning, I was undeterred. I did all the exercises I was allowed, following the doctor's protocol systematically. The only thing I didn't do was take the prescribed pain medication. I took one pill the night of the surgery, but vomited almost immediately. After that, I stuck with over-the-counter medicine.

Winning the
100 meter dash,
Field Day, 1988

Evans family
photo circa 1994

Bryan holding my blocks for the
400 hurdles at the Junior Olympics

Dr. Michael and me at my
commencement from Notre
Dame College

Nichole and my
wedding day, 2004

Me and my marathon support crew
(Nichole, Jyll, and Blake) after the
Philadelphia marathon

Shamus's first
Boston Marathon

Shamus loved his new
baby brother, Simon,
from the start

The first ten miles done
with Joe Orth by our side,
only 3,200 miles to go!

Our first race together, FireCracker
Four Miler, Saratoga, New York, 2013

A hug to end a day of long miles
on the road in Washington
during our run across America

Simon taking care of his daddy's feet
after another fifty-plus mile day

Sweltering Summer
Six-Hour Champions,
Shamus's BIG
dream was born

Chair presentation to Hailey in Sioux Falls, South Dakota

The completion of
Day 8 had us feeling
like superheroes as we
crossed another state
line and a new time
zone into Montana

Brotherly love after a long day on the road

Shamus walking across our journey's halfway point in Presho, South Dakota

Day 6 brought us many obstacles but also led us to the completion of our first state as we crossed from Washington to Idaho

Peggy and Freeda, my daily oasis

Lucas and his family at an impromptu chair
presentation in Iowa

Shamus telling our story to a
reporter at the Rock & Roll
Hall of Fame in Cleveland as
we close in on the East Coast

We made it to Mount Rushmore!

Simon learning to ride a two-wheeler with me cheering him
on close behind

The best pit crew ever!

Rooster and Ainsley join Shamus and
me providing some extra inspiration
for some miles in New Jersey

A journey of over 3,200 miles
begins with Shamus's first few
steps out of Puget Sound

Field of Dreams

Together, we made it to the
Atlantic Ocean!

A celebration of our
successful transcontinental
run at Citi Field with the
New York Mets!

I went back to work on Tuesday after the Memorial Day holiday. I was determined to heal quickly. I had my follow-up with the doctor the following week, and he showed me internal pictures of the work he'd done. I told him recovery was going well, and asked to schedule the next surgery. Knowing I had kids at home to care for, the surgeon wanted to ensure my right leg had fully healed before he'd operate on the left. We decided to schedule the second hip for the end of September, with my sports hernia repair scheduled for early September. Therefore, summer was spent rehabilitating my hip and preparing for my upcoming surgeries. I went to the pool every day before work for some aqua-jogging and stretching and committed to my recovery and strengthening with as much dedication as I had done for my marathon training.

The sports hernia surgery went well, as the doctor inserted a mesh into my lower abdomen, eliminating my groin and stomach pain. A few weeks later, I was under the knife again, getting my final surgery of the year on my left hip. The surgeon said it was in much better shape than my right, and after seeing my recuperation up to that point, he was optimistic about my return to distance running—just what I needed to hear!

TWENTY-SIX

ONCE AGAIN, I RESUMED WORK FIVE DAYS AFTER SURGERY. I felt good and was hopeful about my return to running. Nichole managed everything at home for those first few days, but I wanted to help as quickly as possible. As my post-surgical pain subsided, I appreciated being able to move comfortably. Just two weeks after my final surgery of 2012, I wrote the following entry in my training journal:

Just jogged to the mailbox. I almost had my full stride with minimal pain in my hips. I'll take it! Time to hit the stationary bike and do some rehabilitation. I'll test the legs again soon! Mini goals: run a little further each attempt.

Our mailbox was only one hundred yards from our house, but I valued even the shortest run. I continued to use the stationary bike, go to the pool, stretch, walk, and strengthen my core. I jogged periodically to assess my legs, feel my stride, and dream about getting back to my goal.

In mid-November, I went to a local track to run a timed mile. I wanted a baseline as I returned to training. Previously, I'd go to the track and crank out mile repeats at a sub-five-minute pace. I tried not to think about all those speedy miles, knowing the memories would haunt me. Instead, I focused on the moment, the joy of being able to run, my lungs craving the cold air, and my legs wanting to feel that familiar burn. I was apprehensive as I set my watch to zero. I knew I shouldn't expect too much, but I desperately wanted to know if I was really back. *I'm fit enough, but how will I really fare in my own personal time trial?*

The imaginary starter's pistol fired, and I rounded turn one, glancing at my watch as I hit the straightaway: twenty seconds for one hundred meters.

Keep that pace, I thought. *Maintain it and you'll hit a 5:20 mile.* I charged on, huffing and puffing, a solitary figure striding around the oval. That's how I wanted it—just me, alone. I didn't want anyone else there to witness my success or failure.

I gave it my all. My pace faltered a little each lap. I couldn't turn my legs over any quicker, and my speed declined. Where a 4:40 mile had been easy a year prior, I struggled to finish with 5:45. While I was happy to be under six minutes, I came to the realization that I had a *lot* of work to do. That was okay with me. Hard work didn't scare me, but not being able to regain my speed did. As I pushed myself, I noticed my hips became increasingly sore as my pace quickened. I had been able to run slowly before—and even between my surgeries with minimal pain—but the stress of running faster was where I started to suffer.

The weather turned cold. Ice and snow were frequent that winter which made training difficult. I spent lots of time on the treadmill, but felt I wasn't able to recover my quickness. Years earlier, I'd set the treadmill at maximum speed and run for ten miles. Post-surgery, I'd set it at six-minute pace and labor to keep up for one mile before having to slow down. Despite having told my physical therapy patients for years that the hardest part of recovering from surgery is being patient, I had difficulty heeding my own words of wisdom. I was expecting too much improvement too quickly.

I got discouraged and needed something to pull me out of my self-pity. *What better cure than to sign up for a race?!* However, I didn't want to register for a marathon. While I felt my endurance was decent, my speed wasn't where I wanted it to be. I didn't want to run a marathon in a time that would feel disappointing. I felt the best path toward chasing my goal of the Olympic trials was to try something different.

After much discussion with Nichole, I decided to sign up for my very first ultramarathon in 2013. Nichole wasn't excited about me running my first fifty-miler, but I was adamant. I needed a goal to work toward. To give myself plenty of time to train, I looked for fall races ten months away. As I searched, I found the Canandaigua 50 Ultramarathon in Central New York. Even though I'd never run farther than 26.2 miles, *and* had two recently repaired hips, I registered for the event. I was excited to train and built my mileage quickly. I wanted to get my legs used to more distance, but the temperature dropped, the snow piled up, and all winter, I never ran further than a twenty-mile run.

When April arrived, I felt like I wasn't making much progress with increasing my distance, and I needed to more than *double* what I was running in a single run! Again, I started to have doubts, and was frustrated with myself about signing up for such an ambitious goal while recovering from multiple surgeries. To her testament, Nichole never once said, "I told you so."

Meanwhile, Shamus had been watching closely as I'd go for long runs each Saturday. He frequently asked if he could join me. Each time, I said no, typically because it was too cold and slippery on the roads. As the temperatures rose in the spring, my excuse was no longer valid. One particularly sunny and warm day in late April, Shamus again asked if we could go for a run. His request was the remedy I needed to get out of my funk. I retrieved Shamus's jogging stroller and carried Shamus outside. I hugged him close, thanked him for being persistent in asking to run, and held him for a minute as we planned our route. We agreed on a five-miler that ran near the creeks and small waterfalls we both admired as we ran.

As I began to place Shamus in his jogging stroller, it became obvious he would no longer fit. He was seven years old and hadn't run with me since he was six. He'd grown a lot during the year, and we realized we wouldn't be able to go for our jog. We were both disappointed, but opted to take a walk with me pushing his wheelchair. We'd been running partners for Shamus's entire life, and as we walked that day, he looked up at me and asked, "Daddy, will we still be able to run together?"

My heart broke. I didn't have an answer. I knew there was a father and son duo—Rick and Dick Hoyt—who ran the Boston marathon together. I had seen them each time I'd run in Boston. Rick was the adult son of Dick, who pushed him every year in the marathon and in countless other road races and triathlons. I knew the chair they used could accommodate a larger rider, but I had no idea if our family could afford one of those chairs or how long it would take to get one.

When we got home from our walk, I searched Team Hoyt on the internet. I quickly found their contact information and sent an email. I'd been following the inspiring duo for years and didn't expect them to get back to me right away, if at all. Much to my surprise, by day's end, I had a response asking me to call to give some more details about Shamus.

I called the next morning and spoke with Kathy Boyer, Dick's significant other. She was extremely kind. She told me about their chairs and while they *could* get me one, the price tag of nearly five thousand dollars might be prohibitive. With Shamus still growing, she indicated it would make more sense to get a chair that wasn't customized, but could accommodate riders who were too big for a baby jogger. The price of such a chair would be about one thousand dollars.

While our young family didn't have a thousand dollars to spare, the price seemed within our reach.

"That sounds great!" I replied. "What do I need to do next?"

"We can't get you a chair like that, but we know someone who can. He leads an organization called Ainsley's Angels. Email him and he'll help you. His name is Major Kim Rossiter, but he goes by 'Rooster.'"

PART THREE

"So many of our dreams at first seem impossible, then they seem improbable, and then, when we summon the will, they soon become inevitable."

—*Christopher Reeve*

TWENTY-SEVEN

I EMAILED ROOSTER IMMEDIATELY, hoping I'd eventually get a response and be able to get the chair before the summer passed. To my surprise, I received a reply within the hour. Rooster presented me with options for getting new wheels for Shamus. One option was to write a one-thousand-dollar check and he could ship the chair straightaway. Another option was to set up an online fundraiser for Ainsley's Angels, ask family and friends for donations through email and social media, and he'd ship it when fundraising reached eight hundred dollars.

Nichole and I thought the fundraising idea sounded great. Family and friends were always wondering what they could do to help on Shamus's behalf. I provided Rooster with background information and photos of Shamus for the fundraising page, and Rooster provided me with information about Ainsley's Angels of America. I learned Ainsley's Angels was an organization created to get individuals with disabilities included in endurance events by pairing able-bodied runners with individuals with special needs to roll in races. I was astounded to discover there were hundreds of families across the US who wanted to give their children the opportunity to participate. It was awakening for me to recognize there were so many other kids out there like Shamus who wanted to be a part of the action. He wasn't alone in wanting to roll with the wind. For us, fundraising for Ainsley's Angels made perfect sense.

By the end of the day, Rooster had built our fundraising page. We began to share the donation link the next morning. Rooster texted within an hour and asked how we were getting so many donations so quickly. Our friends and family rallied, and within a few hours, we'd exceeded the fundraising goal, ending with over $1,300. We were overjoyed when Rooster let us know the extra funds would help provide another running chair to another family.

Our joy was even greater when Shamus received his brand-new Freedom Chair a few days later. Less than a week after initial contact with Ainsley's Angels and Rooster, the enormous box arrived. It was waiting for Shamus when he got off the school bus, and he couldn't wait to give it a try. He helped me take it out of the box, put it together, and inflate the tires. Assembly was quick and easy, which gave us plenty of daylight to give it a test run. Shamus knew right where he wanted to go. We took our five-mile route past the bubbling waterfalls and over the rolling hills nearby, past grazing sheep and some chickens wandering in the road. We rolled along and Shamus exclaimed how fast his new wheels felt.

We were both soaring on the adrenaline of the moment, in awe of the incredible support we'd received. Some of the contributors were people I hadn't seen in two decades. They'd never even met Shamus. Nichole and I anticipated family and close friends would make donations, but we felt truly blessed to know so many people cared about our son.

When Shamus and I returned from our run, Simon was waiting for us. He wanted to go for a run with me, too! Shamus was happy to share with his little brother, and I had plenty of adrenaline to carry us for another five miles. We took the same route so the boys could compare notes when Simon and I returned.

As soon as Simon and I pulled into the driveway, Shamus said he wanted to go again! He had a twinkle in his eyes when he asked, and I knew I couldn't say no. It had been too long since we'd run together. We went for another few miles, and as we rolled, Shamus presented me with a great idea.

"Dad, can we run in a race . . . together?" he asked.

Shamus had seen me run lots of races, but he wanted an opportunity to experience race day *with* me in his new ride. I thought it was a fantastic suggestion. Over the next few days, Shamus and I looked at various local race options. One of those races was a four-mile race on the Fourth of July, in the neighboring city of Saratoga. Shamus thought it sounded like a fun way to spend the holiday, and I agreed.

I reached out to the race director to inquire about Shamus being able to join me. I didn't want to presume wheels would be allowed. The race director emailed me and said they'd be happy to have us, but they thought it would be best if we started at the back of the pack for safety reasons. I knew the race was very popular, typically drawing four thousand runners. I knew if we started at the back, it would be hard for us to do any real running, as we wouldn't be able to navigate through the massive number of runners on the streets of Saratoga.

I replied to the race director that Shamus and I wanted to try to go fast, and didn't want our wheels to pose a hazard for other runners. Luckily, some friends were on the race's volunteer committee and they indicated to the race director that Shamus and I would be able to hold our own on race day. The race director quickly responded that we could start up front with the elite runners. He simply asked that we stay to the side to not interfere with anyone. Shamus and I were on cloud nine. For the next several weeks, we trained together as often as possible. We covered between five and ten miles every time we ran, and we knew we'd be ready for race day.

As we ran, I knew I still had an ultramarathon to get ready for in the fall. Shay and I trained diligently and he helped motivate me, but I didn't feel I was running enough miles to be able to endure *fifty* miles. As a result, I decided to sign up for *another* ultramarathon in August as a way to gauge my fitness. The race I signed up for was a six-hour timed event, hosted by one of my high school friends who had relocated to Pittsfield,

Massachusetts. I added it to our summer calendar: "The Sweltering-Summer Ultra" in August.

As June concluded, Shay and I were energized for the upcoming race and I attempted some longer runs on my own. The weekend of the summer solstice, we were scheduled to go to New Hampshire to visit Nichole's family. On a whim, I informed Nichole I was going to leave at five o'clock in the morning, on foot, and head east toward New Hampshire. I told her she and the boys could get up whenever they wanted, leave when everyone was ready, and I would run until they caught me. We briefly discussed the route we'd take, and I was up and out the door early. I ran alone in the quiet dawn with a CamelBak loaded with water and snacks. I watched the sunrise and pondered the upcoming race with Shamus. I'd run for just over five hours when I looked over my shoulder and saw Nichole and the boys approaching. I'd covered forty miles, had run through many villages, and crossed several county lines. Nichole picked me up just shy of the Vermont border. It gave me a boost of confidence . . . until the next day when I was so incredibly sore, I could barely walk from the hotel bed to the bathroom. I knew I still had a lot of work to do, but first, Shamus and I had a race to run.

By the Fourth of July, we'd logged hundreds of miles in his new chair. We rolled to the starting line amongst thousands of other runners. By race time at nine o'clock, the air was extremely hot and humid. I typically wouldn't run with Shay in such scorching weather conditions, but I knew there was no way he was going to sit it out.

We nosed into a spot on the side of the starting line, and Shamus looked at me with a huge smile. I handed him two water bottles—one for him and one for me—and pushed the sun canopy of his chair down to give him some shade. I was surprised by my pre-race jitters, but it was the first race I'd run in over a year, and my very first race with my son. I hoped we could handle the heat. I also hoped I'd be fast enough, after having received permission to start up front.

I shook my legs out one last time, and together, we were off. I sprinted to the front, not worried about conserving energy, but wanting to avoid tangling Shamus's wheels with any runners' legs. We cruised at a steady pace and were in the lead until we hit our first big incline after a half mile. We climbed the hill with the sun beating down on us. I was already exhausted when we got to the top. I couldn't believe how much I was sweating! Our first mile was run in 5:40, but we still had three to go. Just as I felt like I was overheating, we turned a corner and were greeted by ice-cold sprinklers from someone's lawn. A few strides later, around another bend, spectators were spraying runners with garden hoses. For Shamus, our run quickly turned into an amusement park water ride and *I* was glad he wanted to be drenched by each and every spray.

The cool water and Shamus's smiles and laughter kept us moving through the next couple miles. The final mile of the race was a long, steep incline leading to the finish. My legs were tired since they were still recovering from my forty-mile experiment two weeks earlier. I leaned into Shamus's chair, shortened my stride, and pushed with all my might. We crested the hill and sprinted toward the finish with Shamus's beaming smile leading the way. We crossed the line in just over twenty-four minutes. We were ecstatic! Nichole and Simon greeted us with big hugs, and I could tell by the look on Shamus's face that he was hooked. He loved being a part of the running community. We had some post-race popsicles as Shamus told Choley and Simon all about the race—the sights he saw, the water sprayers, and how fast we zipped down the hills.

We relished in the moment, and as we headed back to the car to drive home, Shay looked up at me and requested, "Can I run your next race with you, Dad?"

I gulped. My next race was set to be the Sweltering Summer Ultra!

TWENTY-EIGHT

My initial reaction to Shamus's request was, "That doesn't seem like a great idea, buddy," mostly because I'd never participated in an ultramarathon myself, let alone pushing him. He and I had done some long runs, but they were all twenty miles or less, and not much more than two hours. I knew how my body had reacted to some of the marathons I'd run: cramps, dizziness, dehydration, and pain. I wasn't sure having him along for the ride in a *six-hour race* made sense!

The more I thought about it though, the more it seemed doable. The race would take place on a closed course. In fact, it was scheduled to occur on a .355-mile cinder track at Clapp Park in Pittsfield, Massachusetts. Since the race was a timed event, we could stop at any time. Shamus could hang out with Nichole when he got bored of running in circles in the August heat, and I assumed boredom would set in quickly for my seven-year-old son. Whenever Shamus wanted, I could drop him off with Nichole and I'd continue alone.

The race director, Benn, was a friend of mine, so I reached out to him and explained our situation. He was excited about Shamus wanting to roll and was on board with the plan we'd established. He notified volunteers there would be some wheels periodically circling the track on race day and we were welcomed to the event with open arms.

I continued to run lots of miles and ran as much as possible with

Shamus, but we hadn't spent much time running in circles, so we went to the track to run some laps. I quickly discovered how exhausting it was to repeatedly turn left. The running chair had a fixed front wheel, so whenever we wanted to turn, I'd lean to the side, pop a wheelie, and angle the back two wheels to turn. Shamus enjoyed the added movement and we had fun whizzing around the track. I soon realized it wasn't going to be easy to turn for six straight hours! Again, I reminded myself that Shamus was bound to get tired or bored after running a few laps with me.

On race day, the fog was thick as we gathered at the starting line in Clapp Park with one hundred other runners that mid-August morning. We couldn't see much more than fifteen feet in front of us. Nervous energy filled the air as runners and their families made final adjustments to their aid stations, which were set up on a table at the north end of the park. The cinder was damp from the morning dew and stuck to my knees as I gave Shay's chair a final check and adjusted his position to ensure he was comfortable. Despite the early morning wake-up call, Shamus was bright-eyed and ready to roll.

We wheeled to the front of the starting area, cautious of hitting runners' legs on the two-lane track. We were given the one-minute warning, and I leaned down and gave my little man a kiss on the forehead.

He gave me a fist bump and said, "We got this, Dad!"

I was glad *one* of us was confident. As we waited for the starter's pistol, my last thought was, *What did I get us into?*

Luckily, my legs remembered what to do, and together, we sped into the fog. Many experienced ultramarathoners started at a walk or slow jog. I had no idea how to pace myself for a quarter-day of running, so I ran at a pace that felt comfortable. I knew Shamus didn't want to be out for a leisurely stroll, so we settled in at 7:30 per mile. I realized many participants had no intention of being on the track for the whole six hours, and instead planned to stop at a set goal distance of their choice. While my intention was to be in it for the long haul, I still figured Shamus would last about ten laps.

As those laps ticked by, Shamus entertained me by describing the latest chapters he was reading in *Harry Potter*. I'd read the books several times, but loved hearing it from his perspective. The details he gave provided me with a welcome distraction from running in circles. I periodically interrupted Shamus's storytelling to check on him.

"Shay, how's it going? Do you wanna take a break?" I asked.

He gave a quick no, and then proceeded with his conversation. After an hour, and many more than ten laps, I could tell he was getting irritated with my interruptions. Together, we rounded the track. Shay chatted and enjoyed the warm wind on his cheeks, and I listened as I put one foot in front of the other.

The sun burned off the fog and, although the temperatures were rising, we found a steady rhythm. I noticed as time went by, most runners were resting, rehydrating, refueling, stretching, and finding shade. Shamus kept a water bottle for each of us in his lap. He was happy to be our private water station, and handed me the bottle over his shoulder whenever I asked. I also fueled on the run, grabbing what I needed as we passed the aid table. I knew many of the runners were much more practiced at ultra-running than I was, but I was feeling okay and decided not to stop.

Finally, after four and a half hours of running, Nichole stepped in and told Shamus he needed to take a break to eat, stretch his legs, and use the restroom. He reluctantly agreed, but insisted I keep going. It was ninety degrees, and I was exhausted. I would have loved to lay down in the shade, but I obliged my teammate's request.

There was no respite from the sun on the track, and my legs were screaming at me to stop. Without Shamus to entertain and encourage me, I had a hard time finding a groove. I plodded along, took some walking breaks, and tried to keep moving in a clockwise direction—one step at a time. Fortunately for me, Shamus took only a thirty-minute rest. Nichole loaded him in his running chair, and we were together again. I leaned on him for support. I worked through muscle cramps, aches, and sore feet, and did my best to continue. I found motivation in knowing that stiff, sore, cramped legs were a daily occurrence for Shamus as he persevered through each day despite the physical limitations imposed by his cerebral palsy. I quickly found my stride with him in the pilot seat. We trudged on, mostly without words. Only an occasional grunt by me broke the silence, to which Shamus would respond, "You're doing great, Dad, we got this!"

My feet scuffed the cinders as it got harder to lift them. Shamus's wheels maintained a steady *whiiiirrrr*, and left a familiar trail that we followed all day long.

As the race clock neared six hours, we decided to squeeze in one last lap. The sun was high in the sky and we were both drained of our early morning energy. Yet, as we completed our 125th and final lap of the day, we felt accomplished, realizing we'd covered forty-five miles! It was the farthest I had ever run. Even more surprising was that no one else had run more than 115 laps. Shamus and I had *won* our very first ultramarathon (and only our second race ever) by *ten* laps and nearly *four miles* more than our closest competitor. Onlookers and runners were impressed with our feat. They patted me on the back and congratulated me for pushing Shamus lap after lap. I felt the need to correct them immediately because there was no doubt in my mind, Shamus was the one *pulling* me. If it hadn't been for his encouragement, I would have been content to stop much sooner. His spirit fueled me when my body was spent. I had him to lean on when I wanted to collapse. With Shamus leading the way, we had done it. We had *won* an ultramarathon—together!

TWENTY-NINE

WE CELEBRATED WITH A BIG FAMILY HUG AFTER THE RACE, and enjoyed the post-race camaraderie as we visited with other runners. Everyone was drained from the heat and running in circles all day, so the celebration was short-lived. I was still in a slight state of shock. Going into the race, I had no delusions of winning. I'd trained conscientiously, but had never run that long without stopping. Shamus had propelled us to victory with his positivity.

I was glad Nichole was there to drive. I couldn't imagine driving the ninety minutes to get home. Shamus sat in the backseat beaming, proud of our accomplishment. I sat up front, feeling dehydrated, cramped, and with salt-caked temples from a day's worth of sweat.

As soon as Nichole pulled out of the park, I closed my eyes and thought to myself, *Maybe I should retire from running while on top, having won an ultramarathon with Shamus leading the charge.*

The thought was fleeting though, as Shamus piped up, "I had a lot of fun today, Daddy!"

"Me too, bud," I replied, eyes still closed, already dozing.

"We should run that far every day," he thought aloud.

"Ha," was the only response I could muster as I yawned.

The conversation quieted for several miles, and I drifted to sleep. Nichole, who was tired from her own ten-mile run that morning and emotionally exhausted from supporting us, focused on the road. Shamus sat in the back, watching the trees go by, with the wheels in his head spinning.

A few minutes later, I woke up to his sweet, little voice asking, "Mommy, how far could Daddy and I go if we ran that far every day, for the whole summer?"

My eyes opened. I sat up, smiled sleepily at Nichole, and shook my head.

"You had a fun day, huh?" Nichole replied.

"Yeah, it was awesome," he said. "How far could we go?"

Shay had just finished first grade, so we helped him with the math.

"Let's see," I said, "you have about ten weeks of summer vacation, and we ran forty-five miles today. How many days are in a week?"

"Seven," he grinned.

"Yup, seven days per week, forty-five miles per day, times ten weeks . . . Shay, we could run over three thousand *miles* if we ran that far every day of summer vacation!"

"Wow! That's a long way!" Shay smiled.

"Sure is!" Nichole said as I nodded off.

Five minutes later, Shamus piped up again and asked, "Where could we go if we ran three thousand miles?!"

"Good question, Shay," Nichole responded. "We'll look at a map when we get home. For now, let's get some rest, okay?"

I slept for the remainder of the ride, and before I knew it, we were pulling into our driveway. I opened the door to get out of the car and transferred Shay into his wheelchair. I was stiff from sitting, but not overly sore.

We rolled into the house and Shamus exclaimed, "Let's get the map!"

Choley found a map of the US and brought it to the dining room table. She unfolded it and laid it in front of Shamus and Simon. We stood behind the boys and pointed to where we lived, where Nichole grew up, where we just drove home from, and the scale on the map showing how far one hundred miles was.

"So, how far could we go on this map?" Shay asked. "If we ran three thousand miles?"

"Well, buddy, we could go all the way from this ocean," I pointed to the Pacific, "to this ocean." I drew an imaginary line to the Atlantic.

"The whole country!?" He raised his eyebrows and then paused. It was silent until he proclaimed, "We gotta do that!"

Nichole and I looked at each other, shook our heads, smiled, and laughed.

"That would be awesome, Shay," we said as we gave the boys hugs and settled into our routine of dinner, baths, and reading at bedtime.

Nichole and I went to bed exhausted. We figured Shamus would forget about his big dream by morning, but we were overjoyed that he had a great day.

I was sore when I woke up at sunrise, realizing I had just six weeks until my next ultramarathon, the Canandaigua fifty-miler. I was even more sore a day later. I knew I wouldn't be able to train right away. I jogged a little and took Shay and Si for a few walks with the running chair. We all decided Shamus would be spectating for the Canandaigua race, because the roads were not conducive to me pushing him in his chair. He, Nichole, and Simon would be at the checkpoints to offer support.

As training resumed and my legs started to feel less like stones, I often thought about Shamus's big dream of running across the US.

My thought was always the same, *There is NO way I can do that.*

I had read books about people who had run across the country—some of them even faster than ten weeks—but that didn't make it feel any more realistic to me. I couldn't fathom running that kind of distance (or even a marathon) every day, day after day, while pushing Shamus. In fact, I was getting nervous about having to run fifty miles in just a few weeks.

I wasn't scared of the distance. After all, Shamus and I had just run nearly fifty miles. I also didn't care how fast I ran. I just wasn't sure what to expect from the whole race experience. My only ultramarathon had been with Shamus, on a closed course, running in circles all day with support whenever I needed it, and with water and fuel available every few minutes. *This* fifty-mile race was basically one *big* circle around Canandaigua Lake with minimal support and some *enormous* hills. I trained with a CamelBak to prepare for hauling my own hydration, plotted out aid stations, and studied the course to ease my mind.

Before we knew it, it was Columbus Day weekend and race day was upon us. My legs hadn't fully recovered from our ultramarathon in August, but I was looking forward to the event and was glad to have the family there as my pit crew.

The race started at dawn in the chilly, fall air. I bummed a ride to the start with another runner so Nichole and the boys could get a few extra hours of sleep. Just over a hundred other runners gathered as the sun rose over the mountains.

We jogged into the morning, our breath visible with every exhalation. The views of peak foliage and reflections of the trees on the lake did not disappoint. I soaked in the breathtaking scenery and felt strong for about twenty miles of incredibly steep hills. Then, I hit the wall—the metaphoric brick and mortar that I had tried so desperately to avoid since my encounter with it in Philadelphia.

I couldn't imagine that I'd run only twenty miles, not even half of the race, and my legs were already spent. I quickly slowed to a walk and slogged along as I tried to stretch my tight, cramping legs, take in some nutrition, and rehydrate. It had gotten warm, every step was a struggle, and I still had thirty miles ahead of me!

I played games in my head. *Get to the next mailbox,* I thought, then I'd figure out what to do next. *Jog ten steps, walk twenty.* The process persisted for several miles until Nichole and the boys pulled up next to me. Their smiling faces and cheers gave me a much-needed jolt to get my legs moving.

The spark they provided lasted for several miles and carried me up and down several hills. I'd muster some strength to climb the hills, and then simply let my legs fly on the descents, hoping I wouldn't fall as the pain shot through my legs into my lower back. My legs were beat, my motivation waning. I pressed on, inching my way toward the finish. Downhills became more painful than uphills, as I just let gravity carry me down. I stayed on my feet, but just barely. My legs and back took a pounding. While the descents were painful, at least I was moving forward. Each time I got to the base of a slight incline, it felt like Mount Everest staring down at me. I looked at my feet to avoid seeing what lay ahead. My posture deteriorated as I slouched deeper with every step. I told myself to keep going, no matter how slow. I grasped my upper thighs as I climbed, allowing my arms to help in the work.

Finally, with most of the hills behind me, I made it to mile forty. It wasn't pretty as I shuffled along, hardly lifting my feet enough to clear a sheet of paper. The scenery that had seemed so beautiful during the early morning became blurry. My legs were toast and my lower back was shot. The only thing keeping me going was getting to see my blondies at the finish.

After eight hours and thirteen minutes, I finally could see their smiling faces and hear their cheers as I arrived at the merciful end of the fifty miles. I was completely depleted, but was proud to have not given up. My back had never been so sore during or after a run, and I knew I had damaged my body. I went into the bathroom to clean up. I also wanted to make sure I could urinate and hadn't become completely dehydrated. I stood at the toilet, relaxed, and was shocked when I noticed my urine was red. I wasn't sure if I was delusional. I called Nichole in to get her opinion. She glanced at the toilet, gave me a stern look, and stated, "You are *not* doing this again," referring to running an ultramarathon.

At the moment, I couldn't disagree with her. I laid down that evening and closed my eyes, but was haunted by hills. Every time I closed my eyes, another incline was there to greet me. I barely slept that night, but admittedly felt content in having covered fifty miles on foot. I had pushed my body to its limits. Nichole was right, once was probably enough. For the next three days, I peed blood.

THIRTY

I CELEBRATED WHEN MY URINE NO longer had a reddish tint to it. I began jogging a little each day to stretch my legs. Of course, Shamus wanted to join. I was happy to have him to lean on, as my legs weren't sure they wanted to support me after I'd abused them so badly with fifty miles of hills.

As we jogged along, we'd visit, with Shamus intermittently asking, "When can we start planning our run across America?"

I would respond to him each time by saying, "Let Daddy recover a little, and we'll figure out a plan," though in the back of my mind, it seemed too overwhelming to even ponder. I didn't see how it would be physically possible for me to complete the task.

I could barely run through the hills of Canandaigua, New York. How could I possibly survive the Rocky Mountains? Despite our success in our first ultramarathon, the Canandaigua 50 Ultramarathon completely humbled me. I couldn't fathom running far enough every single day to actually make it across the US in a year, let alone during summer vacation. In addition to the physical toll of a transcontinental run, I considered several other excuses: *How could we afford it? How will I get the time off from work? How does one plan for such an endeavor?*

Shamus was never put off by my response. He never became irritated or impatient. He simply persisted. Almost every night as Nichole and I would tuck him into bed, he would inquire about running from ocean to ocean. He looked forward to running with me whenever possible. To him, a 3,200-mile run from coast to coast would be a dream come true. Those miles together are what he thought about as he drifted off to sleep each night. The routine was the same for the next month. I increased my mileage, if for no other reason than to enjoy time on the road with Shamus. I had no specific goal race in mind. We were running for the joy of being together.

November arrived. The weather was colder, and as a result, we were running less together, but the questions at bedtime continued. On Thanksgiving Eve, after his bedtime story, Shamus's inquiry changed slightly.

"Daddy, when we run across America, can we give running chairs to other kids like me so they can feel what it's like to go fast?"

Nichole and I stood silently, looked at each other, and smiled. We leaned down, gave him a big hug, and whispered, "That's a great idea, buddy. Get some rest."

We shut off his light and left the room with tears in our eyes. We both knew we needed to try . . .

The following Monday, I walked into my CEO's office and asked how she felt about me taking the summer of 2015 off to run from coast to coast. I explained Shamus's goal and his idea to donate chairs. I rarely took vacations, and when I did, it was never for longer than a few days. I had weeks of vacation time accrued, but never imagined I would ask to use it all at once. I was nervous as I posed the question to my boss, Millie. I oversaw two departments and it was a big ask for me to leave for ten weeks. I knew it would take full commitment from our entire agency to make it work. Despite having known Millie for several years and knowing how much she cared about her employees, I had no clue how she would react. I figured Millie would take some time to think about my request and process it with the management team. I was wrong—she didn't hesitate at all in answering. Her response was simple, kind, and I'll never forget it.

"Of course. We'll make it work," she said, before standing up to give me a hug.

I exited her office in disbelief. Shamus's dream of running from coast to coast suddenly became a possibility. Deep down, I never expected Millie to agree. I figured I would have to go home and tell Shay I tried, but wasn't able to get the time off. Instead, I had the opportunity to deliver him hope.

I immediately called Nichole to share the news. Her response was a lengthy silence, followed by, "Are you serious?!" I think she, too, was expecting an unclearable hurdle.

"I can't believe it either," I replied. "Here we go!"

At home that night, I delivered the news to Shamus. I told him it would still be a while until we were actually able to embark on the journey. It was December 2013, and we'd be making our attempt in the summer of 2015.

He took it in stride and said, "Awesome! Let's start planning!"

He was right. While June 2015 was eighteen months away, we had so much to figure out. It was hard to know where to begin. We decided to start by determining our route. For insight, we turned to Simon. Shamus had come up with an epic plan, and we wanted Simon to be a part of it too.

At dinner, we questioned, "Si, where in the US would you wanna go? Is there any place you've learned about that you'd like to visit? You can think about it and we can see if we can work it into our route!"

His immediate reply was, "Oh, I already know! Mount Rushmore!"

He'd recently read about it in school, and loved learning about history and the presidents. I unfolded our map of the US and placed it on the table. I pointed to western South Dakota. I was secretly relieved Simon had selected a landmark in the northern part of our country, avoiding the southern deserts. We started to look to points west and east, toward the coasts, aiming to make the mileage as short as possible. As a family, we'd rarely traveled outside the Northeast. Most of our trips were to New Hampshire to visit Nichole's family, an annual trip to Pennsylvania to visit Sesame Place, and occasional weekend trips through New England. The boys were good travelers, but this would be a whole new level of travel—for all of us.

To make the run across America official, Shamus decided he wanted to begin and end the journey with his toes in each ocean, taking the first and last few steps of the journey with his walker. As a family, we resolved to run left to right; agreeing that running toward home made the most sense. We scoured the map and landed on Seattle as a starting point on the West Coast. As we looked at the northern coast of the Atlantic, we decided the shortest distance would be the shoreline near New York City.

With a general route planned, the most basic work was done. As we started to review details, Nichole and I were overwhelmed by the seemingly infinite number of tasks. We needed money, not only for the journey, but also for the cost of the chairs Shamus wanted to donate. We needed a safe route, a vehicle spacious enough to be our home for the summer, campgrounds to stay at, locations of hospitals in case of emergencies, families to donate chairs to, and on and on. Our minds were swimming as we envisioned every detail in places we'd only seen in books, maps, or TV. As Shamus and Simon dreamed of all we'd see, Nichole and I laid in bed and made lists of logistics to be coordinated. As Choley dozed, I stared at the ceiling and tried to figure out how in the world I was going to be able to train my body for a 3,200-mile run.

THIRTY-ONE

WHEN IT CAME TO TRAINING, I had no idea where to start. I'd trained for two ultramarathons, but what Shamus was proposing required an ultramarathon every single day, all summer long. It also included running at high altitudes through the Rocky Mountains. I'd read numerous books about *marathon* training, but as far as I knew, there were no books about training for a transcontinental trek on foot, while pushing a hundred pounds in a running chair. The best I could do was build up my mileage and work on sustaining that mileage day after day after day. Even still, I wasn't sure how much to run, how quickly to build, when to rest, and how to coordinate it with my work schedule and other commitments. Not to mention, I had constant doubts, as the struggle of the Canandaigua 50 Ultramarathon was still fresh in my mind.

When in doubt, turn to Shamus. He was the one who dreamed up the adventure. He'd spent hundreds of hours and thousands of miles with me in his jogging stroller and running chair throughout his childhood. *Why not ask him for training advice?*

So, I did. After a few weeks of fifteen-mile runs each day, I turned to Shamus as my transcontinental coach. After all, he would be there, pulling me each step of the way.

I'd wake up in the morning, get Shay out of bed, and ask, "How far today, buddy?"

He'd think for a second before replying, "Twenty-two miles."

Fair enough. That's what I'd do. I'd run five to seven miles on the treadmill before work, squeeze ten miles in at lunch, and then finish what was left of the twenty-two when I got home. After several days of twenty-two in a row, I realized it must be Shamus's new favorite number.

After a grueling week, I went to Shamus and said, "Hey bud, I need a little break. How many today?"

He furrowed his brow, calculated, and came back with, "Twenty."

I raised my eyebrows, pleading for mercy with my facial expression.

"Okay, okay, eighteen," he announced.

I laughed, and then I obliged. I knew I needed more rest, but I also knew there were days ahead which were going to be much harder, and much farther. Training became equally important as a mental exercise as it was physical preparation. It wasn't easy, but I persisted.

As the weeks went by, I started asking Shamus about mileage before I went to bed so I could squeeze some miles in before getting him up in the morning. It quickly progressed to me waking up at four in the morning to get treadmill miles under my belt and not miss out on family time. I'd often run for two or more hours in solitude in our basement before the sun rose, long before the rest of the family's eyes opened for the day. I was surprisingly not exhausted. I thrived on Shamus's enthusiasm. It had become contagious, and Nichole, Simon, and I were all equally excited. That excitement got me out of bed in the wee hours of the morning and propelled me through the day, where every free minute was spent plotting and planning our journey.

Of course, I had many free, mindless moments as I churned out morning miles on the treadmill. It was during those moments I tried to wrap my head around how we were going to make the dream a reality. I trained like a man possessed. Running was something I could control. Yet, there was so much beyond my control, and much of it boiled down to how Nichole and I would finance the mission. We had a small savings, but also a lot of debt from student loans, our mortgage, and car payments, in addition to monthly bills. We were doing okay, but we wouldn't be able to fund it alone. We needed to do a lot of fundraising, find some big sponsors, or both.

While we'd been discussing Shamus's dream run as a family, we'd kept it fairly quiet from the public. My employer knew our plan, but other than that, very few people were informed about our adventure. By January 2014, we decided it was time to share the news. After all, we were never going to be able to fundraise or find any sponsors if we didn't tell anyone. However, we had some trepidation in telling the rest of the "world." It would make it much more real, and I remained apprehensive about my physical ability to run over 3,200 miles in two months.

I wasn't much of a social media user, but I did have a Facebook account. In January 2014, just before Shamus' eighth birthday, I made a public post about his dream for our family to run from coast to coast, and that we'd be making our attempt to make it a reality during the summer of 2015.

As word trickled into the community, most people's responses were phrases such as, "That's crazy," "It's impossible," and, "Know when to say no to your kids!"

Very few people believed we'd actually try.

Amongst all the pessimists—some of whom were close friends and family—there was one optimistic response, which will forever give me chills. It came in the form of a private message from Major Kim Rossiter, Rooster, the president of Ainsley's Angels who'd helped us get Shamus' running chariot the previous spring. His message was, "You and Shay are planning to *run* across America?! That sounds amazing, what can we do to help?"

While I'd constantly heard we were foolish, senseless, or irrational to attempt such a feat, Rooster provided a beacon of light and buoyed my resolve with one simple phrase: "What can we do to help?"

Someone actually wanted to be a part of what we were doing! What better way to bring it full circle than to involve Ainsley's Angels, the not-for-profit that allowed Shamus and I to keep rolling together when he'd outgrown his jogging chair?

We messaged frequently over the next few days. I joyfully shared the story of how Shamus's new wheels led to him having his *big* dream of a continental crossing in that chair. As we began to formulate definitive plans, Rooster's background allowed him to treat our projected journey as a military mission. His enthusiasm for our goal was obvious, and an incredible partnership was born. Our family's mission was dubbed "Ainsley's Angels Power to Push." We were honored to represent the mission of Ainsley's Angels. Rooster and I collaborated on ways to raise money, how to find families for chair donations, and how to make the journey a success. We brainstormed about logistics regularly, and although Ainsley's Angels was a relatively new nonprofit, his passion for our mission and compassion for humankind let me know we were in good hands. I had never met Rooster in person, and had only briefly spoken with him on the phone, but his caring nature, sincerity, and genuine positivity were apparent in all of our communication. His military leadership was welcome, as it removed a great deal of stress around the planning process from Nichole and me. We suddenly had someone who was as absorbed in the project as we were. It was clear that he could aid in the coordination of the endless to-do list.

As the weeks went by, he guided us through social media tasks, which allowed us to reach a greater audience. As a nonprofit, we'd be able to more easily reach out for sponsorships and solicit donations.

On Valentine's Day 2014, we launched a fundraising page through Ainsley's Angels with a target goal of seventy thousand dollars. The goal was the amount of money Nichole and I estimated would be required to purchase Freedom chairs, secure lodging, rent an RV, cover food and fuel costs, et cetera. We could hardly fathom raising that kind of money in a little over a year, but we had a plan—and we had support. We understood that our team, which had consisted solely of our family, had grown astronomically with the addition of Rooster and Ainsley's Angels of America. We instantly had help, encouragement, and "family" across the USA!

THIRTY-TWO

WITH OUR SPIRITS BOLSTERED BY THE BACKING OF AINSLEY'S ANGELS, it was time to get to work raising money. With the fundraising web page established by Rooster, and the hefty target goal of seventy thousand dollars, we spread the word via social media and email. Donations began to roll in. Support from family, friends, and acquaintances was excellent, but we knew we would have to reach more people. Friends of friends began to hear about Shamus's dream, the mission of Ainsley's Angels, and the adventure we were planning. They joined the fundraising team by setting up their own pages. The term "crowdfunding" gained significant meaning to our family, and we were humbled by the outpouring of well wishes and monetary donations. Many contributions were less than a hundred dollars, but they added up and were greatly appreciated.

Even still, we felt we wouldn't be able to do all the fundraising online in the year remaining before the journey started. Shamus and Simon decided they wanted to be active participants in the process too. So, what do any six and eight-year-old brothers do to raise money? Set up a lemonade stand, of course!

As the weather turned warm and summer enveloped Upstate New York, the boys launched their business at the end of our driveway—Evans Brothers Lemonade. The boys were diligent about setting up their stand whenever the sun was shining. During the first week, there were days when several cars would stop, and days when no one other than our next-door neighbors (my parents) would support the business. The boys weren't deterred by slow days, but decided they needed a sweet treat to accompany their refreshing lemonade.

Shamus loved to bake with us and would hunt through cookbooks to find recipes. Each night, he selected a treat for the next day. We spent time each night after dinner baking a new cake, cookie, or brownie. The sweet treats were a great addition to the stand, and business began booming as passers-by would see the boys waving their signs and calling, "Lemonade! Sweet treats!" They were hard to resist.

Simon and Shamus were excellent little businessmen. They made change, tracked sales, set aside money for supplies, put out a tip jar, and told patrons about our plans to run across the US. Of course, on our busy road, and being only six and eight years old, they ran the business with constant adult supervision. Neither Nichole nor I had ever set up a lemonade stand as kids, so we had a blast helping them and waving cars into the driveway. It became a great bonding experience for the family as we chatted during slow business and worked together during the rushes.

The sweet treats became a hit as the summer passed. The boys tracked which treats sold best and returned to those recipes, offering a variety of their best sellers on any given day. In fact, they developed their own cookie recipe, which was quick and easy for them to make. As business thrived, Evans Brothers Lemonade earned repeat customers, many of whom would come back just for the cookies. We couldn't have imagined how fun and successful their little business would be. The boys even pledged to donate *all* their earnings to Ainsley's Angels Power to Push.

Of course, there were some interesting moments along the way. There were several people who would get out of their car, order their lemonade and treat, and visit with us. On more than one occasion, a customer would look at Shamus and ask, "What happened?" insinuating he was using a wheelchair because he'd sustained an injury.

To look at Shamus without his wheelchair, you wouldn't know or think he has a disability. You can't feel his muscle tightness, or see he has difficulty balancing. He spoke clearly to customers and looked at them with his bright eyes. Obviously, the people who asked those questions hadn't had much experience with individuals with special needs. I couldn't fault them for thinking he had broken his leg, but it led to some awkward moments. The first time he was asked, Shamus couldn't guess what the customer was asking about. She proceeded to inquire, "Why the wheelchair?"

I looked at him and nodded that he could tell her.

"I have cerebral palsy," he said.

She didn't know what to say, and wasn't sure if she should believe him. I could tell she was thinking, *Wait . . . but you don't look like you have CP.*

Although uncomfortable for everyone, it was a fabulous opportunity for Shamus to educate a whole new group of people on what disability looks like.

Conversely, there were also a myriad of positive moments for all of us. There was the day a group of cyclists riding from Niagara Falls to Saratoga stopped. They bought lots of lemonade and cookies, and one of the cyclists gave Shamus his United States Air Force cycling jersey, a treasure Shamus has hanging in his room to this day. There was also the day Santa Claus pulled into our driveway on his motorcycle and asked the boys what they wanted for Christmas. Another motorcycle stopped and let the boys sit in their sidecar. A news crew even caught wind of the boys' business story and came to interview them! Shay's dream was catching fire!

As summer ended, the boys counted their earnings and tips. Together, they'd raised over $2,500—an enormous contribution to Ainsley's Angels from our two little philanthropic entrepreneurs! It was a huge success, even if the story had ended there . . . but it didn't.

After the boys went back to school in the fall, we still had people stopping by on the weekends and leaving us notes in our mailbox, asking where they could get some cookies.

Shamus thought that was great, and his response was, "We should start selling them in stores!"

While I thought that was a neat idea, I had no idea how to pursue it and didn't think it seemed realistic. Nichole and I were busy with our full-time jobs, the boys' extracurricular activities, and of course, planning and training for a 3,200-mile run from sea to shining sea.

In typical Shamus fashion, he persisted, "People *love* the cookies. We could sell a ton of them! We could raise even *more* money for our run and Ainsley's Angels!"

He had a great point. The cookies were undoubtedly an enormous success. People genuinely loved them. I decided to look into it and found out we could be considered a "home processor." I contacted the New York State Department of Agriculture and inquired about the necessary steps. After a simple water test, filing paperwork with the county and state, creating a small business, and setting up our kitchen, we were ready to go! Nichole reached out to some local grocers, with cookie samples in hand. We worked out a quick contract and the boys were in business!

They delivered cookies on Wednesdays and picked up checks payable to *Evans Brothers* the following Fridays from three nearby stores. Orders poured in for holiday cookie platters. We were up to our eyeballs in cookies most nights of the week, but teamwork and persistence, once again, paid off. By Christmas 2014, the boys' business had contributed another $5,500 to the mission!

THIRTY-THREE

AMIDST THE BUSY SUMMER FOR THE BOOMING Evans Brothers business, I was still feverishly training. For a good fitness test, Shamus decided we should go back to the Sweltering Summer race, the race that had inspired his dream to run across the US. In 2014, the race increased to an eight-hour event. It truly was what we needed—a full day of running together in the sun, in a controlled environment where we knew we would have constant support.

Race day for the Sweltering Summer Ultramarathon started like most race days. I was awake early, hopped in the shower while the family rested, had a bagel and banana, slathered myself in sunscreen, lubricated to prevent chafing, and donned my race gear. I went through my checklist of aid station supplies: nutrition, hydration, fresh sneakers, and fresh socks.

Shamus, Simon, and Choley wiped the sleep from their eyes as we loaded up the cars and checked out of the hotel. Since the Evans Brothers were an official sponsor of the race, we drove two vehicles to the event. One was loaded with all of *their* gear, including a tent, coolers, hundreds of cookies, five-gallon jugs of lemonade, banners, tables, tablecloths, and T-shirts to sell to benefit the Ainsley's Angels Power to Push mission.

We arrived at the park and Shamus reminisced about how he liked running in the fog at the race the year prior. We were back for more as part of our training for the 3,200 miles that would consume the summer of 2015. With the new eight-hour timeframe, we'd run from seven in the morning until three in the afternoon, and cover as many laps/miles as possible in the allotted time.

After unpacking the Evans Brothers' gear and assembling Shamus's running chariot, Shamus and I headed for the start line a minute or two before seven o'clock. On our short walk, I asked Shamus what the goal was for the day.

His answer was clear, concise, and direct: "Fifty-plus miles, Dad."

I said, as always, "We'll do our best," but I knew we'd run lots of miles together the previous week—nearly a hundred miles in the six days leading up to race day. My legs were sapped but I figured it would be great preparation for the rigors we'd encounter in 2015, when obstacles like the Rocky Mountains and continuous fifty-mile days were upon us.

The race director gave the cue to start and Shamus and I hit our stride. We cruised through the early miles and chatted as we rolled. We talked about the warm morning, the fog over the field, and the sun which was starting to burn its way through the mist. We talked about summer vacation and all the fun things we'd done. It felt good to visit as other runners and spectators cheered. Shamus said he was comfortable. He wore arm warmers and tucked his hands into a blanket to keep them toasty. He stuck his little index finger out as we passed the start/finish line to indicate our bib number—number one—to the officials as they kept track of our laps.

Two and a half hours into the race, the sun was blistering, and I'd already stopped sweating. That was *not* a good sign. My legs cramped, my will was fading, and Shamus said he needed a break. I dropped him off to help manage Evans Brothers Lemonade. After a few solo laps, Simon was waiting in the chariot to provide me with a little motivation. Shortly after, I was discouraged as I was forced to walk. The year prior, I'd run the entire *six* hours, and this year I hadn't even made it to three. I tried to rationalize my need to walk by considering all the miles I'd run that week, but I was still disappointed. The thought of dropping out never crossed my mind, but the thought of walking the remaining five hours pervaded every painful step. Runners we'd passed several times began passing us repeatedly. Shamus and Simon alternated in the chariot, taking turns boosting me, pulling me along, and encouraging me to run. Choley met me on as many laps as possible, all but forcing me to eat and drink as she looked into my pain-filled eyes.

At the fourth hour, the halfway mark, Nichole looked at me with concern and asked, "Shauni, do you really think you can do this every day next summer?"

Even though I was having the same thoughts, I couldn't handle Choley not believing in me. It was all I needed to light a fire in my belly. As the race DJ pumped Eminem's "Lose Yourself," Shamus and I caught a second wind and started our comeback with a vengeance. After lots of water, electrolytes, and a salt tablet, I started sweating again, and was cruising as Shamus clapped and repeated the words, "Go, Daddy, go!" over and over.

The comeback lasted nearly an hour as we gained ground. We pushed hard until a short time later when I stopped sweating again. The boys took a lunch break and I started walking. I overheard fellow runners say, "That stroller makes him go faster. He only walks when he's not pushing." They were right . . .

When I had one of the boys with me, I had a better pace. When I was alone, I stumbled and struggled to find a rhythm. They were truly pulling me with their reassurance and positive attitudes.

After five and a half hours, as Shamus and I pushed onward, he said, "Dad, now you just need to get your third wind." I desperately tried to will a third wind upon myself, but the pain was growing. Shamus took a look at the lap counter the race officials were displaying and saw we were in second place, but we were several laps behind. We'd been behind as many as twelve laps (which equaled about four miles), and Shamus said, "We can catch him, Dad."

I kept repeating that I'd do my best, but I didn't think my legs had enough in them to make up the distance.

Shamus kept up his constant, "Go, Daddy, *go!*" and, "We *can* do it, Dad. Just keep going!" We kept at it for a while longer.

Six and a half hours into the race, Shamus and Simon needed a break and my legs needed one too. I took a quick pit stop at the bathroom and was reminded why I hadn't been feeling well. As I pulled down my compression shorts, the pain radiated. I had been diagnosed with a testicular cyst a month earlier. The best way to describe the pain was to say it felt like being kicked in the "family jewels" repeatedly. It was not an easy pain to breathe with, let alone run with, and I still had an hour and a half to go. I jogged back to the start/finish line to have my lap counted, and I continued with tears of pain in my eyes. I forced my legs to keep going and asked Choley to get me an ice pack. We discretely taped an ice pack to my lower abdomen, into my compression shorts, and alternated it with fresh ice packs every few laps as I jogged. The packs weren't providing enough relief, and jiggled around uncomfortably as the tape didn't hold on my salt-caked body. I asked Choley for some ice cubes in a cup on the next lap—just some "ice on the rocks," I joked.

Choley ran a cup of ice across the field to me and I dumped it directly into my compression shorts when no one was looking. It provided great, albeit brief, relief; a little jolt of shocking energy; and my much-needed third wind. We found a recipe to keep me going.

By hour seven, I'd pulled within a couple laps of the male leader, Jake, and the overall leader, Danielle. Nichole kept the ice coming for over thirty laps. Late in the day, all modesty was gone. She handed me a cup and I'd dump it down my shorts as fast as I got it. I no longer waited for a "private" moment. Nichole was left to explain to race officials and spectators (including the boys' principal) what was going on—lucky Choley! In truth, I was the lucky one. I wouldn't have been able to continue without her assistance or patience.

I ran on and Jake said he was done as I passed him and pulled within one lap. I offered him encouragement to keep going. He was walking, but kept moving. As I pulled even with him a lap later, he pointed to Danielle and said, "Go get her."

I kind of laughed, thinking I'd already used everything I had left. *Can I find one last "wind" in me?*

As much as I wanted to stop and walk, I knew if I did, I'd also be done. Shamus sat in his wheelchair and shouted as I passed him. Deep inside, I remembered his goal for the day: "Fifty-plus, Dad." He'd said we could do it, and I hadn't believed in myself as much as he had. My body was saying it wasn't possible to push on, and here was a little boy whose body tells him "*no*" every day. Shay was inferring *it might not be easy, but keep trying.* The thought propelled me to pick up my pace.

Get to fifty-plus. That was my goal. I asked the lap counters how many laps constituted fifty miles. I hadn't memorized it on the lap sheet the race director had provided, and I was in no position mentally to perform even the simplest of math. Every ounce of mental energy was being used to remember how to put one foot in front of the other while blocking out the pain.

The race volunteers looked at their charts and informed me 141 laps was the number required to reach fifty miles. At that point, I was on lap 136. All I'd have to do was keep moving forward. I passed Danielle with a half hour left, and a race volunteer stepped in to pace me through a few laps, including my 141st. As the time ticked by, I knew Danielle could put in a charge, and I wasn't sure I could respond. I knew that if I stopped to walk, she would surely catch me. She had been so consistent *all* day long.

With about five minutes left, I picked up Shamus in the chariot for one final lap and let him pull me to the finish. Nichole and Simon ran in front and gave me a target to run toward. Just one more lap's worth of steps remained. I hoped my legs wouldn't seize and Danielle wouldn't have a sprint left in her as I maintained a half-lap lead. Danielle completed her lap and realized she wouldn't be able to complete another in the remaining two minutes. She stepped off the track. We simply had to finish one half-lap in those two minutes, and we'd defend our title as Sweltering Summer Champions.

Against the odds, we did just that! Despite having an extremely difficult, dehydrated, and painful morning, and an even more excruciating afternoon full of "ice on the rocks," *we* did it! Simon and Shamus pulled me through, and Nichole tended to my nutrition, hydration, and medical needs. It was a family victory in more ways than one. Not only did we take home the first place prize, but more importantly, we gained confidence that with teamwork, maybe we'd *actually* be able to run from coast to coast the following summer. With Simon's enthusiasm, Nichole's support, and Shamus's optimism and "never quit" attitude, all I would have to do is provide the leg power. I knew that alone, I couldn't succeed, but *together, anything* was possible.

THIRTY-FOUR

As 2014 ENDED, logistics for summer 2015 began to fall into place. We'd settled on the route and, as a result, had a target number of miles we'd be covering. Through countless hours spent viewing internet mapping services, bike paths, and road maps, we found a 3,205-mile route that would carry us through fifteen states. In addition, we determined our starting point would be Golden Garden Beach in Seattle. Nichole and I searched for finishing locations during a holiday visit to New York City, and we found the perfect place: Orchard Beach at Pelham Bay, in the Bronx, New York of all places.

Simultaneously, Rooster and I communicated regularly to discuss our transportation and support vehicle needs. Nichole and I initially thought we'd be renting an RV to fill those roles. Instead, Rooster thought it made more sense for Ainsley's Angels to purchase an RV on the West Coast. We could then use the RV for our mission, and deliver it to him on the East Coast. Rooster's vision was to have the RV serve as a mobile headquarters, not only for our journey, but also for Ainsley's Angels events in the future.

Pieces for the mission were definitely coming together. Nichole spent much of her time after school booking campgrounds and hotels. I double-checked our route to ensure RV passage would be safe. I tried to plan locations where Nichole and Simon could rendezvous with Shamus and me, since we'd sometimes be running in places the RV couldn't travel.

Since Shamus thought it would be great to donate at least one chair in each state as we made our way from coast to coast, Rooster worked on finding potential chair recipients along our path. Meanwhile, Simon flipped through travel guides to investigate attractions we'd pass, and I continued to train in earnest.

Although everything was coming together logistically, we were still well short of our fundraising goal in December 2014. Online donations were coming in steadily, Evans Brothers business had been a huge help, but we were still lacking a large donation or sponsor to ensure the mission could actually happen.

On a whim, my mom reached out to a couple she'd met as a bartender in Saratoga. She remembered the husband saying he was the coordinator of a nonprofit in Brooklyn, and that he could potentially support a project such as ours. After a phone call explaining Shamus's dream and the mission we were planning, it was agreed we should apply for a grant. I spent the next several days perfecting the application requesting funds that would be used to purchase running chairs for individuals with disabilities. The aim was inclusion, inspiration, and to help our son's dream come to fruition. I sent the application with hope in my heart. A week later, we had an envelope from the nonprofit in our hands.

Over the preceding twelve months, I'd written *hundreds* of emails requesting sponsorships, grant money, donations, and funding, but with no significant success. I desperately hoped this one, with the lead from my mother, would be different. I figured the abrupt response couldn't possibly be good news. They were either denying it because our goal didn't fit their mission, or they needed more information. We sat down to dinner as a family, and I pulled out the envelope. My hands shook as I tore it open. I quickly looked down to see a single sheet of paper, with no more than a paragraph written on it.

Another rejection, I thought. I must have frowned a little as I looked around the table, because Nichole diverted her eyes to avoid witnessing my disappointment. I glanced down and started to silently read the words on the page.

"We'll keep trying," Nichole optimistically vowed. "It'll happ—"

"We *got it!!*" I interrupted. "We got it! It says, 'Congratulations, we have approved your request!'"

I was in disbelief as I read the paragraph aloud. Not only were we approved for the funding, but they had *increased* the amount of the award. I was astonished. The check was attached, made payable to Ainsley's Angels—for *twenty thousand dollars!*

We hugged, laughed, and cried joyous tears for several minutes. We knew we'd received a game changer, our own golden ticket. Although we still had plenty of fundraising to do, the sizable grant confirmed we could make a legitimate attempt at our transcontinental run.

Shamus and Simon couldn't wait to let "Mr. Rooster" in on the excitement. Shay wheeled over to the Christmas tree, and Simon followed close behind. They placed Santa Claus hats on their heads and smiled proudly. Simon was missing a front tooth which made their sweet little grins all the more adorable. Nichole grabbed her cell phone to record a video to send Rooster. They delivered the good news as follows:

Simon: Dear Mr. Wooster.

Shamus: You must've been a very good boy this year!

Nichole zoomed into the check to show the "pay to" and "amount" lines, revealing the extremely generous donation. She sent the video to Rooster, and within seconds, my cell phone was ringing.

"I'm flying around the house right now!" Rooster beamed through the phone.

We all deeply understood, at that moment, our epic mission and Shamus's dream of running across America was one *gigantic* step closer to reality.

THIRTY-FIVE

WITH THE ADDITION OF THE SIGNIFICANT FUNDS and the calendar turning to 2015, my level of anxiety increased exponentially. We were mere months away from *actually* beginning the journey, and there were still seemingly endless details to coordinate.

Rooster and I contacted an RV dealership in Washington State and started the process of purchasing the RV for Ainsley's Angels. Simultaneously, we determined we'd need a trailer to haul the chairs we'd be donating. Rooster worked with the RV dealer to coordinate finding a trailer, as well as someone to vehicle wrap the RV so it would be a rolling Ainsley's Angels billboard. The biggest challenge was that Nichole would be the one driving the RV and hauling the trailer. She'd never driven anything larger than her Honda CRV, and had never towed a trailer in her life. Yet, in a few months, she'd be driving the twenty-six-foot RV and twelve-foot trailer from coast to coast.

Nichole was undeterred by the unnerving task and set up a test drive for herself at a local RV dealership. They were happy to review the basics of RV driving and maintenance with her, and she took it in stride, shining as she test-drove a Winnebago. She looked tiny sitting behind the wheel of the behemoth vehicle, but she was amazing from the start at driving the RV—even navigating turns and parking like a professional. A few weeks later, she made time to do some trailer hauling with our friend, Mark, who towed a twenty-foot trailer with his pickup truck. She practiced hitching and unhitching the trailer, then pulled it around tight turns and roundabouts, and even attempted backing it up! After that lesson, she made sure all of the campsites we'd booked for the summer camping were pull-through sites so that no backing up would be required. There was no doubt we were rookies when it came to RVs and trailers, but Nichole was confident.

As components came together, my biggest concern shifted drastically to training. I'd been meticulous about keeping my weekly mileage in the range of 100 to 140 miles. It was a challenge with a full-time job, boys involved in lots of activities, and day-to-day household tasks. Not to mention, I was constantly working and reworking our proposed route. Shamus and Simon, both baseball aficionados, had become fans of the movie *Field of Dreams*. They knew we'd be running through Iowa, so we added Dyersville, Iowa, home of the famous field, to our itinerary! It was exciting for us to have those stops to look forward to, but I knew detours could add lots of miles, and we couldn't get delayed. Chair recipients needed to know when to expect us in their towns to present them with their new wheels.

To select those recipients, we accepted online nominations and before we knew it, we had recipients for nearly every state on our route. I was motivated by the proposition of meeting kids and their families, and by the thought of being able to provide them with gifts of mobility. I understood the inclusion opportunities those wheels would provide. The inspiration of those families along our route propelled me through hours of daily training. I also knew the motivation of wanting to get to the next chair presentation would inspire me from town to town during the summer.

As the route came together, the time frame became paramount. We decided we'd start our journey from Seattle on the Fourth of July, the second anniversary of Shamus's and my very first race together. The early-July start date would allow Shamus and Simon to attend their annual overnight summer camp the final week of June. While the date was fitting, it also meant one week of summer vacation would already be behind us when we started running. Though we knew we needed to finish before school started, the end date was still up in the air. We wanted to push our final day of running as close to Labor Day as possible, to allow us more time to cover the 3,205 miles on foot. Labor Day was September 7, and we figured that would be a perfect day to end our run . . . until we were contacted by the New York Mets.

My friend Josh had a contact in the Mets organization and informed him about our mission. Knowing we'd be finishing in New York City, Josh asked if there was anything they could do to be a part of it. The Mets, enthusiastic about the opportunity, reached out to invite us to their home game on September 1, where they'd recognize us on the field prior to the game.

It was a no-brainer. We immediately accepted their invitation and began condensing our trip from seventy days down to sixty! The reduction resulted in eight additional miles each day. We'd need to run fifty-four miles for sixty consecutive days. It was formidable, to say the least. I'd run more than fifty miles in eight hours, and much of that was done pushing Shamus or Simon, so the one-day distance was doable. Repeating it every day for two months straight was the scary part. My heart and soul wanted to be able to make it happen, but how would the rest of my body hold up? The fifty-plus miles we *had* done was on a cinder track, running in circles with constant support. What intimidated me most was that the first thousand miles of our transcontinental journey would be spent running through the Cascade, Rocky, and Big Horn mountain ranges, at elevations up to ten thousand feet!

I'd never done any running, or even spent much time, at elevation, but I had done a lot of reading about it. I wanted to be as prepared as possible, so to help my body acclimate, I used a mountain air generator. The apparatus looked like an oxygen concentrator, but did the exact opposite.

Rather than supplying oxygen to breathe, the generator depleted the oxygen being inhaled. It simulated oxygen levels up to the elevation of Mount Everest. It was an extremely useful piece of equipment in getting my body ready to endure at altitude. For the final few months leading up to "go time," I turned the machine on and put the mask over my face as I laid in bed at night. Unfortunately, it was a noisy piece of machinery, and Nichole had to tolerate sleeping next to "Darth Vader."

Simply resting in bed with the mask on was exhausting, but as the days went by, I could feel it getting easier. As my body adapted, I extended the tubing down to our basement so I could run on the treadmill with the mask. I cranked the incline of the treadmill to its maximum level and ran with depleted oxygen, mimicking the altitude of the highest mountains on Earth. Nichole remained nearby, for fear I might blackout. Luckily, I never did. I continued to get stronger and felt I'd be ready when the time came to ascend into the thin air of the mountains of the western US.

With a strong running base and confidence regarding running at elevation, I knew I had to prepare my body for ultra-long distances every day. Most of the spring, I increased my training volume as my schedule allowed. A few days each week, I would wake up early, run a marathon on the treadmill before work, run ten to thirteen miles at lunch, and then another thirteen when I got home. Thursdays were my day off from work, so I'd put the boys on the bus at 7:30 a.m., start running, and then make it home just in time to get them off the bus at three in the afternoon. I'd cover forty to fifty miles during the seven to eight hours. Saturdays and Sundays would be spent pushing Shamus for three to four hours in his running chair, occasionally stopping to stretch his legs.

I was gaining strength and endurance, but hadn't had the chance to run multiple, consecutive fifty-mile days. As Memorial Day weekend approached, I saw an opportunity in my schedule to make that happen. I was off work from Thursday through Tuesday, and set a goal to cover fifty-five miles each day, on foot. It would provide me a trial for nutrition, hydration, and to see how my body would respond. I'd been working with a nutritionist, who recommended I should consume twelve thousand calories every single day during the proposed run across America! Memorial Day weekend gave Nichole and me the chance to test how my digestive system would respond. Nichole prepared meals, protein shakes, snacks, and supplements for the six days, and we began to learn how much I could actually ingest.

We learned a lot during the holiday weekend: when to eat, what to eat, how to eat on the run, how to hydrate, what to wear, when to change sneakers, and how to recover each night. Most importantly, we learned all my training, preparation, Shamus's coaching, and Nichole and Simon's support had paid off. I made it through Tuesday's long run, having covered over 330 miles in six days. For the first time, the little voice in my head began to believe what Shamus had believed all along. Together, we really did have a shot at running from coast to coast!

PART FOUR

"We may not have it all together, but *Together* we have it all"

—Unknown

THIRTY-SIX

THE NEXT MONTH FLEW BY WITH FINAL PREPARATIONS. We shipped gear, maps, running chairs, non-perishable food, and supplies to an Ainsley's Angels ambassador, Sarah, in Olympia, Washington. She would store, then deliver these items to us upon our arrival in Seattle. School ended for the boys and they were immediately off to their week of summer camp, which gave Nichole and me a few days to review plans and finalize logistics. We confirmed flights and coordinated last-minute details, including locations, times, and dates of chair presentations. We even did some live, local TV interviews as our "launch date" drew closer.

On June 29, Nichole and my mother flew west to Pasco, Washington, the location of the RV Rooster had purchased. They were picked up at the airport by the RV saleswoman, Suzan, who provided them the first look at the Ainsley's Angels RV. Over the previous several weeks, the RV had transformed from an everyday beige Winnebago into an Ainsley's Angels spectacle. It had been wrapped in Ainsley's trademark pink and black, complete with images of Ainsley's Angels runners and riders from across the nation. Nichole squealed in delight as she unveiled the RV on social media. There was no doubt we'd be rolling in style!

Suzan gave Nichole and my mother a crash course in all things RV-related. She spent the day teaching them about RV maintenance, water, electric/gas hookups, how to dump waste water, and every last detail of how to operate our temporary home. Suzan even took them to the store so they could purchase linens, dishes, and some necessities for the road. Over the next two days, they learned the ins and outs of RV-living as they slept in and stocked the vehicle for our two-month mission. Nichole then drove the RV, with my mom as her navigator, four hours from Pasco to Seattle where they set up camp at an urban campground. That campground would serve as our staging area as we prepared to embark on our trek across America.

Back in New York, I picked Shamus and Simon up from summer camp on June 30 and we headed to the airport. Despite having shipped much of our gear and clothing to Sarah in Olympia, we still had quite a bit of luggage for the six-hour flight. We each had a carry-on bag, plus Shamus's walker, and one large suitcase to check. I placed a backpack on Shamus's chair and carried two more on my back. Simon rolled the suitcase—which was bigger than him—into the airport where we were greeted by a stream of local news reporters. Each wanted to capture video of us getting ready to fly west, knowing we'd soon be running home.

My sister, Jodie, had set up a press conference at the airport, and several friends and family members came to see us off. Each was granted a gate pass so they could escort us all the way to our departing gate at Albany International Airport. At our gate, an impromptu stage and podium had been erected where I answered questions from the media. I suddenly realized a lot of people were paying attention to what we were attempting. We'd been so busy with planning and training, I hadn't noticed how much the attention to our journey had increased. This wasn't just a family or Ainsley's Angels mission anymore. The entire community was watching and rooting for us.

Shamus and Simon were incredible on the flight. Flying solo with both boys was certainly a challenge, but Simon was a trooper. He stepped in to help whenever he could. With Nichole already waiting for us out west, Simon was an essential part of making the flight and transitions at the airports a success. We flew from Albany to Baltimore, then from Baltimore to Seattle. It was a long flight, and the anticipation of our run gave us all something to discuss as we flew. The flight attendant overheard us discussing the upcoming adventure. She was so enthralled with our mission, she made an announcement about it over the loudspeaker as we neared our destination. Upon our arrival in Seattle, the passengers erupted in cheers and wished us well as we deboarded.

We gathered our carry-on luggage and headed to baggage claim to grab our suitcase and Shamus's walker. Seattle's airport was much bigger than Albany's, but Simon was amazing at keeping up and helping lug the bags around, or pushing his brother's wheelchair when necessary. We were excited to get our rental car so we could get to Nichole and my mom.

The three of us boarded a bus to take us to the rental car agency. I knew they must be exhausted, but the boys never complained as we huddled together on the hot, crowded shuttle. There were no seats available, so I stood, and Shamus offered his lap to Simon so they could both rest on his wheelchair. We waited in a long line for our rental van, which would get us around Seattle for the next couple days. Another half-mile walk to the van, and we were finally ready to rendezvous with the rest of our crew. We excitedly loaded the van and headed to the RV park.

We pulled in and instantly spotted the Ainsley's Angels RV, which shined brightly among the other vehicles. It was Fourth of July week, so RVs were packed tightly and there wasn't a single empty parking space. Nichole and my mother proudly gave us the tour of our new home. They had predetermined sleeping arrangements for everyone. In the rear of the vehicle was a full bed for Nichole and me. Space was tight, with a small closet on each side of the bed, allowing a single foot of walking space around it. The bathroom and shower area were directly in front of our bedroom. Next was the kitchen, with a small countertop and sink across from an RV-sized fridge. Adjacent to the fridge was the kitchen table, which converted into Shamus's bed. Up front were the captain's chairs for a driver and passenger. Behind the passenger seat was a swivel chair. I inspected the area and couldn't find anywhere else to sleep. I knew my mom would be with us for the next few nights, and Simon, of course, would be with us all summer.

I looked at Nichole quizzically. "Where's Simey sleeping?"

She smiled and pointed toward the front of the RV. I couldn't figure out what she was pointing at. I opened the overhead cabinets above the driver seats. I tried to recline and adjust all the chairs. I looked at her again with a puzzled face.

"The dashboard," she grinned.

The RV was a class-A motorhome, so the dashboard was plenty big for a seven-year-old boy to call his bed. Nichole demonstrated how the blinds and curtains of the windshield could be drawn tightly to eliminate outside light. She then unrolled a foam cushion and sleeping bag, tossed down a pillow, and Simon tested it. I laughed as he expressed how awesome his new "bedroom" was.

"What about my mom?" I inquired.

Nichole pointed to the floor. She said my mom had insisted she sleep on a cushion on the floor next to Shamus's table bed.

I offered the bed to my mom, but she maintained I'd need a good night's sleep leading up to the run. I couldn't disagree. I didn't like having her sleep on the floor, but she was adamant.

Nichole then took me out to the trailer to show me what she'd be towing. The trailer was loaded with the first several Freedom running chairs we'd be donating. Another level of reality hit home. The gifts of mobility were there. The preparation had been done. We'd made it to the starting line and our journey was about to begin.

"Just one more thing," Nichole said. "We need to name the RV and trailer. We can't keep calling it the Ainsley's Angels RV."

We sat down for a family dinner around the kitchen table (soon to be Shamus's bed) at the Seattle KOA (Kampgrounds of America), and brainstormed a name. We decided on "Peggy," short for Pegasus—the winged creature of inspiration from Greek mythology. Peggy was also the name of Ainsley's physical therapist. She was the one who introduced Ainsley and her dad, Rooster, to inclusion running. "Peggy" was perfect. We then determined "Freeda" would be the name of our trailer, since it would be carrying Freedom running chairs. We settled in for the night, glad to be together, ready to begin our ambitious journey in a few short days.

THIRTY-SEVEN

FOR THE NEXT FORTY-EIGHT HOURS, in record-setting Seattle heat, we organized and reorganized Peggy and Freeda. The goal was to make everything as efficient as possible, so time and energy wouldn't be wasted on the road. In addition, Shamus and I got acclimated to our new running chair. A Washington-based company, Adaptive Star, had built us a custom chair so Shamus would be sure to roll in comfort. Shamus and I had met one of the owners of Adaptive Star, Teri, at the Louisiana Marathon a few months prior. She was fascinated by our transcontinental attempt and wanted Adaptive Star to contribute. During the lead-up to July, Teri and I worked closely to determine details of a custom chair for Shamus. Rather than ship the chair to us, only to have us ship it back, we opted to receive the chair upon our arrival in Seattle. We figured, over the course of fifty miles each day, we would have plenty of time to get used to it!

Teri delivered the chair to us at the campground and we were in awe. The chair had disc brakes, ability to recline, an attachable sun/rain shield, and cushions designed specifically for Shamus's needs, including pockets for him to put his books or electronics in. The handlebar height was adjustable for my different postures and needs while pushing—uphill versus downhill, fatigued versus fresh legs. Adaptive Star covered every detail and took all our requests into consideration when creating the chair. It exceeded expectations and we couldn't wait to start rolling. Shay had picked the color—turquoise—and he christened his new ride, the "Turquoise Tornado!"

July 3 had finally arrived. Although we'd officially be starting the run the next day, we decided Shamus's first steps and the first chair presentation would be easier to coordinate on the third. In advance, we'd communicated with local media and the chair recipient. We informed everyone that the journey would be launched with a 5K fun-run, starting from the beach at Golden Garden Park on the afternoon of the third, and the *big* journey would begin the following day.

We enthusiastically headed to the beach, and Shamus was excited to kick things off. Prior to our departure from the campground, we detached the trailer, which made it easier for Nichole to navigate through Seattle. When we got near the park, we were glad we did. As Nichole drove down the road to the beach, we encountered an unwelcoming sign: "Overpass Ahead—Clearance 12'." Peggy wouldn't make it under. Unfortunately, there was nowhere to turn around. We had media and a chair recipient waiting for us at the beach, so we decided to park Peggy on the shoulder of the road. A military motorcycle group, the Green Knights, came to celebrate with us and helped us carry gear for the mile-long walk to the shore line.

Our first little bump, the inability to drive to the parking lot, was behind us. Nichole, Shamus, Simon, and I stood on the shore and looked out over Puget Sound. We made our way into the cool water of the Northern Pacific. From that point forward, we'd be headed toward the rising sun each day, until we made it to the "other" ocean. The enormity of the task was not lost on me. It was daunting, but also invigorating. Everything we'd been preparing for was upon us.

Simon jumped the waves with Nichole as Shamus stood in his walker; the cool, salty waves crashed around him. My mother waited on the beach with Teri; the Green Knights; our chair recipient, James; James's family; members of the local media; many passersby who were curious about the gathering; and Joe Orth, a member of Ainsley's Angels leadership who volunteered his time to help us get started. Joe had spent the previous few days with us prepping the RV, assembling Freedom chairs, and organizing them in Freeda. Joe secured GoPro cameras to Shay's walker and greeted media members for us, giving them the backstory on our mission.

Our family turned and looked to the horizon one more time as the sun began to set. We waved our goodbyes to the Pacific, and then turned to the beach. I steadied Shamus's walker, and he slowly lifted his feet and took ten steps on the hard-packed sand. Cheers erupted from the beach as cameramen zoomed into Shay's feet and then panned to his determined face. His dream journey was beginning.

After those monumental steps, I transferred Shamus to his new wheels, and we headed to a running trail with Joe, Sarah, and James in his brand-new Freedom chair. James laughed and cheered as he rolled in his wheels for the first time. We rolled together on the hot, humid July evening and celebrated the moment, knowing there was so much yet to come.

After several interviews and continued celebration, we headed back to Peggy. We loaded up boxes of food and water donations collected by the Green Knights, and tried to figure out how Nichole could possibly turn Peggy around on the busy road. It was the night before the Fourth of July, and the weather was perfect for a beach day, so there was a constant stream of cars blocking our path.

The Green Knights stepped in to save the day. The half-dozen leather-clad riders hopped on their motorcycles and blocked traffic. They gave us a nod to indicate they were in full control of the oncoming traffic, and Nichole spun Peggy's first U-turn in a matter of seconds. We were on our way back to the campground before we knew it, and with a military motorcycle escort. We'd never met any of those men before that day, but they quickly became family to us, and we were grateful for their help.

At the campground, we unwound and cooled off from another hot and busy day. The weather was atypically hot, and we were feeling it.

We sat in Peggy and were happy for the air-conditioning. We turned on the TV, which picked up just a few channels, as we settled in for the night. Much to our surprise, there we were on the TV screen—Shamus taking his steps out of Puget Sound. We changed the channel and saw us presenting James with his chair. It was surreal. It was one thing for us to be on our local news, but we were thousands of miles from home and people were still interested in sharing our story. Shamus's dream was gaining momentum. It was both exciting and terrifying. The dream had started as a family adventure and opportunity for Shamus to pay the "gift of mobility" forward to others. The journey we were about to undertake had evolved into so much more: promoting inclusion, spreading a mission, advocating for individuals with disabilities, and daring to dream *BIG*.

We tucked the boys into their respective beds, and Nichole and I laid down and reviewed our plan for the next day. Despite being excited and nervous for the journey ahead, sleep came surprisingly easy. The nonstop activities of the previous few days had caught up with us, and we were ready to rest. As I drifted into my slumber, I counted the miles that lay ahead.

THIRTY-EIGHT

MY RESTFUL SLEEP WAS SHORT-LIVED. I was full of adrenaline for the mission of running 3,200 miles. The distance seemed incalculable, but I knew I'd done everything I possibly could to prepare for it. The dream was not my creation, but I was fully invested and desperately wanted to succeed. Ainsley's Angels had gone out of their way to support us and get us to the starting line. I was extremely grateful for the support. I knew there would be help along the way, but I couldn't help but feel the burden of pressure. I didn't want to let Shamus down. I wanted to make his dream a reality, to encourage him to keep dreaming *big*, to show him the only limits are the ones we place on ourselves.

The day we had been counting down to for two years arrived: July 4, 2015. The alarm went off at 4:45 a.m., but I was awake well before that. Joe Orth knocked on the RV door, and he and I went through final checklists and preparations as the rest of the family began to stir. The plan was to drive to the University of Washington, our starting spot for the day. Shamus and I were invited to be honorary starters of the Firecracker4 race back home in Saratoga. We were flattered to be included on the two-year anniversary of our first race together, and the Firecracker4 race directors wanted to be a part of our start in Seattle. It was just before six o'clock, local time in Seattle, and nine o'clock in Saratoga, when Shamus and I got the call from the race directors.

We gave some words of encouragement, over a speaker, to the runners lined up three thousand miles away and listened to the crowd roar back in support of our upcoming journey. It felt good to know there were crowds of people cheering us on. The Firecracker4 started back east, and we transferred Shamus into his running chair to begin the first leg of our trek. It was not lost on me that most of the runners of the race back home would be done within the hour, while we were starting a run that would take us all summer.

Our first day on the road would take us from Seattle to Gold Bar, Washington. Joe joined Shamus and me for the first ten miles. It was helpful to have him there to navigate the hilly streets as we weaved our way out of the city to a bike path. We listened to some music and chatted with Shamus as we strode along. I quickly realized I was the one doing most of the talking, as Joe labored to keep pace. When we left that morning, I'd told Joe we'd start easy and get a feel for the day. However, the adrenaline and excitement took over and I was flying along at six-minute pace. Joe called Rooster as we ran so he could join us virtually for a portion of day one, and he laughed as Joe informed him about our "easy pace." At mile ten, the bike path ended and we met up with support vehicle Peggy, loaded with Nichole, Simon, and my mom. We mapped out the rest of the day and realized road conditions wouldn't allow Shamus to roll with me much longer. As much as he wanted to keep rolling, we decided it made the most sense for him to ride in the RV. We knew road conditions wouldn't allow for him to roll the whole way, and we decided, like our ultramarathon, that I would go solo as needed.

We selected our next rendezvous point fifteen miles away, and stayed in contact via cell phone so I could keep them apprised of my location. As I got back out on the road, I missed Shamus and Joe immediately.

The unusual warmth in Seattle persisted throughout the Pacific Northwest. Wildfires loomed in the eastern portion of Washington and temperatures blazed in the west where we were. I plodded along much slower than I had with Joe and Shamus, and tried to process the miles in front of us. We'd covered ten hot, sweaty miles, and we still had about 3,200 miles and sixty days to go. I tried not to be overwhelmed by the distance, and focused instead on getting through day one safe and intact.

I knew Shamus, Choley and Simon had extra support with Joe and my mom there for the day. I had started too fast and I didn't want to pay for it for the entire summer. I decided to go easy for the remaining miles, to enjoy the scenery and the sunshine. It didn't take long for the sunshine to catch up with me. I was used to running fairly long distances without water, and had hydrated fully at the pit stop, but at that moment, as the sweat dripped off my brow onto the pavement with each step, I realized I had forgotten my CamelBak. I had trained with the water-carrying backpack and had used one during the Canandaigua 50 Ultramarathon, but neglected to send it to Sarah or pack one to bring with me. I knew I'd need one as the summer wore on, but after we exited the city of Seattle, it seemed like we were in the middle of nowhere.

At the second pit stop, mile twenty-five, I told Joe about my foolish error. He immediately set out on a mission of his own to find a CamelBak for me. As he recounts the story, he went to a big box store and looked around, but to no avail. Eventually, he asked an employee if they had any CamelBaks, and the employee looked back at him like he had three heads. Finally, after three more stops, he found one, filled it with ice water, and brought it to me on the road with seven miles remaining for the day. With my thirst quenched, I cruised into the campground to the cheers of Nichole and the boys after eight hours and forty-five miles of running. We had survived day one!

The boys were anxious to get into the campground pool, and that's where we went as soon as I finished hydrating and refueling. We relaxed in the pool as the late afternoon sun blazed down. We had dinner with Joe and my mom before they departed for Seattle to return the rental van and catch their respective flights east. Then Choley, Simon, Shamus, and I sat around the table and reflected on our first day on the road. All in all, we felt things went well and we knew, from that day forward, it would be up to the four of us to make our way the remaining 3,155 miles to New York City. We were exhausted from our long, hot day, but also exhilarated about our mission finally being underway. We settled in, watched a movie in the RV, and drifted to sleep with Fourth of July fireworks blazing overhead.

THIRTY-NINE

Day two started before sunrise with me preparing for the day's distance. I shuffled around the RV in darkness to not wake the rest of the crew. I wolfed down two bananas wrapped in pieces of bread like hot dogs. My condiment of choice was protein-rich peanut butter in place of ketchup and mustard. I then ate a few bagels and covered my body in SPF 100 sunscreen in preparation for another long day in the sun.

As the sun peeked over the mountains in the distance, I took a few minutes to reflect on our mission as I watched Shamus and Simon sleep. What an adventure for our family, and all because of our little man's dream. As they slumbered, I wondered, *What is he dreaming about right now?*

I thought about all the miles ahead of us, but not for long. I knew to not overwhelm myself by the distance. One day, one mile, one step at a time. Enjoying the journey was the goal. As Nichole and the boys woke, we went into motion packing up the campsite and reviewing a checklist we'd written. Since we were not experienced RVers, we didn't want to forget any important steps. Over the course of the week, Nichole had been living in the RV, and she had become well versed in all the details. I was amazed by how she went through the list like an expert. While I readied Shamus's chair for the day, Nichole took care of *everything* else. She fed the boys, detached the RV hookups, cleared the kitchen, folded Shamus's bed, packed up Simon's sleeping area on the dashboard, closed vents, moved the slide-outs in, raised the jacks, and we were ready to go.

After giving Choley and the boys big "good morning" squeezes, I transferred Shamus into the Turquoise Tornado. Nichole and Simon rolled out in the RV, and we gave chase on foot. It was a beautiful morning, though I was already getting hot. Despite our best efforts to roll out at sunrise, we didn't leave the campground until 7:15 a.m. Not bad, but temperatures were on the rise, and so was the elevation as we pushed through the Cascade Mountains. The altitude wasn't extreme, but we were ascending and descending significant hills, which put my legs to the test.

After seventeen miles, a little after nine o'clock, we arrived at Peggy. Shamus needed a break and I needed water. I ran out of my supply on the road, and it took me a while to feel well enough to begin again. As I looked at our map, I realized we had fifty-five miles remaining to get to Leavenworth. My dehydrated, hazy brain couldn't figure out how that was possible. I'd mapped out every single run myself, and there were no days longer than sixty miles. I'd spent hours scouring maps, AAA TripTiks, and Google Earth. How could they *all* be wrong? After refueling with one of Choley's special, calorie-dense shakes, we hit the road, but this time with Simon in the chair so Shamus could rest and stretch his legs.

Nichole's shake—loaded with a whole avocado, almond milk, vegan protein powder, chia seeds, and who knows what else—gave me a needed boost. With featherweight Simon in the chair, it felt like we were flying up and down the hills. As Simon read *Harry Potter,* I treaded along and periodically stopped to snap some pictures of the gorgeous mountains. A little after noon, we rendezvoused with Peggy, having covered a total of thirty-five miles. Yet, as far as I could see, we were only halfway finished with our daily total. I was upset about making a mapping blunder so early in our trip. I hoped I hadn't miscalculated more distances, but I couldn't dwell on it. I had to keep moving toward Leavenworth and figure out how to cover the seventy miles so we didn't get behind schedule, just two days into the journey.

The heat was getting to the boys and the roads were narrow, so we decided it was best I complete the final thirty-five miles without the chair. I instantly missed their company. I was on the road, in the middle of nowhere, alone. I reminded myself that Peggy and the crew would be another hour or so of running down the road. I tried to enjoy the scenery and soak in the moment, but continued to get frustrated with the number of miles I had left to run. I woke up thinking I'd be running fifty-two miles that day, yet seventy was the true total.

As the thoughts passed in and out of my mind, I spied something on the side of the road. It was "Ainsley's Angels" pink, in the distance. It gave me something to run to for the next few steps. When I got to it, I quickly noticed it was simply a spray-painted rock on the side of the road . . . bright pink, as if left there by Ainsley. It didn't seem to mark anything. There were no houses anywhere within sight. I snapped a picture of it and immediately texted it to Rooster. I didn't give any explanation, just texted him the picture of a pink rock on the side of Route 1 in the middle of Washington State.

Without missing a beat, he instantaneously replied, "You found it!" as if he and Ainsley had delivered it there for me. In my fuzzy mind, as I trudged onward, and I found myself debating whether he and Ainsley had really been there (even though I knew it would have been impossible). Then, I found myself wondering if Rooster had put someone up to leaving the rock for me. I wouldn't have put that past him—he had connections everywhere! Regardless, it gave me something to ponder as I trekked eastward.

I didn't delay at the next RV break. I only stopped long enough to hug Nichole and the boys, rehydrate, and eat a couple of Lärabars. I tried not to ruminate on my mapping mistake and the miles ahead. I'd beaten myself up enough, and fortunately my legs were feeling good enough to make up for my error. The pink rock helped me refocus on the journey and remember to enjoy the time on the road.

For the final twenty miles, we decided to split the distance into ten-mile intervals, the first of which I went solo. For the final stretch in the early evening, I was joined by Shamus as we rolled into the Leavenworth KOA for the night. Much to our surprise, we were greeted by a great fanfare from the KOA employees, including signs welcoming us as we neared the campground. When Nichole had made reservations months before, she'd told everyone she booked with about our mission. The Leavenworth KOA had taken note and went out of their way to make us feel welcome. They had goodie bags ready for the boys, snacks and water ready for me, and told us our stay that evening was on them.

It was refreshing to be surrounded by people who genuinely cared about our mission. Even though they were strangers, it was evident Shamus's dream had impacted them, and they wanted to be a part of it any way they could. We had a great visit with them, and then we reunited with Suzan (the RV sales rep), who had driven from Pasco to show her support. Although we were thousands of miles from home, love and support of the community made us feel as if we were in our hometown.

As we settled in, I took time to delve into the maps and look at our route in detail. I was determined to find my miscalculation in planning, and wanted to ensure it wouldn't happen again. While we had successfully made it seventy miles, I wasn't sure I'd be able to repeat it. As I cross-referenced my route map with the campgrounds, and then revisited a TripTik I'd created, I quickly realized my gaffe. It hadn't been an inaccuracy in planning at all. In the margin of my spreadsheet for the day, I had noted there were no campgrounds within fifty miles of Gold Bar, where we'd stayed the night before. I indicated we'd run the majority of the way to Leavenworth, drive to the campground, and then backtrack the next day to pick up where we left off!

In the heat of the day, in a slightly dehydrated state, I'd completely forgotten my plan. I had just logged an extra twenty miles due to a silly oversight. I couldn't help but laugh at myself for the ridiculous slipup. I'd spent hundreds of hours creating the route for our journey. I was meticulous about checking and rechecking to ensure "manageable" distances. On day *two*, that planning went out the window when I ran the longest single-day run of my life: seventy miles in eleven hours. I laughed as I told Nichole and the boys. Although it would make the next day's run a little shorter, I knew it was a mistake I wouldn't, and *couldn't*, make again!

FORTY

OVER THE NEXT FEW DAYS, we settled into a routine as a family by finding a balance between all of the running, some sightseeing, and family fun. We focused on savoring each moment. One of the boys was with me as often as possible, seeing the countryside and visiting as we ran. The other was in the RV with Nichole, finding safe spots to pull off the road, prepping and planning for the day, and reading or playing cards as they awaited our arrival. As the first few days passed, we learned it didn't make sense for us to run fifteen-mile increments.

Part of our daily routine was a morning weigh-in for me to check how I was doing with nutrition and hydration. I started the run at 140 pounds, and we wanted to keep me as close to that as possible. After three days, we realized we were failing. My weight had dipped below 130 pounds, and we recognized I wouldn't be able to keep running if I was withering away to nothing. I knew I'd rapidly be headed toward injury or worse, so we altered our plans and acknowledged more frequent pit stops would be more effective. I always carried water and snacks with me, but I couldn't keep up with my rate of sweat in the heat of July, and found it difficult to eat on the run while pushing the chair. We opted for a stop every five miles so I could hydrate regularly, reapply sunscreen as needed, and the boys could swap out of the chair more often to get out of the hot sun. It was a great decision. We kept the breaks brief whenever Nichole could find a spot to pull Peggy to the side. I'd pop in and out of the RV quickly and get back on the road. At midday, we'd pause for a little longer and eat lunch as a family. Although my lunch typically consisted of a "power shake by Choley," I was happy to sit at the table with them as they gobbled down sandwiches, mac 'n' cheese, or whatever else Nichole whipped up in the RV kitchen.

We were finding our groove on the road and although it was stressful, we were making progress and were off to a phenomenal start. We made it to Spokane in five days, averaging nearly sixty miles per day! Despite having a long way to go, I truly started to believe we could make it. The routine of running, resting, and refueling was working. The months of logistical planning and relentless training were paying off . . . until day six.

We encountered numerous obstacles on day six, beginning with a late start. Typically, we began our days close to sunrise, but on day six, we had the chance to donate a chair in Spokane, live on morning TV. We were in the TV studio with the recipient family, and it was fun for us to see behind the scenes of local morning news. It was also an excellent opportunity to share our mission and spread the word about Ainsley's Angels. The only downside was we started running four hours behind our typical schedule, and would now be running even more miles in the hottest part of the day.

Meanwhile, an old high school friend who recently relocated to the area asked if he could run a few miles with us. We were happy to have the company. Regrettably, he overestimated his ability and wasn't able to keep up for more than a few miles. We slowed to jog with him, and then had to increase our pace after he left us so we could meet some media waiting for us with Nichole and Simon. We were always excited to share our story with newspapers, radio, and TV, but it was tricky to coordinate timing. They often wanted specific times of arrival, and when you're running fifty to sixty miles daily, precise estimates are challenging.

We eventually arrived at the meeting point, with temperatures rising nearly one hundred degrees. Nichole and Simon entertained the reporters and camera crew in the air-conditioned RV while they waited. They reviewed our day-to-day procedures and showed them around Peggy. While our support crew was being interviewed, one of the reporters accidentally bumped into the RV stove, inadvertently turning on the propane. By the time Nichole realized what had happened, she already had a migraine from the fumes. She quickly shut off the propane, evacuated the RV, and opened the vents to air it out.

Shamus and I arrived and finished the interview outside of the RV. After an eventful morning, Shamus was a little overheated. We took a break and found some shade. We decided to let Simon have a turn in the chair for the next four miles. It would be a short leg to Peggy, but that was okay with me. Per our route for the day, the short leg ahead of us would take place on a bike path. So, when Simon and I realized we forgot my cell phone, we opted to not turn back, knowing we'd be back to the RV shortly. I felt confident we wouldn't get lost on a bike path . . . but alas, I took a wrong turn on another paved footpath and ended up running over twelve miles en route to Peggy! We only found our way to the correct path when a ten-year-old boy on his bike led us to the appropriate trail. Needless to say, Nichole and Shamus had been worried sick.

At that point, we were *way* behind schedule with twenty miles still remaining for the day, and a barbeque being thrown in our honor that evening. Shamus and Simon relaxed while I finished the final stretch. I zipped along, simply wanting the day of running to end. I hopped inside Peggy after finishing my mileage, and we drove to the campground we'd booked months prior. We were all ready for a quick rest before heading to the barbeque. Much to our dismay, the campground was closed—permanently! We drove down a long driveway, only to be greeted by a locked gate. With no place to turn around, Nichole was forced to back the RV (*and trailer*) down a half-mile-long road to get back on track. It was *a lot* of stress for our rookie RV family! I scrambled to find another nearby campground with availability.

Finally, after several phone calls, sharing our story, and pleading with a campground owner, we found another place to park, use the RV hookup, and do laundry for the night. I was exhausted, Nichole was migraine-ridden, and Shamus was hungry! With all the events of the day, he hadn't eaten more than a few snacks. Simon, being a great little brother, volunteered to make him a sandwich. He gathered ingredients for a turkey sandwich, began to slice a chunk of cheese, but instead sliced his thumb—and deep!

At the site of the gushing blood, he went into shock, alternating fainting spells with vomiting grape juice. We helped him elevate his hand, applied pressure, and wrapped it. As Nichole and I tended to Simon, Shamus observed his brother with concern. It took several minutes to bandage Simon and calm him down. After the traumatic event, he fell asleep in our bed. Ultimately, everything stabilized enough for us to join the barbeque. Shamus finally got some food, Simon recovered, and we enjoyed visiting with new friends. After a long day, we were grateful for the meal.

Over dinner, we learned of a nearby public water park/sprayground, and thought it sounded like a nice place to unwind after the chaotic day. We happily climbed into Peggy, headed for some fun, when suddenly . . .

Thud! Crack! Bang!

We thought someone, or something, had hit the RV. It took us a moment to realize we'd left the roof vents open after airing out the propane leak earlier in the day. We had accidentally spent the day driving with the vents open, and one was completely destroyed by a low-hanging branch! We patched it up the best we could, then went to enjoy the park.

The boys had a blast, running and wheeling through the water sprinklers and fountains until the sun started to set. When we finally arrived back at the campground, we chatted for a few minutes before bedtime as we readied the sleeping areas. We reviewed the muddled events of the day—the late start, hot temperatures, running behind schedule, propane leak, getting lost, campground debacle, sliced thumb, and broken vent—

and wondered what the next day might bring. No doubt, our voices had a tone of self-pity, disgust, and a little fear. We still had so many miles to cover, and the miles on day six had been a challenge from start to finish. I wasn't sure how we could handle many more days like that.

As we talked, Shamus swiftly chimed in, "Yeah, but we got to give a chair away on TV! *And* we finished running across Washington! We're in Idaho now—a whole new state! Daddy, you saw a friend you haven't seen in *twenty* years! We got to talk to news reporters! That boy on his bike helped you and Simon! *And* we got to go to a barbeque and a *water park!*"

Smiles and hugs followed. Of course, Shamus was right. We couldn't lose sight of what we were doing and the numerous positives we experienced. We had two choices: remember the bad, or focus on *all* the good. It was a lesson we would carry with us. Despite the many obstacles we encountered on day six, thanks to Shamus's heartfelt comments, I genuinely believed it had been a fabulous day.

FORTY-ONE

AFTER FINISHING DAY SIX IN COEUR D'ALENE, we spent all of day seven running on the Centennial Trail as we traveled across Idaho. It was nice to not have to contend with traffic, and the paved path allowed the boys to roll with me for the duration. The most challenging part of the day was after the forty-seven-mile run was completed, we had to drive to the next campground over the border into Montana. The mountain passes we took were simultaneously breathtaking and terrifying. Nichole wound her way up the incline with a mountain face to the left, and cliff drop off to the right. She drove like a pro, but we were all on the edges of our seats on the descent.

We pulled over frequently to give Peggy some respite. At one of the stops, we could see smoke from the heat the RV's brakes were creating. Nichole and I tried to play it cool so the boys wouldn't be worried, and we both breathed a huge sigh of relief as we exited the ups and downs and got onto a level road as we entered a new time zone and drove into Montana.

The worst part was knowing we needed to drive back the next day to get to our starting point. We found a (slightly) better route the next morning, and I ran from Pacific Time to Mountain Time. Shamus couldn't join me because of the insane mountain passes, so I was alone as I crossed the state line and set my watch forward an hour, which caused me to lose an hour of running time. It was an odd feeling, having run from the ocean to a new time zone in just over a week, but losing an hour of running wasn't a stressor because it gave me a way to gauge our progress. It was a *huge* accomplishment. There was no denying we'd covered a great distance on foot and were assuredly making our way toward the rising sun.

Due to the remoteness of the area, we stayed at the same campground for two nights, which was a welcome change. For the first time since our running started, we wouldn't have to settle into a new "home" that night. With days of constant change, we liked having something familiar, and spending two nights at the same campground made it a little hard to leave. Even though we had only been there for a short time, constantly being on the go gave us a whole new point of reference for time. We had to adapt to change nearly every minute. The consistency of two days in one place made it feel safe and comfortable. Regardless, we knew we had lots of miles and many new adventures awaiting us, so we set out, continuing southwest towards Missoula.

Nichole drove me to Plains, Montana where I had stopped my running the previous day. As we looked ahead on the maps, we decided Shamus could join me for the morning miles, but the second half of the day I'd run solo. After running a smooth twenty-nine miles with Shamus, I had thirty-one miles on my own. The highway I'd be running on wouldn't allow many opportunities for Nichole to pull off for support. In addition, she coordinated with another news station to meet us at the campground for an interview, and she wanted to park Peggy, wash laundry, contact some chair recipients to work out details, and look into other media outlets to help us spread our mission. I knew she needed significant time to work on her to-do list, and she needed the Wi-Fi at the campground to make it possible. Nichole was anxious about leaving me for so many miles, and I have to admit, I was nervous as well. We were going against our decision from the previous week—from frequent pit stops to *zero* pit stops. We both concluded it was the best way to tackle all we needed to accomplish. At the very least, I knew the road I'd be running on was well-traveled and led to a major city, so if I got desperate, I could flag down a passerby for assistance.

I loaded up my CamelBak with ice water, grabbed two extra water bottles filled with electrolytes, and stuffed the extra pockets with Lärabars, gel packs, and basic first aid supplies. I gave everyone big hugs, and then slathered on as much SPF 100 as possible. Nichole let me run for a bit while she and the boys had lunch. She cruised by me forty-five minutes and 6.5 miles later, as I steadily jogged down the highway. She honked and drove slowly as she approached. I gave her a big thumbs-up and blew a kiss to each of my blondies as they passed, giving Choley faith I was feeling strong and confident for the marathon left to run to Missoula.

As the sun burned above, I consistently drank from my CamelBak and stopped twice to pull some fuel and electrolyte bottles out. I focused on rationing the fuel and hydration I had, keenly aware I didn't want to run out. As the sweat poured off my body, I checked the distance remaining on my GPS and began a routine of hydrating every ten minutes. It was a good game for me to play to keep me focused on drinking, but it also gave me something to look forward to at regular intervals. I felt my CamelBak supply dwindling as I approached fifteen miles remaining, but I also sensed myself desiccating. The salt from my sweat dried on my skin. One of my electrolyte drinks was empty, and the other was down to four ounces. I knew I couldn't space my sips any further, so I plodded on, drinking only a gulp every ten minutes. By five miles to go, my water supply was completely dry.

I remember thinking five miles wasn't that far, and that I'd have no problem making it without any more to drink. I'd completed many runs back home while training with minimal hydration. Of course, I wasn't thinking clearly. Dehydration was setting in. I foolishly decided I shouldn't bother Nichole, because she had so many things she was trying to get done. All I had to do was plod along. I slowed down to conserve energy, but the sun was relentless and there was no shade in sight. I decided to speed up, figuring I'd get to water sooner. That didn't work well either, and my legs started to cramp. I slowed again, trying to set points in the distance to run to, knowing each step was bringing me closer to hydration. I was desperate for water at ten-minute intervals. Over the course of the day, I had conditioned my body to thrive on those six swallows every hour. I looked at my phone and reviewed the distance remaining—less than three miles. I should have called Nichole, but in my delirious state, I kept talking myself out of it. I figured she was getting ready for the news station, or maybe the reporter was already there. The thought of the reporter waiting made me more frantic, and a shot of adrenaline carried me for another few minutes. By the time I was a mile away, I remember looking at puddles on the ground and wanting to get down on my hands and knees and lap them up like an animal. Luckily, I didn't! In retrospect, I don't know if there really were any puddles or if I was hallucinating. I was so thirsty and out of it, if someone had offered me a glass of gasoline, I think I would have chugged it.

Finally, I could see the campground in the distance and as I turned the corner, I immediately saw Nichole and the boys waiting with a camera man. Instinctually, I sped up and gave the best smile I could muster. Nichole saw my white lips and salt-caked skin and gave me water. She had one of her super shakes ready for me too, but all I wanted was water. I could feel it permeating every cell of my body and I couldn't get enough. She gave me salt tabs and electrolytes, and I absorbed all I could. My stomach was bloated. I poured more over my head, which brought me back to life like a wilted plant. I finished the media interview and ran a mile or so with Shamus to provide the news with some footage of us in action.

I ended the day feeling lucky; lucky I'd made it, lucky to have Nichole and the boys waiting for me, and lucky nothing *really* bad happened. I had dodged a bullet and could *not* let it happen again.

FORTY-TWO

WE REGROUPED OVER THE NEXT FEW DAYS as we worked our way through Montana. After two solid weeks of running in some isolated areas, my sisters, Jen and Jyll, were set to fly into Bozeman and drive out to meet us. We were excited to get a little taste of home. Knowing we'd be seeing them soon helped me recover from my dehydration. Luckily, I hadn't done any serious damage, and my fluid intake got back on point.

We cruised through the back roads until we reached the town of Anaconda and our next campground. It was another beautiful day, and the heat wasn't quite as oppressive. Excited to see family, we'd departed early so we'd have more time to hang out with my sisters. As a result, we arrived at the campground early in the afternoon, and had some time to rest before "Aunt Jenny and Auntie Juli" would arrive.

The Big Sky RV Park was beautiful, nestled in a basin surrounded by rocky mounds. The scenery and prospect of my sisters coming to visit inspired me to hike an embankment adjacent to our campsite. It looked like a great opportunity to get some aerial photos of Peggy, while also observing the nearby area from a high vantage point. After having my post-run snack and refuel session, setting up the RV for the afternoon, and leaving the boys to nap, I jogged out the door and climbed up. The views did not disappoint. From the top, the quaint town of Anaconda was fully visible below. In the distance loomed the *big* mountains I knew we'd soon have to tackle, but for the moment, I soaked in the view and snapped a few photos before I headed back to Peggy.

A short time later, Jen and Jyll arrived to a gigantic family hug. We were eager to show them around Peggy and tell them about our first two weeks on the road. After we visited, we then decided to do some sightseeing together. We discovered we were close to Lewis and Clark Caverns and made the short drive together. My sisters had rented a car, and it felt odd for us to ride in anything other than Peggy. We tossed Shay's wheelchair in the back and the six of us crammed into the SUV.

We drove up the mountains to an elevation of five thousand feet and found the state park and national monument caverns. Although most of the caverns weren't reachable with Shamus's wheelchair, we were over-joyed that the most breathtaking area of the caves, "The Paradise Room," was accessible, and an easy mile-long walk on a paved path. The room was spectacular. Upon entering the caves, we were suddenly surrounded by limestone formations of gorgeous stalactites, stalagmites, columns, and helictites. We spent an hour exploring before we headed back to Anaconda for dinner. After our family meal, Jyll and Jen drove to their hotel with the plan of meeting us early the next morning to spend the day with us as we ran.

In the morning, we decided Jen would stay with the boys and Nichole, and Jyll would be my support crew for the day with the SUV. We knew several back roads and steep, winding, mountain passes lay ahead, and Shamus wouldn't be able to safely run with me. With Jyll as my support, Nichole could take the easy route to the next campground via the highway. The boys were excited to spend time with Aunt Jenny in Peggy, and I was equally excited to have my "best man" as reinforcement. I knew she could stop as often as I needed, compared to the RV and trailer, which required much more space for a pit stop.

We started with Jyll finding a local store to help me restock my SPF 100. Ironically, the day was overcast, and I wore a long-sleeve windbreaker in the higher elevation. Regardless, running errands was exponentially easier in a regular-sized vehicle, and it was nice knowing I'd be well stocked in sunscreen for the rest of the journey.

The day started smoothly. For most of the morning, I ran up switchback roads and, conveniently, the rental car had a GPS device that included elevation data. As I climbed, Jyll quickly provided me with our elevation, and I could judge how my body was responding to the increasingly thin air. As I climbed to over six thousand feet, it became evident that the elevation simulation training I'd done with my mountain air generator had worked. We were cruising, and my body was adapting well. I had no difficulty breathing and I felt strong. I knew there were much bigger mountains ahead, but I was certain I'd continue to acclimate successfully.

As my confidence grew, my pace increased. I couldn't wait to get back to the family, who had set up camp in Bozeman. Surely bolstered by having Jyll and Jen in the same state, I was on cruise control as I descended from one of my final climbs of the day. Unfortunately, as I trod downward, my right foot slipped off the side of the pavement, and I rolled my ankle.

I hobbled down the road until I could meet Jyll, who had pulled off to the side of the road a short distance ahead. She could see my gait had altered. I was no longer striding smoothly. Instead, I labored as I favored my right side and tried to limit the weight I put on that foot. As usual, I'd been wearing my compression socks all day, which kept most of the swelling down. I only had five miles left for the day and figured I could walk or jog that distance. My fear was what would happen when I took my socks and sneaker off at the completion of those miles. Due to previous injuries, my right ankle had a tendency to rapidly swell to the size of a softball, and sometimes larger. For the first time since we started, I feared we might need to alter the schedule so I could take a day off. As I went through scenarios in my head, I realized we had too many deadlines, with chair presentations en route and the Mets at the finish, to be able to make any significant changes.

Luckily, I remembered to toss my first aid kit in the SUV when Jyll and I left that morning. I quickly taped my ankle over my sock to give it some added stability. I pushed through the discomfort as I staggered for the last few miles, and my mind continued to play out scenarios. I wanted the miles to be done so I could take inventory of the injury. I limped into the campground with Jyll close by for every step. I arrived to hear Choley, Jen, and the boys lamenting in their own story from the day. Choley supported me like a crutch and walked me to the trailer where she showed me two big dents in the front.

While I had my misstep, the pit crew had been experiencing their own. She and Jen went on to tell me of a wrong turn they made while nearing the campground. They ended up on a narrow, dead-end road with no place to turn around. They politely asked if they could use someone's driveway, but the homeowner quickly said they could *not* turn around there. The boys giggled as they imitated how the lady had waved her finger in the air and said, "*Nooooo way!*"

Nichole was left with only one option: to back Peggy down the long, narrow road, just as she had done in Idaho. Unfortunately, this time the road was much longer and much narrower. The trailer jackknifed twice as they retreated, which left deep dents in the trailer's front end. There was no other significant damage, and it left them all with a good story, but Nichole felt horrible about denting the new Ainsley's Angels trailer. She hastily let Rooster know about the incident, and he put her mind at ease by saying he'd take care of it when we made it to the East Coast.

After her trying day, I felt bad that she then had to deal with my ankle, but we headed into the RV where she helped take off my sneaker, the tape, and my sock. My ankle had already started to bruise and swell. Nichole quickly grabbed one of our ice packs from the RV freezer and wrapped it around my foot and ankle. I laid with my foot elevated, hoping one wrong step wouldn't ruin our chances of covering the remaining two-thousand-plus miles. I tried to put it out of my mind as we drove into town for a phenomenal dinner, but as dinner wore on, my ankle throbbed.

The boys thought it would be fun to stay with their aunties in the hotel, and Jen and Jyll were happy to have them for a sleepover. While my sisters took Shamus and Simon, Nichole and I discovered our campground was next-door to natural hot and cold springs. We went there to relax and recover. I decided to try some contrast baths on my ankle by alternating between hot and (freezing) cold springs for two hours. By the time we headed back to Peggy, the pain had subsided and the swelling was minimal. We were lucky to be in the right place at the right time. I taped my ankle with some Kinesio tape before going to bed, and I woke up the next morning feeling pain-free and ready to go.

FORTY-THREE

THE NEXT MORNING, MY SISTERS DELIVERED the boys back to us and stayed for the first few hours of the day before they had to catch their flight back to New York. We were sad to see them go so soon, but had plenty to keep us busy with the miles and chair presentations ahead. Over the next few days, we made our way into Wyoming and Yellowstone National Park. On July 19, the temperature was thirty-five degrees as we prepared to depart West Yellowstone. It was the only day I wore long pants while we ran. However, the sun abruptly warmed things up and by the afternoon, we were enjoying the national park after finishing our miles. We made time to see Old Faithful, the sulfur springs, waterfalls, and to observe the bison. We appreciated the beauty that encompassed us in every direction. We couldn't spend as much time there as we wanted, but we cherished the afternoon and made a promise to return in the future.

As we ran across Wyoming, the terrain was remote and desolate. We were surrounded by mountains, which made us feel isolated. We had little cell service and minimal opportunity to access the internet. The entire journey had continued to strengthen our bond as a family, and with no opportunity to communicate with anyone else for several days, we were glad to have each other.

After finishing our miles each day, it became tradition for Simon to massage my feet. We started the routine after I sprained my ankle, and

Simon loved being able to help. He was also the only one willing to touch my feet after I spent eight to twelve hours running. There was no better feeling than when seven-year-old Simon would squeeze my toes, rub my feet, and massage my ankle. At the end of each day, he was my hero, and the few minutes he spent squeezing my feet felt like heaven. When people saw pictures of him pampering me, they jokingly asked him, "What do Daddy's feet smell like after running all those miles?"

Simon would respond, without delay, "Oh, it's not bad. They smell like pepperoni and cheese!"

We had also begun to establish other summer traditions, like playing Uno or Trivial Pursuit after dinner, taking walks together around the campgrounds, and swimming every chance we got. Simon wanted to become an independent swimmer, so we took every opportunity we could to practice with him. We purchased a bike for Simon while we were in Idaho since he'd also made it a summer goal to learn to ride a two-wheeler. We took the bike out of the trailer at campgrounds whenever we could. We were genuinely making the most of every moment.

Despite the exorbitant number of miles we were covering, the days passed quickly. We had plenty to occupy us, and every day was a new adventure. We never knew what a day would bring in terms of roads, terrain, obstacles, or the new people we'd meet or sights we'd see. We soaked it in on a daily basis and sat around the dinner table each night reviewing and digesting the highlights. Each evening, we also made it a tradition to take a picture to indicate what number day we had completed. We had started at day one by each holding up one index finger, but as the days went by, we became more creative—locating numbers on road signs as we ran, making numbers out of fruit, using numbers from playing cards, and anything else we could find. It was a fun way to remember the day, and as we continued our journey, followers enjoyed our daily number photos on social media. In fact, folks along the way began creating their own number signs for us as we ran through their towns. It was amazing to see the support we received in the smallest municipalities. Places we'd never heard of had welcome signs and gifts for our family, and we were surprised every time.

Of course, one of the main motivators compelling us forward every day was our mission of donating chairs and spreading the vision of Ainsley's Angels; promoting inclusion for individuals with disabilities. We hadn't donated a chair since the two we presented in Washington State. We were unable to find a family in Montana, and though we had a family lined up in Wyoming, it wasn't until the eastern portion of the state. While that allowed us ample time to prepare and communicate with the family, we also couldn't wait to get there to celebrate. To make it, we had to climb the Big Horn Mountains and achieve the highest elevation point on our journey. Once again, my training paid off, and I tolerated the elevation better than Peggy. While Peggy sputtered and labored at ten thousand feet, I shortened my stride and kept putting one foot in front of the other. We climbed more switchbacks and ran uphill for entire days. The good news was, once we hit the highest point, it was all "downhill" from there!

Finally, on July 25, we made it to Gillette, Wyoming, where we had a huge celebration waiting for us. The family of our chair recipient, Emily, had rallied the entire community to welcome us! We were greeted by a fleet of emergency vehicles that were lined up to lead us into town. Shamus and I ran in the parade of vehicles, which also consisted of Nichole driving Peggy and Simon aboard a fire truck. When we got to the town park, a mass of people were there to greet us, including the mayor of the city. As we rolled in, she presented Shamus with a key to the city! We then granted Emily her chair and I gave her a spin in her new wheels. She squealed and smiled with delight, reinforcing the significance of our mission. We were making a difference in the lives of those we were giving gifts of mobility to, *and* to those people we were inspiring to dream *BIG* as we made our way from coast to coast.

Over the next few hours, we feasted and visited with our new friends.

They gave us several gifts, including gas cards, potpourri for Peggy, and donations of snacks and water. We were humbled by the outpouring of support and the feeling of family amongst all of those in attendance to celebrate Emily getting her new ride.

While we ran across Washington in six days and the bottleneck of northern Idaho in two, it had taken us eight days to run the eastern border of Montana, and then another eight days to get across Wyoming. Day twenty-five brought us to South Dakota. It had been the epicenter of our journey when we mapped out our route, which made it a milestone to cross the state line. Simon had selected Mount Rushmore as a sightseeing destination, and after nearly a month of running, we had arrived! After completing our miles, we set up camp and met some friends of friends who lived in the area. They brought us dinner and were generous enough to let us borrow their car so we could drive it to Mount Rushmore. Although we were tired, we were excited to visit the historic site.

As we pulled into the parking lot, it began to rain. It was the first time it had rained during our journey, but we didn't let the weather dampen our spirits. The rain kept many other tourists away, so we had most of Mount Rushmore to ourselves.

We were in awe of the mountain before us. We loved the museum and descriptions of how the faces had been carved. As it poured, we went inside to view the memorial from an observation area. As the rain dripped down the presidents' faces, they soon looked like they had runny noses, and we all chuckled. The rain had made our visit even more memorable. After all, how many people get to see George Washington with the sniffles?

While driving back to the campground, the rain turned into a massive hailstorm. The sides of the road looked like they were covered in snow. We'd never seen so much hail accumulate so fast. We took our time as we drove back to Peggy through the storm. When we got there, we discovered the hail had damaged another of the RV's vent covers. Once again, we patched it up for the night to keep everything and everyone dry. We didn't let it get us down. After the damage sustained in Idaho, we knew exactly how to fix it and we found a repair shop to go to the next morning. Another momentous day was in the books, and another dream—seeing Mount Rushmore in person—was fulfilled.

FORTY-FOUR

AFTER A QUICK STOP AT AN RV DEALER TO GET A NEW VENT COVER, we continued our run across South Dakota. We had remarkable scenery as we rolled through the Badlands. There was minimal vegetation, but the lack of trees was more than made up for by the magnificent striations of reds, browns, and oranges in the rocks. It was as if we could see every layer of history, each marked by a different hue. We absorbed it all at eight miles per hour as Shamus and I strode along, and Peggy, Nichole, and Simon led the way.

As we made progress across the state, we arrived in Presho where a sign welcoming us read, "Population: 500." Although we'd never heard of the tiny town, Presho marked the halfway point of our journey. It didn't matter to us that there would be no fanfare or public celebration. We were just amazed we'd already traveled over 1,600 miles in twenty-eight days—*on foot!*

The night before starting our run to and through Presho, Shamus decided he wanted to walk across the halfway point. At just over 1,600 miles, Nichole and Simon pulled over, parked Peggy, and hopped out with Shamus's walker in hand. As Shay and I approached, we saw them waiting with big "HALFWAY ACROSS AMERICA" signs they'd made. I teared up at the sight of the word "halfway" as I transferred Shamus from the running chair to his walker. He labored as he raised each leg and steadied himself with his walker. He took ten steps on the rocky shoulder and beamed as he helped us obtain another milestone in our journey—midway to the Atlantic, and halfway to Shay taking his finishing steps into the ocean.

We plugged along and prepared for a flurry of chair presentations. The first would be in Sioux Falls, at the eastern border of South Dakota, followed by another the next day in Worthington, Minnesota, and *another* in Estherville, Iowa. We'd be running through three states in three days and donating chairs to three new families. It was hectic as we planned and ran nonstop.

Each chair presentation was unique. Some families organized big gatherings, while some were smaller and more private. Some had parades and media, while some welcomed us with a family dinner and offered to do our laundry. Each was incredibly special and something we looked forward to and cherished.

On the way to Sioux Falls, we were greeted by a young reporter who wanted to share our story. He met us at a pit stop and said he wanted to drive ahead and get some footage of us running. He took off in his car and underestimated the pace Shay and I were maintaining. He was still setting up his camera and gear as Shamus and I cruised down the hill past him. He threw the gear in his car and leapfrogged us again, this time giving himself more time to get video of us running by. He met us again, as we presented Hailey with her chair in front of a large gathering of her friends and family.

Hailey's smile radiated as I took her for a spin around the hotel parking lot, where the presentation took place. A special treat for us was getting to spend the night in the hotel. While a break from Peggy was appreciated, and allowed us to stretch out and take a "real" shower, we all quickly realized how much we missed our RV when we didn't have her. Simon was so conditioned to being in the RV that he woke up in the middle of the night to ask Nichole to turn off the RV generator. She had to tell him that he'd actually been awakened by the hotel air conditioning! While *we* rested in the hotel, Hailey's dad provided Peggy with her own indulgence by taking her to a truck wash—her first bath since our journey had started. Peggy had been covered in dust, dirt, and bugs for thirty-two days of our journey. It was astounding for us to see her sparkle again when he brought her back to us the next morning.

With a fresh RV, we headed toward the sixth state of our adventure—Minnesota. Hailey's family had set up a police escort to get us from Sioux Falls to the state line. It was nice to be surrounded by police vehicles for the ten miles we had to run to the border, and the officers were happy to assist and be a part of the mission. Unfortunately, as we ran, I realized I wasn't feeling well. I'd been keeping up with my nutritional requirements, but the constant consumption of calories had been hard on my stomach. The adrenaline of the police support in the morning kept me going in the early hours, but as soon as they left, my status quickly deteriorated.

As the pain and cramping in my stomach worsened, I had Shay ride in the RV because I didn't want him to be stuck with me slogging along. I slowed to a walk, then stopped to vomit. Nichole stayed close with Peggy and thought I should take a break, but I knew we had another chair presentation, and I didn't want to be late. We were scheduled to arrive in Worthington to present Tori with her chair at three o'clock that afternoon, and I didn't want to delay the festivities. I knew they'd organized a big celebration with lots of friends and family. In addition, they organized another half-marathon police escort for us to finish our day. The police would lead us to the celebration, and we were scheduled to meet them thirteen miles out from the destination at one o'clock—that would give us two hours to do the final stretch. There was little room in our schedule for me to walk, let alone stop and rest. I needed to cover distance . . . and I was hurting.

I focused on getting some fluids into my body to replace what I'd lost, and after a few more miles, I was keeping everything down. My body didn't want to continue on the road, but my spirit didn't want to give up. Tori and her family expected us to be running when we got there, and I wanted to do everything I could to oblige. At every pit stop, Nichole pleaded for me to rest. I was pale, dehydrated, and my posture slumped as I ran. It didn't take a medical expert to know I wasn't thriving, and Nichole was looking out for me. Deep down, I knew I could have thrown in the towel. Nichole could have driven me a portion of the way, and no one would have cared . . . but that isn't what we had set out to do.

I kept going, barely convincing her I'd be okay. I completed several miles without getting sick on the side of the road, and was back to jogging again. I was doing everything I could to assure Nichole (and myself) that I was okay. I willed myself to keep running. Shamus periodically hopped in the chair for some miles, and I leaned on him, resting my legs as Shay "did the work."

By midday, I started feeling a little better, but we were running behind schedule. I felt horrible about delaying everyone, but Nichole insisted they'd understand. I knew she was right, but something in me did *not* want to be late. We met up with the police at 1:35 p.m. I'd done well to keep moving forward without losing too much time—a half hour behind schedule wasn't bad. I looked at my watch, knowing I'd run many half-marathons in less than an hour and twenty-five minutes. *Why couldn't I do it again?* Of course, I'd never pushed Shamus while racing a half-marathon, and I didn't know how fast I could run it with him, but we wanted to do it together. The police escort was for *us,* and we wanted to roll into the celebration *together.* In reality, at that point, I *needed* Shamus. Although I'd rallied, it had been a long day, and having him to pull me along with his smile was just what the doctor ordered.

I spoke with the police escort and told him we'd be stopping briefly twice over the final stretch, in five-mile intervals. I loaded Shamus into his chair and looked at Nichole with a determined, yet pleading expression, and said, "We're gonna make it by three."

Ever supportive, she gave Shay and me kisses, and said, "Love you. Be smart—*please!*"

Shay and I chased the police lights in front of us. We ran through the first five miles at nearly a six-minute pace—just over thirty minutes. Nichole pulled off at the five-mile marker and waited outside Peggy with water and electrolytes for us. I thanked her, gave a resolute nod, and off we went.

It felt like we were running uphill the entire time. Shamus and I kept saying to each other, "We must almost be to the top," but the top never seemed to arrive. Yet the *hope* for the top propelled us through the next five miles in just over thirty minutes, once again. I looked at my watch: 2:42 p.m. This time, Nichole simply handed me a water bottle as we ran by, like an aide station in a marathon. My pace quickened. I knew we could make it. Three o'clock was the goal, and we chased it as if we were racing. To me, it was a race . . . against the clock. As I look back now, I recognize it was just another method of fooling myself to keep going. That day, it was what I needed, and it was working. As we pushed the final three miles, we approached a roadside speed limit sign that showed passing cars their speed in flashing lights. I didn't alter my pace as we ran to the end of our fifty-six-mile day. I was shocked as the number twelve flashed on the sign . . . *twelve miles per hour, that's five-minute-mile pace!*

I was dumbfounded. With Simon, Nichole, and Peggy parked in the distance, we smiled as we surged for the finish. When we breathlessly pulled into the parking lot for the celebration, my watch read 2:59 p.m.

FORTY-FIVE

THE NEXT DAY BROUGHT US TO OUR SEVENTH STATE and another chair presentation as we rolled into Iowa. My stomach woes subsided, and Elizabeth's chair presentation was simple and quiet. It was just our family, two news reporters, the recipient's family, and a surprise guest! During the day as we ran, Nichole received a message from Shamus's third-grade teacher, Mrs. Hoffman. She and her family were vacationing in Colorado and wanted to make the drive to northern Iowa to meet us. Shamus and I were stunned to see the familiar face, and it was great to visit with them after finishing the chair presentation and interviews for the day.

As we drove to the campground, we celebrated seeing our friends and our arrival in another state. Iowa emerged with stereotypical corn-fields and soybean crops on each side of the street. We traveled down the country roads, having a difficult time determining where a campground could be, but eventually after some twists and turns through the farms, we arrived at a small, secluded RV park. We were promptly greeted by the kindest man with bibbed overalls and white hair protruding from a well-worn farmer's hat. He directed us to our campsite and asked us about our journey. We gave him the two-minute version of our mission and adventures before telling him where we were headed the next day. The gentleman said how amazed and impressed he was with Shamus's dream. He briefly excused himself and then came back with a bag filled with fresh sweet corn. He then said our night in the campground was on him. Finally, he reached into the front pocket of his overalls and pulled out an old, folded-up county map. He laid it on the picnic table beside Peggy and proceeded to show us the back-country roads to save us a few miles on our run. The roads he showed us weren't visible on any of our maps, but he assured us they were there and would work—even though they were most often traveled by farm equipment. We thanked him, and he said he felt privileged to help.

We loved Iowa from the start. The scenery didn't change much, but at each and every stop, the people were phenomenal. They welcomed us into their towns with hand-crafted signs lining the roads for miles. The campgrounds were all friendly and accommodating, with plenty of room for Simon to practice his bike riding. Each day after completing our run, I'd put in an extra few miles jogging behind him as he worked on losing his training wheels. It was in Iowa where Simon found his balance and became an independent bike rider.

At a campground in Elkader, Iowa, Simon was riding his bike through the campsites—with Nichole following nearby—when they caught the eye of another little boy who was using a walker just like Shamus's. After a few laps of making eye contact, Nichole persuaded Simon to take a little break so they could introduce themselves. While Shamus and I finished up our last few miles on the road, Nichole and Simon shared our story. The little boy, Lucas, was tremendously intrigued by the "running chariot" Nichole told him about. As soon as Shamus and I finished, Nichole asked us to say hello to Lucas and requested we show him our wheels.

Lucas' face lit up when he saw the chair, and I asked if he wanted to go for a ride—provided it was okay with his mom. A few minutes later, I was transferring Shamus into his wheelchair and loading Lucas into our "racing wheels." His squeals of glee propelled my tired legs. The grounds had a pond with a paved path encircling it, so I took Lucas around the half-mile track again and again as he shouted, "Faster, faster!"

While we ran, Nichole, Simon, and Shamus spoke with Lucas' mother, Jill, about Ainsley's Angels and the chairs we were donating during our journey. Jill asked how she could purchase one, since she enjoyed running and would love to include Lucas. Nichole gave her the details, and our family headed back to Peggy for dinner where conversation quickly turned to Lucas and his family.

As we talked, I said, "You know, we have an extra Freedom chair still in its box in the trailer ..."

"Let's do it!" Nichole exclaimed.

Without speaking the words, we knew we wanted to present Lucas with his own chair. We were convinced it would be going to a place where it would get some miles on it—Lucas would *not* let the chair sit unused!

I placed a quick call to Rooster, who answered instantaneously (as always, when we needed him), and I asked what he thought.

He loved the story, and his reply was succinct, "That's the mission—go for it!"

By then it was getting late and the sun had set, but we were leaving early the next morning for another big day so there was no time to waste. Simon and I walked to the trailer while Nichole and Shamus went to visit with Lucas and his family again. Simon held a flashlight as I opened the box, assembled the chair, and inflated the tires. Then we grabbed a copy of the Ainsley's Angels children's book, *Born an Angel,* for Lucas' sister, and jogged to their campsite, hoping we wouldn't be too late.

Fortunately, the family was sitting around a campfire and we were able to present them with their surprises. Tears and cheers of excitement followed as we completed our first impromptu chair donation to our new friends. I then gave Lucas a quick ride in his new chair under the moonlight before heading to bed.

As we laid down, we were grateful for our day, and realized we had more excitement ahead. The following day we'd be running to the Field of Dreams in Dyersville, Iowa! After watching the movie and wanting to include it as a stop, we were all looking forward to visiting the iconic film landmark. Little did we know, *many* more surprises awaited us.

We started early in the morning so we could get to the Field of Dreams before noon. Two contacts we'd met online had set up events for us, and we wanted to be on time. Jeff, a man we met through a running Facebook group, had planned some fun for us at the Field of Dreams. A few days prior, he reached out to Nichole to ask if he could meet us as we ran across Iowa. In his Facebook communications with us, he also asked if he could have the names of the campgrounds we were staying at. Nichole was leery to share that information with *anyone*, and we'd never met Jeff in person. Later that same day, Jeff messaged Nichole to say he'd taken the day off from work and was coming to greet us on the road, and wondered where he could find us. Once again, Nichole didn't respond, since we didn't necessarily want to meet a stranger in a remote area. However, figuring we must be busy, Jeff persisted and decided to come locate us. As I ran a solo leg, Jeff found Peggy and the crew waiting for me, and knocked on the door. Nichole cautiously let Jeff into the RV while she fed the boys lunch, and silently hoped I'd get there soon.

When I arrived, it was clear that Jeff could not have been any kinder. He and Nichole had struck up a quick conversation, and the boys took to him instantly. We discovered he'd wanted to know our campground details so he could pay for them, and he also wanted our trip to the Field of Dreams to be genuinely extraordinary. And that's exactly what it was!

When we arrived at the field, we were greeted not only by news crews and photographers, but an even bigger surprise coordinated by Jeff. As we sat at a table near the farmhouse, our attention was directed toward centerfield amongst the cornstalks. We watched intently and suddenly saw the formation of a ghost player—just like in the movie—making his way onto the field. In fact, it actually *was* one of the ghost players from the movie—a local gentleman, who was an extra in the film and made occasional appearances at the field. We were in awe. Jeff had given the player baskets of goodies to present to us, which included "Field of Dreams" baseball jerseys, baseball gloves, movies, candy, and snacks. He signed movie scripts for the boys and played with them on the diamond. The boys took turns playing with me, and Simon took some swings at the plate with a vintage bat. His pitcher was none other than the "ghost" player. It was both a marvelous experience and photo opportunity. The "ghost" even posed with us as we walked out of the cornfield. We were sad to have to leave to finish our miles for the day, but the day's surprises didn't end there.

Another Facebook friend, Aulanda, had coordinated a group to run with us for the final twenty-mile stretch. When we reached the bike path on our route, we were greeted by dozens of runners, and more would join us as we got closer to our destination. It felt like a scene out of *Forrest Gump* as more and more runners, of all ages, joined in as Shamus and I led the procession. When we finally arrived at our ending point, we were met by fire trucks spraying their hoses, a colossal party atmosphere, and hundreds of people at a restaurant who were waiting to have dinner with us. One of the smallest towns along our journey had produced one of the most massive celebrations, and again, we were humbled.

From the gathering at the restaurant, we headed to a special hotel Aulanda had booked for us. The hotel included an indoor waterpark! As exhausted as we were, we spent the night on water slides and lazy rivers. The next morning, Aulanda booked a hair appointment for Nichole. Nichole had previously dyed her hair Ainsley's Angels pink for the summer, and was now in need of a refresh of color. After a summer with us boys, Choley was ready for some girl time. While Nichole had her hair done, the boys and I ordered room service for breakfast, and celebrated another milestone as we looked out our hotel window at the Mississippi River!

FORTY-SIX

It had been a phenomenal few days. We hated to say goodbye to Iowa, but we'd completed another state, and crossing the Mississippi River was another huge accomplishment. When the girls got back from the salon, we met a police escort Aulanda had coordinated to get us over the bridge, and into Wisconsin. As we crossed the river, it struck me again how far we'd traveled—over two thousand miles and millions of strides. Yet, we still had over a thousand miles ahead of us.

We spent only one fairly unremarkable day in Wisconsin before making our way into Illinois, where we'd begin another streak of chair presentations—three chairs in four days. The chair presentations added excitement to our days and provided a little extra motivation. I couldn't wait to meet another family in person and help provide them with opportunities they might not otherwise have.

The first of the chairs was presented to Alex during a ceremony set up by a sponsor, Lärabar in Schaumburg, Illinois. Lärabar sent representatives and samples to make the event extra memorable. We communicated with Lärabar representatives for months on the phone, and it was a special day to finally meet them in person. It was fantastic to see how truly energized they were about our mission, and how thrilled they were to be a part of a chair donation. They had also coordinated a special ceremony for us the following day at a Chicago White Sox game. Being baseball fans, we were excited to get to see another stadium. And to make it even more amazing, they'd be playing their cross-town rivals, the Cubs!

Before we could get to the game, we had a couple of very busy days. After the presentation in Schaumburg, we picked up a new round of Freedom chairs that Rooster had shipped to my friend, Jason. Jason had saved us a great deal of time by unpacking and assembling all eight chairs! They were ready to roll. We simply folded them and stowed them in Freeda, where they would wait to be delivered during the final three weeks of our journey.

We got an early start the next morning, since we needed to cover the fifty-plus miles from Schaumburg to Chicago before another chair presentation in the city.

After completing the miles, Nichole drove us to Portage, Indiana, which was our stop after Chicago. We realized it would be easier to drive a regular vehicle around the city, so we rented a car there and drove back to Chicago for the chair presentation. The SUV we rented would then be the support vehicle as we ran to Portage the following morning. We drove to our next chair presentation with another one of our sponsors, Fairlife. We had shipped a Freedom chair to Fairlife and presented the chair to Jacob in their headquarters in downtown Chicago.

From the presentation and festivities, we went to US Cellular Field, where we were treated as VIPs. We were taken in via a special entrance and escorted directly to the field, where we watched batting practice and met the White Sox. The players were generous and took time to visit with the boys and sign autographs. We watched the game from VIP seating. We'd never experienced such royal treatment at such an enormous venue. Despite being utterly exhausted, we tried to relish the moment for as long as we could. We stayed for half the game before rejoining Jason, who treated us to a much-appreciated, home-cooked meal. After our dinner, we ended our epic day at a luxury hotel, paid for by Lärabar. The room was gigantic, and the pillows and mattress were the most comfortable I'd ever rested on. Unfortunately, we were only there for eight hours before we had to get up and run to Portage.

In a whirlwind few days, we had crossed another state off our list and made it to Indiana, where we returned the rental car and reunited with Peggy. Chicago was the first big city on our itinerary since leaving Seattle, but as we made our way east, the highways got busier, the roadside shoulders were narrower, and the vast space of the West disappeared.

As we prepared to depart Portage, we did another morning chair presentation like the one in Spokane. We understood we would be getting a later start to our running, but were excited for the opportunity and happy to accommodate the family's schedule. We met at a small park for the presentation, and again were greeted by a large crowd of the chair recipient's friends, family, and community members. The chair recipient, Nick, treasured his new chair right away! In fact, he loved it so much, he didn't want to get out of it! After our few speedy laps to christen the wheels, he wanted to keep running with the "Pinkman," which was his nickname for me because of my pink Ainsley's Angels T-shirt, hat, and socks.

Nichole and I had a quick discussion with Nick's mom and asked if he would like to join us for the first leg of our run that day. She loved the idea and off we went. Shamus was happy to ride with Nichole and Simon in Peggy, as Nick and I treaded down the highway with an emergency vehicle escort coordinated by Nick's family. In Nick's mind, we were in a race following the pace car, and he was in his glory. His joy in the chair reinforced to me why we were doing what we were doing. He just wanted to "go," and I was honored to lend him my legs for a few miles.

After saying goodbye to Nick, we continued our way to another exciting destination—the University of Notre Dame! I'd spent countless hours cheering for the Fighting Irish over the years, in any and every sport they played. Our family was looking forward to seeing the famous campus in person, and some nearby Ainsley's Angels members even arranged for us to stay at the campus hotel, the Morris Inn.

Nichole and the boys arrived before me, as I ran the final stretch to the university alone. Once they got there, they were met by a group of our fans on campus, who cheered me in for my final strides. Again, I was blown away. We were at Notre Dame and people were cheering for *us*! To top things off, Nichole had been contacted by the wife of the campus fire chief prior to our arrival (I had no idea Notre Dame had their own fire department!). The chief's spouse, Jeanne, arranged for us to meet up with the department for a private tour of the campus. As soon as I had given everyone high fives and signed a few shirts, the campus fire truck pulled up behind us and honked its horn. It was driven by the fire chief, who motioned our family aboard. We obliged with childlike grins on our faces, and he proceeded to give us a once-in-a-lifetime tour. It was an experience we will *never* forget. The chief then took us back to the fire station, where we joined the firefighters for dinner and feasted like royalty.

We arrived back to the hotel and were greeted with goody bags of treats and apparel from the university and the campus fire department. I was like a kid at Christmas. It felt like a dream. We hadn't asked for any of these special indulgences. We simply had a mission to run 3,200 miles across the US, and help some families along the way. We were content with the joy gained from all we were seeing and all the people we were meeting. Yet, there were so many people who were reaching out to us, wanting to help, wanting to be a part of it, and wanting to take care of *us*! We were inspiring, motivating, and moving people everywhere.

As we laid in the hotel bed, the previous week flashed through my mind. I looked out the window to the right and had a perfect view of the renowned Golden Dome. Its glow reflected as a beacon of light in the distance, and I couldn't help but think, *This all started with an incredible dream of a little boy. Shamus had been so persistent, and as a result, here we are making a difference in more people's lives than I ever could have imagined.*

FORTY-SEVEN

THE NEXT MORNING, WE AWOKE TO A RISING SUN and the Golden Dome. We headed for another state line as we left Indiana and crossed into Southern Michigan for another chair donation to Rylynn. The Midwest humidity was intense, and the sweat factor was extremely high. Shamus spent most of the day reading a book while in the chariot, shading himself from the sun with his canopy and filling me in on the highlights as we ran. I couldn't help but remember our run two years prior, when Shay told me about his favorite parts of *Harry Potter* as we ran around Clapp Park in Pittsfield, Massachusetts. It was almost two years later, to the day, and we were running across America just as he'd dreamed. While our journey had garnered a lot of attention, and we'd run through all kinds of new places, we were still united, father and son, enjoying a run together. Shamus distracted me from the heat and humidity with his stories, and I was grateful to have him to lean on as we rolled toward Michigan. As we made it to our destination and our chair presentation, we had a parade waiting for us to guide us through the final miles. Rylynn's family and friends made us a delicious dinner to enjoy after the run, as we settled in for another night.

After our day in Michigan, we were onto another new state, Ohio, with more chair presentations ahead. Once we made it to Ohio, we felt like we were closing in on the finish. We also had another visit from family to look forward to as Jodie and Jyll planned to meet us in Cleveland. The visit gave us something to look forward to, however, we still had four days and 230 miles of running before we made it to Cleveland, not to mention our first dual-chair presentation in Perrysburg, Ohio.

The night before our run to Perrysburg, Simon was bitten by an insect on his eyelid and had a colossal allergic reaction. His entire eye swelled shut. We gave him a dose of Benadryl, which helped only a little. As we prepared for our day, Simon looked like he had been in a boxing match. We were set to present two chairs with another town-wide celebration for the recipients, and Simon didn't want to miss it. He was stable, but uncomfortable. He spent most of the day in Peggy with an ice pack on his left eye.

As it turned out, it was a good day to be in the RV. As we ran into Perrysburg on day forty-six, it was the first time all summer we actually ran in the rain. While we had rain *after* we ran and when we were sightseeing at Mount Rushmore, that day in Ohio it poured all morning, and it looked like the chair presentation would be a complete washout. Luckily, by afternoon, the sun broke through the clouds and quickly dried everything out. We met up with a large group of runners for a five-mile fun run to Gibsonburg, where a humongous barbeque would take place.

That parade was perhaps the biggest of our entire run. There were over a hundred runners joining us, and spectators lined the road welcoming us to town. A drone flew above, capturing photos and video of the procession, as we streamed down the country roads. When we made it to the celebration, our family was presented with a special plaque from the mayor, commemorating the day "Evans Family Day" in Gibsonburg. We were humbled as we accepted the honor in front of the crowd. For all the photos, Simon was a true champ as he gave his prize-fighter smile with one heavy eyelid. It was another unforgettable day as we continued to promote inclusion by presenting two more gifts of mobility in the form of Freedom chairs to Brianna and Skylar. To us, it was a simple gesture, and our way of paying Ainsley's Angels' generosity forward to others, but to see the outpouring of support in the communities we were touching showed us it was so much more. We were making a difference beyond the recipients and their families. We were rallying entire communities around inclusion, and the events were genuinely becoming all-inclusive occasions with participants of all ages, backgrounds, races, and abilities. When we'd set out on the mission, we couldn't have comprehended the ripple effects of positivity we were creating . . . and that positivity continued to propel us toward the Atlantic Ocean.

We made it to Cleveland where Jyll and Jodie were waiting for us, and where we'd present a chair at the Rock 'n' Roll Hall of Fame! Nichole coordinated the presentation at the last minute when someone reached out to her on behalf of a family they thought could benefit from a chair. Choley pulled it together with full support from the Hall of Fame. We presented Lauren with her chair at the entrance to the museum, with throngs of people watching as I raced her around the grounds in her new wheels. It provided us with a great opportunity to share our mission with a myriad of new people. News reporters interviewed Shamus as Nichole and I visited with strangers, and Jyll and Jodie kept an eye on Simon. Shamus, while still soft-spoken, was becoming skilled at sharing our story. The interviewing reporter did a great job of putting Shamus at ease and made him feel as if he were simply having a friendly chat. He helped Shamus forget about the intimidating cameras and put focus on the fun we'd been having all summer. It was invigorating to witness the transformation in Shamus from a short distance away, as I spoke with a family who was visiting from Kentucky. Shamus's dream was not only taking us places we would have never otherwise traveled, but was also impacting countless others.

It was the first time my sisters had the opportunity to observe, in person, the power of a chair donation. They could fully appreciate the emotions of the recipient and her family, the joy of the onlookers, and the awe in the faces of those who were hearing our story for the first time. It was exhilarating for them to see us in action. They'd been there for bits and pieces of conversations throughout the planning, training, and logistics. My family members were some of our most prolific supporters, and it was great to be able to share the moment with them. They were so inspired, they decided to change their plans and stay with us an extra day. Rather than flying back to Albany, they kept their rental car and extended their trip, planning to instead *drive* home from Western Pennsylvania. Despite having a blast and loving every minute of our journey, we were all getting a little homesick after living in Peggy all summer. It was nice to have a little part of home with us for a bonus day.

As we crossed into Pennsylvania, my sisters wished us well, and Peggy had a major hiccup. The RV's generator died, which meant we wouldn't have air conditioning during pit stops. If we were plugged in at a campground, we could run the air conditioner, but we wouldn't be able to run it from the road. With the summer heat not letting up, it would be a big change for me on my breaks, and for Nichole and the boys as they tried to stay cool. Although we took Peggy to a repair shop, we were told there was nothing they could do to fix it—the generator needed to be replaced. Luckily, it was still under warranty, but there was nothing to help us for the remainder of our journey. We contacted Rooster, and he set up an appointment for Peggy at an RV shop in Virginia Beach. For the rest of the summer running on the road, I'd be relying on ice to keep me cool.

In addition to the trials of a broken generator, Pennsylvania also presented a challenge in the form of a change in terrain. As we left the flatlands of the Midwest, we entered a land of relentless, undulating hills. Perhaps it was my legs fatiguing from the nearly three thousand miles we had covered, but every hill felt like an attempt to summit Kilimanjaro. A day earlier, Jyll had commented on how small my calves looked. As a competitive bodybuilder and fitness fanatic, she always admired my calves. It was never something I worked at, they simply developed over a decade of distance running and tens of thousands of miles of hills. As we made our way across the country, I hadn't recognized the change, but when she pointed it out, I looked down and noticed they'd shrunk considerably. It wasn't for lack of exercise that summer! Instead, it was due to my body breaking down muscle as fuel. I had zero body fat left. Despite my greatest efforts of eating like a raccoon ravaging a dumpster each night, and Nichole's incredible determination to keep me fed and fueled, I couldn't keep up with the caloric demands of my body. It was literally eating itself to keep me going, and as we hit the hills of Western Pennsylvania, my legs were taxed even more.

Fortunately, one of our sponsors was protein-enhanced Power Surge nut butter. I decided to increase my protein intake significantly in the form of extra nut butter, sometimes eating an entire jar in a day, in hopes it would help me to rebuild, or at least maintain, the muscle I had. We were down to single digits in days remaining on our journey, 450 miles from the Atlantic. In the grand scheme of things, we were almost there, but the way my legs were feeling made the distance much more daunting.

FORTY-EIGHT

THE BOOST IN PROTEIN SEEMED TO MAKE A DIFFERENCE. As Shamus and I tackled the Allegheny Mountains, my legs weren't feeling quite as fatigued or wasted. We had less than a week to go, and we continued taking on every day five miles at a time. Five miles to a brief respite at Peggy for fuel and hydration. Even though we could sense the finish was near, we didn't change our routine. We enjoyed a tranquil day on the road as a family before the fluster of activity that would accompany the final few days of our journey.

We had a quiet chair presentation for a family in Black Moshannon State Park. Although it was one of the simplest chair donations, it was one of our most memorable because we spent uninterrupted time with the recipient family, the Koontzes. They invited a news reporter who spent a great deal of time not only interviewing and setting up the right shots, but also getting to know us all. The little girl who was receiving the chair, Lizzy, immediately won our hearts with her bright eyes and beaming smile. The family had brought food for a barbeque and we ate, ran, and played with Lizzy and her brothers. We took photos, laughed, and smiled as we celebrated inclusion within our two families. As we wrapped up the day, we rejoiced over the new friends we made and one of our last calm days on the road. As we said our goodbyes, Lizzy's mom, Maria, offered to give Nichole a break from our laundry. Nichole was extremely grateful, but wasn't sure Maria knew what she was in for—we hadn't had access to laundry facilities for several days, but Maria insisted with a smile. She wanted to help and felt it was the least she could do. She took multiple bags full of my several-day-old, sweaty socks, shirts, and shorts, in addition to all of the family's clothes. My modesty vanished as we handed over my week's worth of filth, but Nichole was sure to give Maria our extra-strength sports detergent. Maria didn't even flinch, and said she'd get everything back to us the next day at our next stop, another fifty-plus miles down the road!

The next day, we had another chair presentation, but first we were set to meet up with a writer from *Runner's World* who wanted to spend the day with us. He met us on the road, interviewed the family, and ran several of the day's five-mile legs with us. He said he wanted to see if what we were doing was legitimate. We'd been so focused on covering miles that it never occurred to me there were still doubters out there! However, after spending the day with us on the road, the writer was a believer, and was amazed at the pace we were maintaining. While we ran, I explained all the preparation and training we had put into making the journey and Shay's dream a reality. He was excited to begin writing about everything we discussed and everything he experienced on the road with us. He headed to his hotel with a few running segments of the day remaining so he could get started on the article. After he left us, all I could think about as I ran was the fact that some people still didn't believe what we were doing was real. It bothered me for a bit, but I quickly remembered that we weren't doing it for the doubters. My mind shifted to all of the people who *did* believe, who wanted to be part of what we were accomplishing, who were inspired. I couldn't control what people thought, but I *could* focus on the good we were doing!

That thought propelled me to the finish for the day, where we gifted another chair, this time to a boy named Dominic. A friend of Dominic's family coordinated a massage for me at the campground that night. The massage therapist set up her table right next to Peggy. My legs were tender and the pressure from the therapist's hands made them even more sore, so I asked her to ease up a little. Although she said she was hardly pushing, she obliged and reduced her pressure further. Other than Simon massaging my feet and toes, my muscles hadn't been "worked on" at all during the summer. My legs had one job: churning out miles every day. I decided to have the therapist shift her focus to my arms and back, which felt much better. I knew I would continue to need my legs for the final stretch of road. The leg massage could wait until September.

The next morning, I woke up and my legs didn't want to move. The massage had stirred things up just enough to leave them incredibly achy. Despite me thoroughly rehydrating, my legs were sore and lethargic. I ended up walking the first few miles of the day while doing some radio interviews over the phone. Eventually, the soreness worked its way out. I transferred Shamus to his chair so he could pull us along, allowing me to stretch out my stride and be consumed by his conversation. Together, we persisted, with Shay—as always—giving me a much-needed boost.

That night, we talked about how many miles we'd covered—just under 3,100. We realized the next day, we'd pass the 3,100-mile threshold, leaving us less than one hundred miles from the finish. It also meant, in fifty-seven days on the road, we'd cover the equivalent of *one thousand 5Ks!* The distance we'd covered in less than two months seemed surreal, and to celebrate, Shay decided he'd walk us past the "thousand 5K marker." The next day, we took out his walker on a quiet sidewalk, and we cheered for him as he powered us past another incomprehensible milestone. As he walked those steps on a quaint side road, an Amish horse and buggy trotted alongside, providing him with an unexpected audience.

We were closing in on the finish, and we could all feel it as the days got busier! During the previous month, my boyhood friend, Bryan, reached out to say he'd like to meet up with us somewhere in Pennsylvania. I provided him with a list of towns where we'd be stopping. I told him I'd get him more details as we got closer. Via text message, he told me I had enough other stuff to worry about. He simply said he'd find us. I had no idea how he planned to do that, and as we got closer to the New Jersey border, I assumed he wasn't going to be able to meet us after all. In the meantime, another friend, Mark, along with his wife and two sons met us as we made our way through Eastern Pennsylvania. Mark had joined Shamus and me on several ten-mile training runs back home. He wanted to join us during a leg of our run, and we were happy to have the company. Not only did the terrain of Pennsylvania feel familiar as we ran the rolling hills, but we also had a familiar face with us. It truly felt like we were going to make it.

While we ran, Nichole and Simon drove ahead to a gas station to fuel up Peggy. Mark, Shay, and I soon joined them there for our final pit stop of the day. The plan was to do one more five-mile leg, then drive to the campground. Mark and his family were going to stay at the campsite with us for a while, so we started to come up with plans for the evening. Just then, we got a knock on the RV door, and I figured someone from the gas station needed us to move Peggy. Much to my surprise, when I opened the door, I was greeted by a big grin from . . . Bryan! We hadn't heard from him in over a week, but he'd found us, just like he promised. We laughed as he told us his story of traversing all the possible routes we could have taken, until he stumbled upon the unmistakable Peggy at the gas station.

After Bryan surprised us, we altered our evening plans. Mark and his family went to the campground with Nichole and the boys to relax and hang out in the pool. I told Nichole I could run the rest of the way, and Bryan could be my support crew for the remaining eighteen miles. It would save my legs several thousand steps the next day. Bryan had been hoping to roll with me on the road for a while anyway. He'd brought his bike along, and the shock of his surprise appearance gave me a shot of adrenaline to finish out the day. Nichole agreed the plan sounded good, and off we went, Bryan on his bike and me striding beside him. We visited and reminisced about the "good old days" and covered ground fairly quickly. We ended up crossing into New Jersey a day ahead of schedule.

When we arrived at the campground, Shamus and Simon were swimming with Mark's kids. Bryan rode back to get his car, and we settled in for the evening. I studied the map of the remaining few days—the countryside was far behind, and navigating the urban roads would be a new challenge. Near the end of the extraordinary journey, stress levels increased. I wanted to be as prepared as possible. We were so close to fulfilling Shamus's dream and didn't want anything to derail us in the final miles. I rehearsed and reviewed plans over and over in my mind. Fortunately, I knew reinforcements were coming to help with the countless logistical pieces that needed to fall into place for the homestretch. Joe Orth would be returning to bookend our journey with us, and having him there with me would definitely help ease the tension of navigating to and through Manhattan. In addition, Rooster and his family would be joining us for the last few days of our ambitious quest! That night, as we laid our heads on our pillows in New Jersey, we knew Rooster, Lori, Briley, Kamden, and Ainsley Rossiter would meet us on the road somewhere the next day, and we'd soon be together for the push to the finish.

FORTY-NINE

WE STARTED IN THE EARLY MORNING, as we headed toward our rendezvous spot with Rooster and the rest of the Rossiter family. We found
them and exchanged several joyful embraces fifteen miles from the day's
destination. I refueled and rehydrated as Rooster put Ainsley in her running chair. They ran alongside Shamus and me through the busy streets
of New Jersey. We had come a long way from the wide, open spaces of the
West. Rooster and I chatted about the success of the mission as we ran.
He told me about inquiries he'd been receiving from people who wanted
to get involved with Ainsley's Angels after they saw Peggy, or met Shamus
and me. He said he could track website hits along our journey, as people
from across the nation clicked to find out more about the duo wearing
pink and running from coast to coast. Of course, there were Ainsley's
Angels events going on regularly in different locations across the nation as
we ran, but much of our transcontinental run was taking us places where
there wasn't yet an Ainsley's Angels presence in the community. Rooster
and I talked in depth about how the presence could grow after the run.

The streets got busier and traffic more intense as our day
concluded. Shamus and Ainsley joined the rest of the support crew, and
Rooster and I went on to finish the last ten miles of the day together. It
was a privilege to have him by my side—the man who believed in us
when few others did. His positive energy, commitment, and confidence

in the mission was making Shamus's dream a reality and leaving a lasting impression on the world of inclusion.

After finishing our miles, we converged with our families at the hotel and reviewed plans for the next day. Lori, Nichole, and the kids would drive ahead to the campground in Jersey City, while Rooster would support me with his truck. After getting a little ahead of schedule, the final three distances we'd have to run were serendipitously a marathon (26.2 miles), half-marathon (13.1 miles), and a ceremonial 5K (3.1 miles) to the finish. Those final three distances combined wouldn't add up to what we had been averaging daily for the previous fifty-seven days. It would allow more time to coordinate with sponsors for the finish celebration, and to finalize routes for our most tedious portions of the journey through and around New York City. We weren't overly worried about getting around it on foot; Peggy and Freeda would be the real challenge.

Rooster and I departed the hotel on another hot and humid morning. Rooster drove ahead a mile, and then checked in with me and got me whatever I needed. It wasn't long before we crested a hill and Rooster stopped me with a grin. He had seen it before I did. In the distance, the New York City skyline was visible! After fifty-eight days of running, the finish line was finally in sight. We celebrated and made our way to the campground in Jersey City. The term campground is used loosely, because it was simply a giant parking lot with hookups for RVs. Just offshore from the RV park, the Statue of Liberty was visible in the distance. Our plan was to leave Peggy there for a few days to avoid having to drive her through the city. We'd stay in Peggy one night, and then stay two nights in a hotel closer to the finish. When we rendezvoused with Nichole, it quickly became evident we'd made a good decision about not trying to bring Peggy through the city again.

Apparently, getting Peggy and Freeda to the RV park was a nightmare. Nichole had become proficient at driving the monstrosity through all kinds of terrain and traffic, but Jersey City presented a whole new level of tight spaces and stressful driving conditions. She drove to the RV park at peak traffic times on narrow roads, with cars parked up and down the streets, with no more than an inch to spare on either side. Yet, she delivered as she had all summer long. She made sharp turn after sharp turn, with throngs of pedestrians and cars everywhere. She handled it like a professional, but it was not something she wanted to have to do repeatedly.

That evening, everyone else started to arrive. Jyll and her husband, Mark, helped us load a trailer with a summer's worth of our stuff they'd be hauling home for us. We'd drive Peggy to Virginia Beach and fly home just in time for school to start, so we didn't want to have many bags to bring with us. We packed their trailer with nearly all of our gear, leaving ourselves with just enough for the week. The trailer was jammed full.

Joe Orth was there helping to coordinate the run the following day, as he and I would make the trek through Manhattan. We found a pedestrian ferry adjacent to the RV park, which could take us to the city early the following morning. He'd support me from a bike while I ran the length of Manhattan en route to the Bronx, where we would meet up with representatives from Lärabar and Orchard Beach to organize the final day. The rest of my family would meet us later, while Nichole, Shamus, and Simon would drive Joe's truck to the hotel. There, we'd meet up with the final chair recipient, Nick, and his family, as well as representatives from Adaptive Star who would supply the final chair to donate. The many moving pieces were aligning like gears in a clock.

Joe and I set off early the next morning with the intention of meeting up with our Lärabar reps and Jyll at *The Today Show*. I ran and Joe biked through the city sidewalks, and we made it to Rockefeller Center where *The Today Show* was filming. We weren't able to get the ear of any of the producers. Instead, we settled for holding up "Ainsley's Angels—Run Across America" signs in the background. As we stood there smiling and cheering, my phone was inundated with messages from people who were watching live.

After the show wrapped up, Joe and I continued through the city, all the way to Orchard Beach at Pelham Bay in the Bronx. As we arrived, it suddenly hit me—Nichole and I had stood in that exact spot, on a cold December day, as we planned our journey and scouted an endpoint . . . and there I was, unceremoniously at the finish. I was somewhat in disbelief, numb. I told Joe I couldn't go all the way to the ocean without Shamus. We'd save that for the final day.

We spent the next several hours reviewing details for the finish celebration the following day: determining our 5K route, where we'd set the Ainsley's Angels finish arch, where Lärabar would set up their tent, and how the morning would flow. With so many logistics to focus on, it was difficult to process, let alone enjoy the moment. It had hardly registered in my brain that we'd *actually* made it. Although Shamus and the rest of the family weren't there, we had indisputably covered the distance from coast to coast—on foot!

The next day, we all woke up with butterflies in our stomachs, knowing it was the day we'd been gearing up for all summer. We anxiously rode to the beach in Joe's truck and prepared for the final leg of our grandiose mission, and Shamus's final steps into the ocean. Rooster, Ainsley, Joe, Shamus, and I went out to our starting spot for the ceremonial 5K, while everyone else finished setting up and gathered the crowd to bear witness to the finish.

After spending the better part of two years looking forward to that day, I took a minute to reflect on the moments leading up to it. The training, planning, and fundraising events flashed through my mind like snapshots. Our summer journey played as a slideshow in my mind at hyper-speed—the sixty-day journey condensed into a sixty-second blur of highlights and memories.

As my mind whirred, Joe looked at Shamus and asked, "What do you wanna listen to as we roll in?"

Shay responded with a fitting song: American Authors' "Best Day of My Life."

Joe cued it up and, as the song played, Shamus radiated joy and pride in his smile as we advanced toward the finish line. Nichole and Simon jumped in to run the final hundred meters with us. We turned the corner and were greeted by a hundred people applauding and encouraging us to the finish of our epic adventure. As we neared the Ainsley's Angels arch at the edge of the beach, I looked to my left to see posters made by friends, family, and strangers, welcoming us home. One sign in particular, held by Shamus's friend Noah, caught my eye and pulled at my heartstrings. It simply read, "My best friend just ran across America!" Noah held the sign up, proudly praising Shamus's accomplishment.

We rolled Shamus down the accessible mat over the beach, toward the ocean. Rooster, Joe, and I raised his running chair high above our heads for the final few steps across the sand, toward the water. I lifted Shay out of his chair and placed him in his walker at the shoreline. He gripped it tightly, glanced at the waves crashing at his feet, and methodically led Nichole, Simon, and me into the Atlantic on day sixty of our transcontinental crossing. Together, we had actually done it—ocean to ocean in two months, on foot. We'd flown west, and Shamus had propelled us home!

The rest of our time on the beach was a whirlwind. We made our final chair presentation to Nick, gave multiple interviews, and received a seemingly endless line of hugs, high fives, and congratulations. We were overcome with emotion as we delivered our final remarks to the crowd, and were surprised by a presentation from Lärabar, who donated an additional and unexpected ten thousand dollars to support Ainsley's Angels. They then awarded each member of our family a one-of-a-kind finisher's medal for completing our journey from sea to shining sea. It is, without a doubt, the most difficult and most rewarding medal I'd ever been presented with, as it represented both the arduous challenges and the inexpressible joys of the summer.

That night, the Mets welcomed us to Citi Field, where they recognized us on the field during pregame festivities. We had an opportunity to closely interact with Mets players, many of whom told Shamus what an inspiration he was to them as they signed caps, balls, and shirts for both him and Simon. As the stadium filled with fans, pictures of us on our run from Seattle to New York flashed on the jumbotron for several minutes as the announcer read a proclamation about our run across America and the mission of Ainsley's Angels. After completing some final on-field interviews and tipping our caps to the cheers of the crowd, we settled in to enjoy the game with over a hundred friends who had come to support us at the stadium.

As we celebrated the day and the summer, Simon couldn't stop crying. He simply didn't want such a remarkable and exuberant summer to end. My heart echoed his sentiments. Looking back at the adventure, it seemed to pass in the blink of an eye. It was a once-in-a-lifetime journey, and we all understood it. I loved what we'd been doing for two months, the elation we experienced along the way; the joy and inspiration we provided others. It had all started with Shamus's dream, his unfathomable goal of running across the United States of America. Through his persistence and determination, his dream painstakingly became a reality. All summer long, every single stride brought us one step closer. We endured through the hardships and savored every moment from coast to coast. I would never have set forth such a goal for myself, and could never have done it alone, but Shamus inspired us.

In the end, it took the *BIG* dream of a seven-year-old boy to prove to us all, we definitively are *better together!*

FIFTY

WHILE WE WERE STILL DIGESTING WHAT WE'D ACCOMPLISHED and trying to process the places we'd been, we loaded up Peggy and drove south to Virginia Beach, where the RV would reside. Nichole had a hard time handing over the keys to Rooster because Peggy had become an integral part of our family. After arriving in Virginia Beach to deliver Peggy to her new home, Shamus and I joined Ainsley and Rooster for the Rock 'n' Roll Half-Marathon on Labor Day weekend. It was a fitting end to our summer as we rolled side by side with the ones who helped jumpstart our journey.

After the race, we headed to the airport and said our goodbyes to the Rossiter family. We also said farewell to an unforgettable summer, which was packed with amazing moments and people who would forever impact our lives. Upon arriving home, we were welcomed by banners and signs throughout our small town, and the community rallied for one more parade in our honor. It was strange to be back in our house after living on the road for the summer. A day later, I returned to work, and Nichole and the boys were back at school.

I found it difficult to be sitting in my office. My body and mind had been conditioned to being on the move, all day, every day. I had a hard time re-acclimating to my everyday routine. Each day during the summer, we had a big task to accomplish and something amazing to look forward to. There were new places, challenges, and opportunities every day—new sights to see and people to meet. We had felt we were doing something important every single minute during our journey, as we traveled and donated chairs.

In the days and months immediately following our transcontinental run, the most popular question we were asked was, "What do you do next?"

Once we were home, I felt out of place. Everyone was asking what was next for our family, which was an extremely difficult question to answer. We knew what we'd done was extraordinary, and we'd never be able to replicate it. Even if we *did* repeat the accomplishment, it would never be the same as the first time. What we did know was we'd continue to have adventures as a family, no matter how big or small. Shamus and I would continue to run together, and he would continue to have new goals and dreams for us to aspire to, together. So, that was the best answer we could provide. Our journey didn't start or end with our run across America. There would be much more to follow, but at that moment, we couldn't imagine what those escapades might be.

The best I could do was attempt to put our transcontinental run into perspective for *myself.* I reflected on some of my previous goals. I recognized I'd achieved some, and come up short on others. My biggest personal goal had always been to run in the Olympic trials, which happened to be one goal I *didn't* achieve. However, the more I thought about it in the days after our 3,200-mile run, I realized that goal had been a selfish goal. While there was nothing wrong with it, the goal would have benefited no one but myself. As I processed our journey, I thought about how many people had run in the Olympic Marathon Trials since the modern Olympics began. I calculated there would have been *thousands* of men and women who ran in the trials over those hundred-plus years. Then, I turned my attention to what Shamus had inspired our family to accomplish during the summer of 2015. I realized that what we'd achieved by running from ocean to ocean as a team put our family on a very short list of finishers.

More importantly, it was a dream and journey that benefited countless individuals and families across the USA—not only those who received chairs from us, but also those who'd been motivated, inspired, or compelled to dream *big* themselves. Through his vision, Shamus truly showed us all that there are no limits, there is always room for a greater goal, and that *together*, we could accomplish so much more than we ever could alone.

Itinerary

1. SEATTLE, WA
2. GOLD BAR, WA (47 MILES)
3. LEAVENWORTH, WA (52 MILES)
4. WATERVILLE, WA (61 MILES)
5. ALMIRA, WA (60 MILES)
6. REARDON, WA (54 MILES)
7. COEUR D'ALENE, ID (64 MILES)
8. OSBURN, ID (45 MILES)
9. PLAINS, MT (65 MILES)
10. MISSOULA, MT (60 MILES)
11. DRUMMOND, MT (61 MILES)
12. ANACONDA, MT (57 MILES)
13. WHITEHALL, MT (62 MILES)
14. BOZEMAN, MT (54 MILES)
15. BIG SKY, MT (49 MILES)
16. WEST YELLOWSTONE, MT (51 MILES)
17. CANYON YELLOWSTONE, WY (60 MILES)
18. CODY, WY (52 MILES)
19. GREYBULL, WY (53 MILES)
20. DAYTON, WY (49 MILES)
21. SHERIDAN, WY (57 MILES)
22. ARVADA, WY (60 MILES)
23. GILLETTE, WY (56 MILES)
24. UPTON, WY (49 MILES)
25. CUSTER, SD (58 MILES)
26. RAPID CITY, SD (53 MILES)
27. BADLANDS, SD (60 MILES)
28. MIDLAND, SD (52 MILES)
29. PRESHO, SD (57 MILES)
30. WHITELAKE, SD (60 MILES)
31. MITCHELL, SD (61 MILES)
32. SIOUX FALLS, SD (52 MILES)
33. WORTHINGTON, MN (53 MILES)
34. ESTHERVILLE, IA (52 MILES)
35. ALGONA, IA (51 MILES)
36. MASON CITY, IA (57 MILES)
37. NASHUA, IA (50 MILES)

38. ELKADER, IA (57 MILES)

39. DYERSVILLE/PEOSTA, IA (52 MILES)

40. MONROE, WI (60 MILES)

41. SOUTH BELOIT/CHICAGO, IL (61 MILES)

42. CHICAGO/SCHAUMBURG, IL (55 MILES)

43. PORTAGE, IN (64 MILES)

44. SOUTH BEND , IN (50 MILES)

45. STURGIS, MI (49 MILES)

46. HOLIDAY CITY, OH (58 MILES)

47. PERRYSBURG, OH (55 MILES)

48. NORWALK, OH (56 MILES)

49. CLEVELAND, OH (55 MILES)

50. WARREN, OH (57 MILES)

51. HARRISVILLE, PA (55 MILES)

52. CLARION, PA (47 MILES)

53. CLEARFIELD, PA (59 MILES)

54. BELLEFONTE, PA (48 MILES)

55. LEWISBURG, PA (55 MILES)

56. FREELAND, PA (52 MILES)

57. STROUDSBURG, PA (47 MILES)

58. RANDOLPH, NJ (49 MILES)

59. MANHATTAN, NY (42 MILES)

60. PELHAM BAY, NY (13 MILES)

Acknowledgments

THIS BOOK, our mission, and our unforgettable journey across America would not have been possible without so many selfless, helpful, and caring friends, family members, sponsors, and even strangers.

First, to my extremely patient, supportive, and loving wife, Nichole, who has demonstrated more endurance than I *ever* have. You make everything possible! I could never thank you enough for all you have done for me and our family.

To Simon, the only one who would touch my feet during our sixty day journey—the *true* hero of our summer of 2015. Thank you for your compassion, sincerity, generosity, and commitment to all you do and for being a magnificent younger brother to Shay.

To Shamus, the dreamer, the reason, and the motivation for something I never thought possible. Thank you for your persistence, for dreaming BIG, and for showing me that with the right inspiration, ANYTHING is possible.

To my mother, Gail, thanks for being tolerant of my childhood antics and for helping me channel my energy into more constructive areas. To my father, Neal, thank you for instilling the work ethic required to take on even the most daunting tasks. Both of you have helped to shape me into the man I have become, and for that, I am eternally grateful.

To Jen, Jodie, and Jyll, my Golden Girls, your endless love and support are unequaled. I am incredibly lucky to have you three as my foundation. There is no way I could ever repay my debt of gratitude to you.

To Jeff, Bryan, and Mark B., thanks for being the brothers I never had, for always being there in our formative years, and for still being there now.

To Mark C., thanks for the backup in Jersey City and for taking good care of my best "man."

To Blake and Greg, thank you for the countless miles you put in with me on your bikes and for nourishing my body and soul in innumerable training runs and races.

To Notre Dame College, you are greatly missed, but your spirit lives on. Thank you, Dr. and Mrs. Michael, for your guidance and taking me under your wings. Thank you, Lisa D-P and Dr. Burns, for your mentorship.

To Ashely Miller, Chris Onorato, and WNYT, thank you for your time and dedication to our mission and for spreading our message throughout the community.

To Peter and Bob at the Firecracker4 and Benn at the Sweltering Summer races, thanks for letting Shamus and me participate together and for fueling Shamus's love for endurance events!

To Millie and CHC, thank you for your flexibility in allowing me a summer-long sabbatical to pursue my family's dream.

To all of the sponsors of the summer of 2015: Lärabar (Katie), Frederick Foundation (John), Evans Brothers Lemonade, Pro Compression (Eric), Brooks Running (Tamara), Fleet Feet Albany (Charlie), Power Surge Nut Butters (Gabe and Jessica), FairLife (Sydney), Body Glide (Ryan), Jay Bird (Rhyan), Vega, and Purely Elizabeth. Your generosity helped to make our mission a reality!

To Mike at Team Hoyt Running Chairs and Teri at Adaptive Star, thank you both for setting us up with custom chairs that made Shamus's ride across America comfortable, smooth, and safe!

To Suzan and Russ Dean RV, thanks for bringing Peggy and Freeda into our lives!

To Sarah and family, thank you for giving up your garage to store our summer's worth of supplies and for helping us to get ready to roll.

To the Green Knights (Dave), thanks for the supplies and for stepping in to get us out of a jam.

To Jeff, Aulanda, Suzie, LaRae, and *all* of our Iowan friends, thanks for helping to make our trip through the Hawkeye state so special!

To Jason, thank you for taking on the task of assembling and storing a fleet of Freedom chairs and providing us with a much-needed pit stop.

To Jeanne and Chief Harrison, thank you for making our night at the University of Notre Dame so memorable!

To Josh Lee, thanks for facilitating our finish with the Mets, and to Donovan Mitchell, thank you for making our time at Citi Field an unforgettable conclusion to our epic adventure

To the chair recipients and their families, thank you for providing meaning to our miles. The opportunity to give you gifts of mobility provided extra purpose and motivation. Thank you for propelling us from town to town and ocean to ocean!

To editors Tanya and Abby and to Mascot Books, thanks for helping to make this book possible.

To ALL of our supporters and the Ainsley's Angels family, thank you for the donations, love, encouragement, and kindness leading up to, during, and beyond our journey!

To Joe, there are no words great enough to thank you. You constantly put others before yourself without hesitation. We were lucky to have you by our sides at each coast and are forever grateful for your unequivocal generosity. Thank you, brother!

Finally, to the Rossiter family (Rooster, Lori, Briley, Kamden, and Ainsley), thank you for believing in us when few others did. Thank you for welcoming us to your family with open arms. Thank you for creating Ainsley's Angels and allowing us to represent and be a part of such an amazing organization. Together, we shall accomplish so much more!